Consider
David Foster Wallace
Critical Essays

Edited by David Hering

Sideshow Media Group Press
Los Angeles / Austin

FIRST EDITION
ISBN: 978-0-9761465-7-5

10 9 8 7 6 5 4 3 2 1

Manufactured in the United States of America

For Claire

CONTENTS

Editor's Preface

David Hering

AND BUT SO we come to the commencement of what I suppose we should call Wallace Studies. The book you hold in your hands represents the fruits of an event that took place on 29–30 July 2009 in the University of Liverpool during which academics, researchers, and independent scholars from across the world met to discuss the work of David Foster Wallace. To the best of my knowledge, this represented the first international academic conference devoted solely to Wallace's writing, and the enthusiasm was both infectious and overwhelming.

It is an unhappy but true fact that when a writer dies, the fact of the end of their work effectively seals their canon and provides readers and academics with a complete body of literature to digest and analyze. One thing that distinguishes Wallace's desperately sad passing is that many of his readers were vocal in the weeks and months after his death about their belief that, at the age of 46, Wallace still had many great works within him. This led to two things: an immediate return by readers to his canon to re-read and appreciate the works that he did write, and a growing acknowledgement that Wallace produced a body of work in his two decades as a writer of such volume and magnitude that he should be considered a major U.S. writer of the twentieth century. Also revealed during my organization of the July 2009 conference was the sheer number of scholars worldwide who had been working on Wallace before his death. It was also interesting to note that while many were working on what is generally acknowledged as his masterpiece, *Infinite Jest*, others were writing on earlier, critically neglected works such as *The Broom Of The System* or *Girl With Curious Hair*.

The conference itself was hands-down the most passionate and entertaining academic event I have ever attended. There was not only a sense that people were eager to be amongst other Wallace scholars to share ideas and discuss his writing, but also that, to quote one attendee, the event felt like "the gathering of a force," the beginning of a new area of literary studies devoted to Wallace's work. Within this book I aim to present to you some of the finest examples of this new wave of analysis and discussion.

What, then, of existing critical discussion of Wallace's work? We have Marshall Boswell's excellent monograph *Understanding David Foster Wallace*, the clearest delineation of Wallace's agenda and canon up to *Brief Interviews With Hideous Men*. We have Greg Carlisle's sumptuous and astonishingly detailed *Infinite Jest* study *Elegant Complexity*, a *Bloomsday Book* for our times if ever there was one, and another very good monograph on *Infinite Jest* by Stephen Burn. We also have a number of journal articles and theses, many of which have been helpfully collected by Nick Maniatis in his indispensable electronic archive on the Howling Fantods website, a touchstone for Wallace academics across the world.

Indeed, the importance of the online community must not be underestimated when it comes to a discussion of Wallace's work. The Wallace-l listserv and The Howling Fantods website were invaluable resources when it came to the organization of the conference and this collection, in terms of both the apparently limitless Wallace knowledge held by the individuals therein and also the sense of a community, peopled by academics and non-academics alike, dedicated to the preservation and discussion of Wallace's works.

The majority of published critical and academic writing to date has concentrated on Wallace's position in relation to irony and postmodernism, and his status as a "post-postmodern" author. At a Wallace Conference held by the City University of New York in November 2009 there was much good-humored debate over how to persuasively classify his work without ending up buried under a surfeit of "post-" prefixes. Moreover, both the Liverpool and New York conferences held the aim of presenting readings of the work that diverged from this traditional locating of Wallace, or which used this "post-postmodern" reading as a jumping-off point to explore hitherto unmapped regions of Wallace's writing.

Therefore one of the things I hope this collection will achieve is to communicate the vast number of contexts within which Wallace's work can be read. The papers in this book discuss Wallace in conjunction not only with his contemporaries and immediate predecessors but also with more unexpected writers such as Laurence

Sterne, Iris Murdoch, and George Berkeley, and you will also find academic analysis of Wallace's works alongside subjects as varied as trauma, geometry, and autism.

Another of my aims in compiling and editing this volume has been to present critical analysis that, in the spirit of Wallace's own criticism, is lucid, readable and inspires further exploration, and avoids the "obscurity and pretension" in certain variants of academic criticism that Wallace so disparaged in his essay "Authority and American Usage." In fact, and to my delight as an editor, the essays within this book are all examples of how to construct a rigorous and well-argued academic analysis without sinking into turgidity of language or jargon. Of course I realize now that as readers of Wallace, the contributors to this book most likely share that very same discomfort with such language as Wallace himself did.

I have organized the following essays in as broadly chronological order as possible in regards to Wallace's work, and where essays do not fit a chronological order, I have inserted them into the positions most sympathetic with the papers on either side. I feel that Wallace's canon—with its frequently articulated emphasis on personal and authorial development—is best studied chronologically, the better to understand his aims for his fictional and non-fictional project. Moreover, while *Infinite Jest* receives its due there is also, as stated above, extensive attention paid to Wallace's other works of fiction and non-fiction. We begin with Greg Carlisle's introduction, a passionate and very personal advocacy of the value of reading and teaching Wallace's work. I hope you will find this collection as stimulating and engaging as a reader as I did as an editor.

David Hering,
Liverpool
January 2010.

Introduction: Consider David Foster Wallace

Greg Carlisle

What is extraordinary about David Foster Wallace is that his commitment to his readers exceeded even his incomparable intellectual gifts. Wallace took nothing for granted and processed everything through the complex filter of his own high-stakes values: the techniques of postmodern fiction, popular attitudes about television, his motives for writing, hip cynicism, eating lobster, everything. His philosophy of compassion for human beings in general, one of the qualities that makes his work so valuable, is spelled out simply and beautifully in his 2005 commencement speech to Kenyon College, published in 2009 as *This Is Water.* He was aware of the dark water in which we swim and tried to help us become aware not just of the water but of the other swimmers, too.

As early as 1993, his reader-centered philosophy concerning the purposes of fiction was spelled out eloquently in a seminal interview with Larry McCaffery that appeared in the *Review of Contemporary Fiction.* A sampling of quotes from that 1993 interview goes a long way toward justifying the value of studying and teaching Wallace's work. Concerning what fiction should do for the reader, he said:

> I strongly suspect a big part of real art fiction's job is to aggravate this sense of entrapment and loneliness and death in people, to move people to countenance it, since any possible human redemption requires us first to face what's dreadful, what we want to deny. [...] If you operate, which most of us do, from the premise that there are things about the contemporary U.S. that make it distinctively hard to be a real human being, then maybe half of fiction's job is to dramatize what it is that makes it tough. The other half is to dramatize the fact that we still "are" human beings, now. Or can be. (136, 131)

Wallace wanted us to see the complexity of things we take for granted, to remind us that the communication we receive is heavily mediated, and to create work for us to do:

One new context is to take something almost narcotizingly banal
—it's hard to think of anything more banal than a U.S. game
show . . . —and try to reconfigure it in a way that reveals what a
tense, strange, convoluted set of human interactions the final
banal product is. [...]But what [Wallace's game show story
"Little Expressionless Animals," is] really trying to do is just the
opposite of TV—it's trying to prohibit the reader from forgetting
that she's receiving heavily mediated data, that this process is a
relationship between the writer's consciousness and her own,
and that in order for it to be anything like a full human
relationship, she's going to have to put in her share of the
linguistic work. (141, 138)

Wallace's writing was playful and chaotic, but it was also highly
structured; and he believed that good writing required the writer to be
both skillful and open:

There's an unignorable line between demonstrating skill and
charm to gain trust for the story vs. simple showing off. It can
become an exercise in trying to get the reader to like and admire
you instead of an exercise in creative art [...]It seems like the big
distinction between good art and so-so art lies somewhere in the
art's heart's purpose, the agenda of the consciousness behind the
text. It's got something to do with love. With having the
discipline to talk out of the part of yourself that can love instead
of the part that just wants to be loved. (130, 148)

Obviously Wallace is not unique in experimenting with the
structure of fiction and in caring for his readers, but there is a passionate
intensity and sensitivity and self-consciousness about him which
exacerbates both his attention to detail and to fair characterization and
his awareness of the reader. These are the qualities that set him apart
and make his work unique enough to be called by Marshall Boswell a
"third wave of modernism" (*Understanding* 1), changing the scope of
fiction just as Joyce and Barth did before him.

Because of Wallace's super-sensitivity to the needs of the story
and the reader, his fear of showing off just for attention, and his
commitment to his fictional mission, he achieves a more heterogeneous
mix of formal innovation and emotional quality than his literary
forbears. In *Infinite Jest*, Wallace's character Joelle van Dyne,

commenting on the oeuvre of her mentor, experimental filmmaker Jim Incandenza, says that it was "the work of a brilliant optician and technician who was an amateur at any kind of real communication," that it had "no narrative movement toward a real story; no emotional movement toward an audience," but that there were "flashes of something" in the work (740). I do not ascribe to the cliché that experimental artists leave us cold, but I would say that, while both Wallace and his forbears provide a wealth of intellectual pleasures to their readers, the emotional heat of Wallace's forbears does indeed come in flickers and flashes while Wallace's heat is consistent.

For me, Wallace is funnier than his forbears—Joyce, Beckett, Gaddis, Barth, Pynchon, and DeLillo—and also more intense; and funny and intense at the same time. Think of the eschaton scene in *Infinite Jest*, where young children play a nuclear-conflagration game with tennis balls, which is both engaging and hilarious because Wallace has spent pages detailing the set-up of the game with geekish obsession. Then real violence erupts, and the upperclassmen mentors are too compromised by illicit substances to intervene, and the whole thing gets real serious and ominous even as some of the violence becomes farcical and cartoonish. And I am in that game with those kids, and I am watching it with the mentors, and I desperately want to know what happens to everyone, and I am laughing at the cartoonish quality of it, and I am getting a chill from Wallace's description of a whistle, a siren, and falling snow. It's so much fun, I'm not conscious of the work I'm doing flipping from main text to endnotes and trying to follow shifting narrative perspectives, calculus, game rules, and today's game scenario. I see that a paragraph is going on for pages, but I don't stop and think about that stylistically until I take a break from reading. And I don't realize that a sentence has gone on for 200 words or more because it's parsed so perfectly and the syntax sounds so natural in my head that I don't notice its length until I re-read it. I always know what is happening, no matter how convoluted the action. I may have to work to make sense of how the action fits into the larger context of the story, but the action itself is clear (or clearly ambiguous, as Wallace often intends) because the details of the action have been exhaustively described with self-conscious care and yet are still entertaining to a degree I haven't seen before.

After finishing long novels by the authors cited above, I thought "I'd like to read this again someday"; after finishing *Infinite Jest,* I thought, "I want to read this again right now." That's why I decided to write my study *Elegant Complexity*—I would have an excuse to savor that text continuously for several years. It's rare that an author of fiction inspires me to do additional reading, but if not for Wallace, I wouldn't have read many of the authors I cited above. I ordered McCaffery's Vollmann anthology because of the compliments Wallace gave Vollmann in the McCaffery interview I revisited in writing this introduction. I spent 14 months trying to understand Cahoone's 600-page anthology of modern and postmodern thought because Wallace made me want to know more about it. This is his value: he creates work for the reader that is fun and challenging, and he makes you want to research and to explore. His work is both self-conscious and other-oriented, so detailed and so clearly like a conversation he's initiating with the reader—an invitation to collaboration—that when you read his fiction, you identify with the characters so much that often it seems like you're an actor playing the roles that you're reading.

Wallace's ability to create this sense of intense intimacy in his writing is what has garnered him a legion of devoted, obsessed fans. There is a unique quality about his fan base. Wallace's philosophy and writing style prompt both serious literary criticism and regular human conversation. Quite frequently the online listserv wallace-l discusses items of personal interest and offers opinions about general topics that have nothing to do with Wallace's work, not an uncommon practice for internet communities but certainly uncommon for communities devoted to single literary figures that generally stick to more aesthetic topics. There also seems to be more interaction between electronic and academic communities on the subject of Wallace's work than is standard. Wallace's journalism often seems even more intimate than his fiction, given that he is usually directly addressing the reader. This is why Wallace aficionados often suggest that new readers start with one of his essay collections before moving on to his fiction. I don't think we can get a complete appreciation of the value of Wallace's fiction and the relationship he creates with his readers without also considering his other work: his journalism, interviews, and critical and philosophical writing.

To date, Wallace has not been taught extensively in the classroom. There are several reasons for this. First, he is a relatively new author, canonically speaking, his first major work being published in 1987. And although there are several academic articles and theses available on the internet, only a handful of books about Wallace's work have been published, half of them guidebooks for *Infinite Jest*. Perhaps the biggest obstacle to teaching Wallace is that his work is shifting the way we think about reading and writing fiction so much that we don't know how to talk about it yet. Jon Baskin, in the recent first issue of the Chicago-based journal, *The Point*, writes eloquently about this obstacle and ties it to Wallace's conversational approach:

> For Wittgenstein, the point of the philosophical "conversation" was to address confusions intrinsic to his reader's language and way of life. Rather than one "philosophical method," he advanced in the *Investigations* a variety of techniques for addressing various confusions, "like different therapies."

> Wallace attempted to enact such a conversation in his art. He would borrow from the *Investigations* not only themes—solipsism, language, meaning—but also the theoretical bulwark for a literature that was simultaneously challenging and *therapeutic* in the Wittgensteinian sense. The therapy was necessary and even urgent for a readership which, Wallace believed, had internalized not only postmodernism's theoretical prejudices but also its involute habits of thought. The millennial subject was addicted to the same pathologies he was desperate to escape; nowhere was this more evident than in the difficulty literary critics had in responding meaningfully to Wallace's books. What Wallace wanted to "share" most was a way out. But he would start with his readers, in the middle. The maze of contemporary thinking would have to be dismantled from within. (Baskin)

One technique that Wallace has used across his body of work is to leave climactic events unresolved or undefined, a technique I wrote about in the Wallace tribute section of *Sonora Review* 55/56. We can see this technique in his earliest work, in *Infinite Jest*, and in his later writings, too. Although Wallace isn't the first author to digress from the standard crisis-climax-denouement structure, the degree to which he intensifies this lack of resolution is quite unique, working a plot sequence into a frenzy of "chaotic stasis" (*Jest* 996) or truncating the narrative as it makes an exponential rise to a climax that we'll never reach. Far from being a gimmick, this technique mirrors the anxiety we feel in a culture that gives us a "confusion of choices" (*Jest* 752) or when we face an impossible choice. In tragedy, someone makes the impossible choice and nobly suffers the consequences. In Wallace's fiction, self-conscious characters are often frozen with indecision, suffering before a choice is even made. Although Wallace's use of footnotes and endnotes is usually cited as his method of creating work for the reader, those techniques are actually more for reminding the reader that what he or she is reading is mediated. It is this undefined-climax technique that allows Wallace to put the onus of completing or making decisions about the narrative on to each individual reader, perhaps giving them the perspective and practice for making decisions in their own lives.

If there is a way to encapsulate what Wallace was trying to do throughout his writing career, perhaps it is to say that he was honing in on what lies at the heart of the American malaise of the turn of the third millennium and trying to help us see the black and grained spots on our souls, an extremely difficult task because—repeating the earlier Baskin citation—the "millennial subject was addicted to the same pathologies he was desperate to escape" and the "maze of contemporary thinking would have to be dismantled from within" (Baskin). Looking back at Wallace's early work, I'm sure we would be able to articulate the beginnings of this project, although I believe Wallace was still a little distracted with the problem of breathing new life into tired conventions without compromising the truth and immediacy of what he wanted to express. However, with *Infinite Jest* form and content merge perfectly, and Wallace presents an extremely perceptive and funny and obsessive account of the American problem that is also extraordinarily sad. There is a crushing honesty and sense of loneliness about this book, and although chaotic and sprawling, it is immaculately structured; purposefully shifting time, location, and point of view to better mirror our frenetic culture, but with a rigorous thematic unity so subtle that critics have had trouble detecting it. It took me five years and 500 pages to articulate it in *Elegant Complexity*.

With *Infinite Jest*, Wallace takes a big step towards achieving the goals he stated in the McCaffery interview, because *Infinite Jest* has the potential to inspire people to face what they want to deny: their "sense of entrapment and loneliness." A measure of Wallace's success in fighting this pervasive sense of loneliness is evidenced by the number of electronic communities that sprang up in response to his work, many of which have as their exclusive subject the reading of *Infinite Jest*. The highest-profile electronic community to date has been the online group-read at infinitesummer.org. Thousands of people read and discussed *Infinite Jest* at the main site and on social networking sites such as Facebook and Twitter throughout Summer 2009.

I don't see how anyone couldn't identify with the characters in *Infinite Jest*, although most of the characters are extreme personalities: athletes-in-training, addicts, spies, assassins in wheelchairs. In his subsequent work, Wallace creates characters with which a wider range of his readership might identify. In "Mister Squishy" from *Oblivion*, Terry Schmidt is a product-testing facilitator, but he still experiences the same obsession and loneliness as the characters in *Infinite Jest*. Because *Oblivion* is a book of stories instead of a really long novel, there is a narrowing of focus that gives us the impression that Wallace is even closer than he was in *Infinite Jest* to his diagnosis of why we are obsessed and lonely and bored and what has brought about our state of oblivion. From what we know of *The Pale King* from D. T. Max's article in *The New Yorker*, Wallace's stylistic flair becomes even more subtle; and his characters, I.R.S. agents, have jobs that are even more isolating, helping his readers, many of whom perhaps spend their days relatively isolated at their work stations, better identify with the loneliness and boredom of his characters. There are indicators that *The Pale King* may even suggest more clearly and overtly than in Wallace's previous work treatment or therapy for our indecision, loneliness, and boredom; that it may help us choose our way out of oblivion; that it may be Wallace's best effort to "dramatize the fact that we still 'are' human beings, now. Or can be."

Max says that *The Pale King* is about "paying attention to things that matter" and quotes from one of Wallace's notes about the novel's idea: "Bliss—a second-by-second joy and gratitude at the gift of being alive, conscious—lies on the other side of crushing, crushing boredom" (qtd. in Max). Max characterizes the novel's ambitions this way: "It would show people a way to insulate themselves from the toxic freneticism of American life. It had to be emotionally engaged and morally sound, and to narrate boredom while obeying the physics of reading." The theme of the importance of making a choice which was expressed so eloquently by the spies Marathe and Steeply in *Infinite Jest* continues to resonate in *The Pale King*. One of the characters in the novel says, "If I wanted to matter—even just to myself—I would have to be less free, by deciding to choose in some kind of definite way" (Max). And perhaps the best example of the move from crippling indecision to the hope and bliss inherent in making a choice comes from these two excerpts from "Good People," a story that originally appeared in *The New Yorker* and that will be part of *The Pale King*:

> But sitting here beside this girl as unknown to him now as outer space, waiting for whatever she might say to unfreeze him, now he felt like he could see the edge or outline of what a real vision of Hell might be. It was of two great and terrible armies within himself, opposed and facing each other, silent. There would be battle but no victor. Or never a battle—the armies would stay like that, motionless, looking across at each other, and seeing therein something so different and alien from themselves that they could not understand, could not hear each other's speech as even words or read anything from what their face looked like, frozen like that, opposed and uncomprehending, for all human time. Two-hearted, a hypocrite to yourself either way. ("Good People")

Hesse-Steppenwolf

But then Wallace ends the story with this passage:

> There on the table, neither frozen nor yet moving, Lane Dean, Jr., sees all this, and is moved with pity, and also with something more, something without any name he knows, that is given to him in the form of a question that never once in all the long week's thinking and division had even so much as occurred—why is he so sure he doesn't love her? Why is one kind of love any different? What if he has no earthly idea what love is? What would even Jesus do? For it was just now he felt her two small strong soft hands on his, to turn him. What if he was just afraid, if the truth was no more than this, and if what to pray for was

not even love but simple courage, to meet both her eyes as she says it and trust his heart?

We've got to figure out how to get Wallace taught in more classrooms and how to expand the Wallace discussion in those classrooms beyond just a story or two at the end of the semester. I don't think it's presumptuous or audacious to suggest that we make more room in our curricula for Wallace; we still seem to want to characterize Wallace as a young upstart rebel (which is natural given the enthusiasm and passion in his writing), but he was 46 and in his third decade of publication when he died. We've been admiring and eulogizing him, which is of course appropriate, but now the time has come to evolve the critical conversation about Wallace and to champion him for what he is: the most important author of the late 20th and early 21st centuries. I think a world in which Wallace is a household name would be a more mindful, passionate, and compassionate world. It's up to us now to continue the conversation he started.

How do we do this? What tools already exist, and what else do we need? We have a wealth of important and thoughtful commentary on Wallace's work, much of it quite rigorous and specific, but it is spread out in several individual literary journals, a small number of books, and various places on the internet. Nick Maniatis of Canberra, Australia, has done an amazing job of collecting anything and everything about Wallace and providing links to much of the criticism available online at his award-winning site, thehowlingfantods.com.

Most of the commentary previously available has been on the content of Wallace's fiction and his thematic or philosophical interests, and it usually focuses on one work (often *Infinite Jest*) or one theme rather than taking a broad look at recurring themes and motifs across the body of his work. This has been a perfectly acceptable approach so far, because it's taken us a while to catch up and understand what Wallace was saying. I wrote *Elegant Complexity* in part because I wanted to understand and articulate the structure of *Infinite Jest*. I also pointed out as many intratextual connections as I could find and exhaustively identified instances of a set of recurring themes. I hope I've provided a resource that will help each new generation in their study of *Infinite Jest*, and I believe my book is a good resource for identifying themes common to all of Wallace's work. But as I continue to explore Wallace's work, I also want to take a cue from critics like Baskin, cited above, and attempt to discover more of what Wallace was trying to do with his fiction. Responding to Baskin's identification of Wallace's work as a conversation, Marie Mundaca, who did the interior book design for Wallace's collection *Oblivion*, posted this:

> In a way, [Wallace's] readers are putting the sweat-equity into a start-up that will hopefully break free of the cynicism and stagnation of contemporary thought. It really saddens me that I only started to realize this with [*Oblivion*], because *Infinite Jest* and *A Supposedly Fun Thing I'll Never Do Again* were so entertaining I was only processing the deeper message on a sort of subconscious level. I knew there was something there, something telling me how to think about not being trapped in my head, but it was difficult for me to access consciously. (Mundaca, "Posting on Wallace-l")

I think we're all starting to come to realizations like this and that we should begin initiating this conscious access. I've just started work on a book about *Oblivion*, and this time in addition to identifying structures and themes, I want to try and identify how Wallace's tactics for achieving his literary goals change from *Infinite Jest* to *Oblivion* to *The Pale King*. Something else we can do is start taking a closer look at the form and structure of Wallace's writing. In addition to my article on Wallace's unresolved-climax technique, *Sonora Review* 55/56 included a piece by Sven Birkerts on Wallace's style and his use of the sentence.

My favorite approach for teaching Wallace is what Kathleen Fitzpatrick, Wallace's colleague at Pomona College, did in Spring 2009. She taught a course called *David Foster Wallace* in which she assigned her students to read all of his books, one at a time except for *Infinite Jest* which was assigned in 100-page chunks beginning about a month into the class. She created a blog so her students could discuss what they read and expand on what was said in class, and the students created an electronic resource for posterity as the final project of the class. The students provided impressive commentary, and Fitzpatrick's enthusiasm and sense of academic rejuvenation were evident in her

comments about the class online. This is all on Fitzpatrick's website[1] so
we have a model for future classes.

I believe Fitzpatrick's choice to include all of Wallace's work,
fiction and non-fiction, is the right choice. We need to study everything
he published as well as interviews and critical assessments of his work,
and we need to have a forum for generating new critical assessments.
What we must not do, and something that I hope subsides as we get
further away from the shock of his death, is view all of his writings and
interviews through the lens of his suicide. I'll cite from a wallace-l post
by George Carr that makes this point eloquently and succinctly:

> [Wallace] was ill, and he died from his illness. Trying to re-
> imagine his death as a volitional act that bears on his morality or
> his desires about how to live in the world is a misunderstanding.
> (Carr)[2]

We have excellent online resources with Maniatis's site,
thehowlingfantods.com, and the wallace-l listserv and various blogs
and other sites devoted to Wallace, but to focus and centralize and
cross-reference the wealth of critical ideas that are out there, I think we
need to start generating more print resources as well. We know that a
volume of Wallace's uncollected work is coming after *The Pale King*,
which will give this material a wider audience and perhaps prompt
more discussion of the evolution of Wallace's project. When Bonnie
Nadell, Wallace's lifelong literary agent, mentioned this upcoming
collection in May 2009 at the Wallace tribute event at the University of
Arizona that coincided with the publication of *Sonora Review* 55/56,
Marshall Boswell made a plea for a *Wallace Reader*, a sampling of his
published work that would bring Wallace a wider audience, citing the
boost in readership this type of anthology gave Faulkner. I think that's
a great idea. We should collect Wallace's interviews, too. We should
collect the best of what is online in print format, too. Finally, we should
have a *Wallace Quarterly*. It is not too soon to have this. A *Wallace
Quarterly* would give us a regular forum for continuing the critical

---

[1] http://machines.pomona.edu/166-2009/

[2] See Works Cited for full reference.

conversation about Wallace's work and would provide a central, structured locus for that formal conversation.

If our responses to Wallace in our electronic communities can spill out into our classrooms, into more print resources, and into conferences like this one, I think we stand a good chance of bringing Wallace's conversation to a wider readership. The Wallace events and conferences in 2009 are a great start to what I hope will be regular face-to-face meetings of the Wallace community that strengthen our long-standing academic and electronic connections. This community is vital to continuing and expanding the conversations Wallace started with his readers. Let's keep talking.

The Book, the Broom and the Ladder: Philosophical Groundings in the Work of David Foster Wallace

Clare Hayes-Brady

Introduction

"Some words can literally make things real" (285). So says Rick Vigorous, one of the more voluble characters in David Foster Wallace's *The Broom of the System*. Rick is a character obsessed with words, like his paramour, the befuddled protagonist Lenore Beadsman. This quixotic first novel has been critically overlooked, with only sundry reviews and a single chapter in Marshall Boswell's *Understanding David Foster Wallace* (2003) in its critical retinue. It is certainly less of a heavyweight, both literally and figuratively, than its mammoth successor, *Infinite Jest*, which appeared in 1996, but was in many ways a crucially important text—more important, arguably, than *Infinite Jest*—to understanding the trajectory of Wallace's career and its importance for American and international literature. Wallace wrote *The Broom of the System* as an undergraduate at Amherst, where he was double majoring in Philosophy and English. *Broom*, it appears, was his attempt to get to grips with the challenging branch of linguistic philosophy known as modal logic. Developing and perfecting a philosophy of language through his writing was of primary importance to Wallace as an artist and philosopher. Wallace had previously studied mathematics, and the elegant clarity of mathematics as a universal language appears to have attracted him to the study of modal logic, which sought to discover a way to refine ambiguity out of human communication. In one guise or another, this pursuit was an important influence on Wallace's writing right to the last.

The purpose of this essay is to try to bring *The Broom of the System* out of the critical shade by outlining its vital place in Wallace's corpus. It is my contention that the primary importance of *Broom* is in the way it explores the philosophy of language that so intrigued its author. I further contend that this exploration of philosophy introduced many of the central philosophical concerns that would occupy Wallace over the whole course of his career. This early engagement of Wallace's with varying theories of language will here be explored with reference to three twentieth-century philosophers of language: Ludwig Wittgenstein, Paul Ricoeur and Richard Rorty. The theories of these influential thinkers provide a useful starting point from which to consider the development of Wallace's ultimately unique philosophical standpoint. The relevant ideas of each philosopher will be outlined independently, then investigated for their relevance to *The Broom of the System*. It will also be briefly shown that the ideas articulated at this early stage of Wallace's writing persisted in his later work. Finally, an argument will be advanced for recasting *The Broom of the System* as more than a precocious first novel, and viewing it instead as a self-aware declaration of artistic intent.

Wittgenstein

The major, or at least most visible, philosophical influence in *Broom* is of course Ludwig Wittgenstein. Wittgenstein appears as a shadow character, with Lenore's great-grandmother and namesake allegedly having studied under the illustrious philosopher during his last days at Cambridge. The issues of truth and authenticity—and clarity in particular—that occupied Wittgenstein are visible in *Broom* at every turn. Wittgenstein's early work, the *Tractatus Logico-Philosophicus*, claimed to offer an approach to language that avoided ambiguity altogether. Wittgenstein later repudiated this claim and more or less reversed his position on language. Where his early work saw language as simple and direct, his later work assumed a much more nuanced view, in which multiple meanings were inevitable and enriching, and in which the function of language changed with circumstances. Wittgenstein's influence on *Broom* is pervasive, partly because it is explicit. It is hard to avoid thinking of Wittgenstein's confused and self-negating attitude to language as we read about the linguistic struggles of Lenore Beadsman and her cohorts. However, while it is true that Wittgenstein is everywhere in this novel, there are three specific points of his philosophy that underlie and inform *The Broom of the System*.

Firstly, it is important to look at the way in which Wallace use' names. Wittgenstein founded his original theory of language on th concept of ostensive naming—i.e., that we learn language by means of names and build systems of communication around names. This was developed into the meaning-as-use concept, which Wittgenstein—and Wallace, in the novel—explained with the analogy of a broom: what is the essence, he asks, of broomness? What is its fully-analyzed proposition? It is the fact, he argues, that we use it as a broom. If we use a name for something specific, that name comes to signify the use of that something. Its use *becomes* its meaning. Lenore Beadsman's shared name is no coincidence, and in Wittgensteinian terms indicates that the two Lenores occupy a shared philosophical space, meaning that Lenore Jr.'s name, and by extension her meaning, belongs to and is mediated by someone else, namely her great-grandmother. This is highlighted early in the text, when Lenore Jr. visits Shaker Heights Nursing Home and offends the receptionist by insisting that her name is Lenore Beadsman. The receptionist thinks that Lenore is making a joke in very poor taste, given that Lenore Beadsman (Sr.) has just disappeared (*Broom* 29). The doubling of Lenore's name, while it is used here to comedic effect, highlights the fact that her identity is undifferentiated, and her great-grandmother's disappearance provides her, in a roundabout way, with the means to assume her name. Lenore Sr.'s life in the nursing home is one without meaning, as Lenore Jr.'s father points out. As such, she does not need her name. By literally disappearing, then, Lenore Sr. abandons her name to the meaningful Lenore (that is, the younger Lenore), who is then free to take it on and mould her autonomous identity.

However, things—as ever with Wallace—are not quite that simple. Where Wittgenstein's early logic would allow Lenore's identity to be confirmed by her mere possession of the name, Wallace challenges the simply ostensive. Lenore has to stabilize the set of features to which her name becomes the referent—i.e., she has to establish her Lenore-ness before the name will rest comfortably and the mystery of the whereabouts of Gramma Lenore, as Lenore Jr. significantly nicknames the older woman, can be solved. Important to note here is the fact that Gramma Lenore does not return to the narrative, leaving Lenore in sole possession of the title. It seems that Wallace will not allow his characters to appropriate terms they have not fully earned. This is something he will use later, particularly in the short fiction, where the narrators often misappropriate a tone or register, to the detriment of their narrative, which will be explored a little later.

In contrast to Lenore's double—or perhaps half—name, her brother LaVache takes on several names: Stoney, which he renounces, LaVache, and the Antichrist. When Lenore visits him at university, he explains that he uses these nicknames to distance himself from Stonecipher, his given name. By means of the nicknames he uses, he is able to demarcate clearly his own identity, as Lenore finds herself unable to do at the book's opening. "As the Antichrist," he explains to Lenore, "[...] it's gloriously clear where I leave off and others begin" (*Broom* 250). His plethora of nicknames indicates his absolute comfort in his own identity, and his ability to accept the mutability of language. It is he who suggests most explicitly that Lenore should cease her quest for linguistic certainty when they discuss the two antinomies that Gramma Lenore has left in the wake of her disappearance. He explains to Lenore that the antinomies demonstrate the basic unreliability of language and that to consider too deeply the significance of certain problems is at best futile and at worst dangerous. "KA-BLAM," he says. "There go the old crania" (248). In this sense LaVache represents the later Wittgenstein, who accepted that language is unstable and that it is necessary to move with it rather than seek to pin it down as Lenore does. This, I believe, is central to Wallace's philosophy of language as a whole: the pluralist nature and inherent instability of language is something to be celebrated rather than resisted. It is this, I think, that accounts for Wallace's great variety of narrative voices: he respects the various cracks and hollows in his characters' vocabularies. In this regard Wallace's development as a philosopher mirrored Wittgenstein's: he moved from seeking the order of the mathematical in language, as in his undergraduate thesis, to embracing its pluralist potential.

Besides the crucial position of naming to making sense of the world, two other ideas of Wittgenstein's are necessary to an understanding of *The Broom of the System*. These are language games and family resemblances. The two concepts are intimately connected. Language games, introduced in *Philosophical Investigations*, were Wittgenstein's solution to the problem of ostensive definition, a logical extension of the meaning-as-use paradigm. If meaning comes from use, he argued, then context must be important. The ostensive approach, which did not look at context, falls short at this point. Language, therefore, in Wittgenstein's later view, was predicated on games, in which the different uses of words establish different but connected sets of rules. Wittgenstein gave the example of a chessboard, with a player who is unfamiliar with the game. If this player is shown a piece and told "this is the king," that statement, in order to have any utility at all, must presuppose a familiarity with the rules of the game, the context within which the "king" exists. Wittgenstein gives a list of examples, and it leads to the question of what they have in common, these language games. Here Wittgenstein proposes the idea of "family resemblances": there may not be one defining feature of language. Instead, language uses resemble each other in a wide variety of ways but with no central *sine qua non* feature. Wittgenstein also suggests that language itself—the whole panoply of language functions and aims and uses—be regarded as a language game in itself, a sort of multi-athlon of all the sub-games.

In light of these two theories, it is worth noting the narrative importance of both games and families in *Broom*. The two antinomies that appear in the text, for example, the linguistic puzzles that appear at important points in the novel, are distinct nods to language games that function as signposts on Lenore's meandering path. Games and artificiality are heavily emphasized throughout *Broom*, and Lenore's progress towards comprehending the rules of the various games by which she lives her life maps on to the philosopher's journey towards understanding the workings of language. Family is also a dominant feature; Lenore's family owns most of the city in which she lives. Family looms inescapably throughout the text, while Lenore struggles to free herself from its oppressive influence as LaVache has done. Wittgenstein's presence is therefore both implicit and explicit in the novel, and his theories are explored in both form and content. While much of the exploration is tongue-in-cheek, it is clear that Wittgenstein was a figure of great importance from the earliest days of Wallace's writing career.

Ricoeur

In 1985, Paul Ricoeur gave a series of lectures entitled "Oneself as Another," which were later published as a three-volume book. While Ricoeur is by no means as clear a presence in *The Broom of the System* as Wittgenstein, his ideas about of narrative identity, which were bound up in his overarching theory of language, were profoundly important for Wallace's emerging theories of language and self, and influenced his writing both stylistically and philosophically. Ricoeur challenged the idea of a unitary self, without reference to the world around it, but did not suggest that the self was entirely contingent, either. Instead, he proposed a dual identity, a self that found a balance between the *idem*, which provides the self with its spatio-temporal identity, the anti-Cartesian element that is a function of its culture and surroundings, the inherited and imposed, and the *ipse*, which is the unique, spontaneous element of the character, the creative and self-determining. In Ricoeur's conception of the self, "the narrative constructs the identity of the character" (Ricoeur 195); we use stories about ourselves to make sense of the world and our place in it. The concept of narrative identity as identified here is suggested and complemented by the idea of a dual-self in constant conflict. The *idem* takes its cue from the Latin for "same," and it is the part of the individual that relates to other people, the commonalities that give rise to societies, and indeed the need for language. The *ipse*, by contrast, is self-sufficient and self-referencing, the element of character that makes us different from each other. There is a common platitude in English: "what unites us is greater than what divides us." If we look more closely at this conventional phrase, we can discern the truth of Ricoeur's statement, though he referred to the French language. While it may be the case that the one outweighs the other, it is imperative that there should be elements of both similarity and difference. If the self consisted only of *idem*, the similarity that unites us, individuality would be a non-concept, and there would therefore be no use for the concept of other. By the same token, if the self consisted purely of *ipse*, the spontaneity and difference that divides us, difference would be a useless concept because there would be no similarity to impose hierarchy on difference. The salient point is that self and other are not purely oppositional. Quite the contrary; they are rather interdependent and mutually defining.[1]

The latter strand of this dual identity, the *idem*, is visible in Lenore Beadsman early on, in the form of her obsession with story. In the absence of a solid *ipse*, Lenore is trying to compensate with the strength of her *idem* by seeking story after story with which to identify. Her lover, the paranoid editor—a significant job, under the circumstances—uses narrative to control and possess Lenore. He, too, uses narrative to compensate, in his case for his inadequacy as a lover. Rick seeks to position himself as the necessary other to Lenore's self by supplying her with endless narrative. Unable to fulfill Lenore sexually, and thus achieve the meaning he desires as Lenore's lover, Rick seeks to impose a meaning on her with him as the referent, and so to possess her. Rick's influence over Lenore wanes as the story progresses and is superseded entirely by the figure of Andy Lang, who does not tell Lenore stories but listens to her talk about herself. Lenore's removal of herself from Rick's sphere of influence indicates that she is achieving a balance between *ipse* and *idem*, thus allowing her to use narrative rather than depend on it. Lang's non-literary listening ear makes him a "bestower of validity" (*Broom* 346) as Lenore's pseudotherapist calls him. The progress of their relationship is appropriately silent. This Ricoeurian theme of self-construction is visible in Wallace's later work, where he tends to avoid omniscient narration in favor of dialogue, first person narration, or internal-monologue-style third-person narration, never giving away more than his characters would. As such, he allows his characters the freedom to form their own narrative identities, rather than imposing his authorial will on them. This respect for his characters is a large part of what makes them so memorable and so plausible. An important effect of this style is the capacity mentioned earlier of stories to fall in on themselves owing to Wallace's absolute mimesis of flawed voices. This narrative structure—what I call Wallace's "skeletal narrative," which involves the undermining and eventual collapse of a

---

1 Such an idea holds peculiar resonance for an American writer, living in a country whose creed is E Pluribus Unum, which celebrates both unity and diversity. The formation of American identity concerned Wallace consistently throughout his career. This is an aspect of Wallace's writing and American writing in general that merits further consideration, given its bearing on the exceptionalist paradigm.

surface narrative to reveal the "true" or "real" story, by means of jarring elements planted within the narrative voice itself—was something that Wallace would develop and refine over the whole course of his career, and was one of the great innovations of his writing.

Rorty

Richard Rorty, a fashionable thinker in the late twentieth century, distinguished between philosophy as a pursuit, of which he approved, and Philosophy as a discipline, of which he was critical, even scathing. This position earned him criticism, along with the label of Anti-Philosopher for his objection to the academic isolation of philosophy. Rorty held that philosophical thought should be for everyone, claiming that the problems of academic Philosophy were in fact problems of language. Rorty's incurably populist attitude was one that would have held great appeal to the democratically-minded Wallace, as the most cursory look at his essays will attest. Rorty believed that truth was a matter of construction, social and personal, and that language was critically important to this construction. His best-known work is on contingency, which he held to be the foundation of society. The influential 1979 book, *Philosophy and the Mirror of Nature*, which of course provided the title for Wallace's short story of the same name, challenged the tradition of thinking of the mind as a mirror of reality, extending the argument to challenge the idea that language should in some way represent the world exactly as it is, if such could be discovered. He found fault with the idea that Philosophy could seek this sort of representation at all, claiming that as Philosophy evolved, "philosophical problems appeared, disappeared, or changed shape, as a result of new assumptions or vocabularies" (*Philosophy* xiii). To put it simply, philosophical problems are the direct offshoot of Philosophical vocabularies. Since vocabularies are incommensurable, Rorty proposes the term "edification" to mean the project of finding new and better vocabularies, which "may consist in the hermeneutic activity of making connections between our own culture and some exotic culture or historical period [...] but may instead consist in the 'poetic' activity of thinking up such new aims" (*Philosophy* 360). The point of this project of edification, he goes on to suggest, is "to keep the conversation going rather than to find objective truth" (*Philosophy* 377).

The Broom of the System does not reveal any intelligible truth at its close, does not tidy up neatly in a "what really happened" scene. Instead, the characters, and also the readers, are left to construct their own version of what happens. This may be said to follow Rorty's hypothesis of contingent, constructed truth.

Coping with a world of constructed truth is a challenge that Wallace sets his characters. Some succeed and some fail. Those that succeed, as Lenore Beadsman learns to do, meet the criteria set out by Richard Rorty for liberal ironism. Rorty proposes this as the only way of dealing successfully with the contingency and mutability of the world and of language in the book *Contingency, Irony and Solidarity* (1989). While Lenore develops over the novel to a point at which she can be called a liberal ironist, the best example of this in *The Broom of the System* is LaVache, as we have already seen, who could be regarded as an avatar of sorts for Wallace himself; the brilliant, difficult student of philosophy at Amherst, manipulating language and nomenclature to fit in with his surroundings. Later, in *Infinite Jest*, Orin Incandenza demonstrates these same characteristics. There are many characters who do not display comfort within the shifting boundaries of language, such as many of the narrators of the short stories, particularly the narrator of "Philosophy and the Mirror of Nature" and the narrator of "Oblivion." These serve as good examples of the skeletal narrative structure already mentioned. Where the characters are unable to manipulate language skillfully, language betrays them. In both of these stories, something important is being concealed, and the narrators' lack of mastery of themselves and their vocabularies allows the subtle revelation of what they seek to hide. "Oblivion," a study in dubious consciousness and the pitfalls of perception, deals with what we think we know and how our mind can play tricks if we try to hold too tightly to stability and certainty. "Philosophy and the Mirror of Nature," the most overtly Rortian of Wallace's stories, explores the individual construction of truth and the means by which we betray ourselves in language. This story was originally published in 1998, two years after *Infinite Jest*, in the quarterly magazine *McSweeneys*, under the title " Yet Another Example of the Porousness of Certain Borders (VIII)." While Wallace's philosophy parallels Rorty's quite tidily in the earlier part of his career, it begins to depart from Rortian thinking during what has come to be regarded as Wallace's middle period, beginning around the publication of *Infinite Jest* in 1996, and notably with the original publication of the spider story in 1998. The subsequent alteration of the title to "Philosophy and the Mirror of Nature" serves to highlight Wallace's engagement with and departure from Rorty's ideas. Where Rorty rejected outright the possibility of any sort of truth, Wallace began, at least implicitly, to espouse a philosophy of his own, which allowed that there are truths we do not wish to share which will nonetheless reveal themselves despite our best efforts. As regards ineffable or cosmic truths, Wallace did not fall clearly on one side or the other, but he took account of deceit, making his philosophy more realistic than Rorty's, which, along with both Ricoeur and Wittgenstein, more or less glossed over the philosophical implications of willful or attempted deceit.

Conclusion

While the short stories mentioned in the foregoing sections, along with *The Broom of the System*, highlight Wallace's literary innovation, it is arguable that they also serve a second and more important purpose. These stories mirror more accurately than most literary forms the way in which stories are imparted and developed in real life. It is, for example, difficult to imagine the narrator of "Philosophy and the Mirror of Nature" sitting on the bus and explaining in a calm and linear way to a stranger that he accidentally killed a child, but it is perhaps more plausible that such a life-changing event should weigh on the mind and emerge in fits and starts in an otherwise innocuous conversation or monologue. While neither the narrators' interlocutor nor the stories' circumstances are made clear, the story is written in a pseudo conversational yet slightly stilted style that would suggest a conversation with a stranger or relatively new acquaintance. The tone of the piece does not match the more classical diary-style story of confession like, for example, Tobias Wolff's "Hunters in the Snow" and others like it. As such, the story, which appears to be part of a conversation or attended monologue, emerges in a much more lifelike way than Wolff's elegant, context-less stories. Lenore Beadsman's erratic progress towards equipoise and self-reliance is similarly anti-linear, in a way that accommodates the theories of

Ricoeur and Rorty. Interestingly, Wallace tends to be unclear as to the background of his stories, particularly short stories: is the narrator talking to someone specific or to themselves? Where an interlocutor is acknowledged, they are often silent, acting as sounding-board or therapist, a trait particularly visible in *Brief Interviews With Hideous Men*. It seems that Wallace, like Hemingway, sought to lay bare the act of communication, free from context or prejudice. Wallace's explicit definition of writing as "an act of communication" (*Supposedly* 144) is therefore significant indeed. It suggests that Wallace was not so much fine-tuning the craft of storytelling as he was investigating the reality of communication.

While the theories Wallace investigated in his work are clear and useful, they are not presented uncritically. As earlier suggested, Wallace moved quite decisively beyond the philosophers whose work informed his early writing. Besides the different levels of truth discussed in the section on Rorty, Wallace magnified and examined the reality of language games and rules, taking their existence out of the philosophical realm and exploring their practical application. He also explored the implications of Ricoeur's theory of narrative identity. While this was not found wanting *per se*, it seems clear from *The Broom of the System* that Wallace regarded narrative identity as potentially dangerous, begging serious questions of identity and reality, such as the concerns expressed by Lenore in her therapy sessions about the nature of reality and the impossibility of a knowable, decisively real self. Another area in which Wallace engaged with the challenges of these ideas was in the case of liberal ironism. Where LaVache arguably exemplifies liberal ironism, he also hints at its darker side, which Sartre termed "meta-stability," in which sufferers become so inured to the contingency of life that they cease to take even their own existence seriously. I would argue that this could be termed the problem of post-modernism, and has artistic as well as existential repercussions. Wallace engaged with this issue as it affected both characters and literature right across his career, from *Broom* to *Oblivion*, and most directly in the early essay "E Unibus Pluram: Television and US Fiction." The challenge, as he saw it, was to halt the inward spiral of post-modern thought and stop literature turning into a closed system of endlessly self-referential trivia. This was a mission statement, made twice at the beginning of his career, in the character of Lenore and in the essay above, that Wallace would always follow.

In the *Tractatus Logico-Philosophicus*, Wittgenstein suggested that the philosophy of language he espoused was like a ladder (*Tractatus* 6.54, trans. Anscombe), which should be used to attain a clear view and then discarded. It seems that Wallace took this advice quite seriously. By engaging with the philosophical issues outlined here, he laid the foundations for a career that would investigate linguistic philosophy in a satisfying and interesting way, and finally move beyond investigation into original philosophical thought. Moreover, by challenging the ideas with which he engaged—by, as it were, discarding the ladder—Wallace was able to supersede the philosophical issues at hand, to rescue literature from a slow, circular death and revive it. Using the tenets of mutable language, Wallace was able to engineer a new and richer form of realism, a sort of liberal ironist's literature, which was at home with its own limitations. By embracing contingency, Wallace was able to represent the felt reality of the world in a new way, which has since been emulated by a number of millennial writers, most obviously Dave Eggers. Finally, by allowing and exploring the suggestion that much of what we know is constructed and contingent, Wallace was able to show that there are certain kinds of truth that are *not* created, and that while ineffable truth may well be beyond the grasp of the human mind, there is hope for at least some human truth in language, even if objective or cosmic truth is permanently out of our reach. This hope allowed literature to emerge from its cocoon of paralyzing postmodern meta-stability with the prospect of moving towards valid and valuable communication, a goal Wallace indisputably regarded as the highest aim of literature.

To conclude, I hope to have demonstrated here that this new project of realism is founded on the search for human truth and linguistic honesty, guided by the principle of communication and aware of its own necessary fallibility. It is further hoped that the writing of this generation will come to be seen not as the undirected hysteria of a generation bellowing to be heard above the noise, but rather the carefully modulated representation of world where noise has become the inescapable background, a world of what Wallace called "Total Noise" ("Deciderization" xix), in which to silence the constant hum would be to misrepresent reality. I contend that this representation is based upon a carefully developed philosophy that has its origins in Wallace's earliest work. To conclude, it seems clear to me that *The Broom of the System* deserves to be considered not as the juvenilia of a potentially talented author, but as the self-assured declaration of an artistic and philosophical project that would give rise not just to an impressive career, but also to a rebirth of American fiction.

A Blasted Region: David Foster Wallace's Man-made Landscapes

Graham Foster

Alan Bilton writes in his *Introduction to Contemporary American Fiction*, "The wilderness has always functioned in American literature as a trope of possibility or salvation, liberation from a corrupt and mercantile civilization" (13). Traditional American ideas of the wilderness depict the space as being devoid of cultural influence and as a location that can provide an escape from the rigors of the modern world. Characters are drawn to rural spaces on voyages of self-discovery, pilgrimages to experience nature in all its unrestricted glory. The "real" and sublime are available, if the city is fled and the mall is vacated. As Leo Marx writes,

> One has only to consider the titles which first come to mind from the classical canon of our literature—the American books admired most nowadays—to recognize that the theme of withdrawal from society into an idealized landscape is central to a remarkably large number of them. Again and again, the imagination of our most respected writers—one thinks of Cooper, Thoreau, Melville, Faulkner, Frost, Hemingway—has been set in motion by this impulse. (Marx 10)

To this list, we can add writers of the late twentieth century, such as Kerouac, Auster, McCarthy, Proulx and Coupland.[1] However, David Foster Wallace does not sit comfortably in the same list. My purpose in this paper is to discuss some of the ways in which Wallace defies theoretical ways of conceptualizing pastoral and deserted spaces.

The best example of this may be found in *The Broom of the System*. The Great Ohio Desert (The G.O.D.) has been constructed by the governor of Ohio in order to be "a point of savage reference for the good people of Ohio. A place to fear and love. A blasted region.

---

1 While Douglas Coupland is Canadian, it can be argued that he is documenting the American experience in his novels. Indeed, a great many of them take place in American locations and detail the lives of American characters.

Something to remind us of what we hewed out of" (*Broom* 54). The
governor's reasoning for building this desert in his native state chimes
with traditional literary ideas about the power of the American
landscape. He says:

> Guys, the state is getting soft. I can feel softness out there. It's
> getting to be one big suburb and industrial park and mall. Too
> much development. People are getting complacent. They're
> forgetting the way this state was historically hewn out of the
> wilderness. There's no more hewing. (*Broom* 53)

This quotation brings to mind the lure of the wilderness as a
literary theme, in novels such as Jack London's *Call of the Wild* or
Twain's *Adventures of Huckleberry Finn*. The wilderness, to the American
people, not only represents their historical struggle to tame the
landscape and settle, but also provides a provocative counterpoint to
the luxuries of modern living, a place with a seductive promise of
adventure and escape. As Jonathan Raban writes, "the true American
will not be long content with a life of rubber bones in the doghouse.
The unfettered prairie and our wolf-ancestors beckon" (Raban 36).
The governor of Ohio's view of the desert is atavistic, a space where
the people of the state can be reminded of their pioneer roots, and be
inspired to transcend their soft, suburban lives. His very idea is to
challenge the success of a state in which, "unemployment is low,
inflation is low, taxes haven't been raised in two years, pollution is way
down" (*Broom* 53).

However, despite using black sand to increase the "blastedness
aspect" and having "cacti and scorpions and the sun beating down,"
the desert does not end up fitting with the governor's atavistic ideals.
Later in the novel, Wallace presents the desert as a commercialized
space, countering *Baudrillard's* theory that the American desert has "a
radical lack of culture" (*America* 126). Baudrillard goes on to describe
the American desert as "void of all meaning, arbitrary and
inhuman", (*America* 127). In *The Broom of the System*, the desert is
constructed from the culture, built on the established ideals of the
American wilderness yet becoming a hyper-real version of them. At
the climax of the narrative, Lenore and Rick head to the desert, while
being followed by Obstat and Lang, but the desert is described as

having a "Boat Rental Center" where people can rent a "Great Ohio Desert Fish License" for a "truly criminal amount of money" (*Broom* 420). Earlier the desert is described as having "concession stands at the rim" (46) and it is necessary to purchase a "Wander Pass" in order to experience what the desert has to offer (143). The characters also seem to be disappointed that the desert does not offer an opportunity to experience authentic wilderness. Lenore states that, "the really desolate areas can get pretty crowded, of course, sometimes, so it's good to get there early, get as much wandering as you can in before noon" (143). Wang-Dang Lang is frustrated because "the whole thing's just gettin' too goddamn commercialized" (421). The desert is no longer "liberation from a corrupt and mercantile civilization," but merely another marketing opportunity—the last space that could be sold to the American public.

The G.O.D. is a theme park, a constructed fake designed to placate the American lust for wilderness, just as Disneyland is designed to placate the American lust for fantasy. Both the G.O.D. and Disneyland allow the customer to experience adventure without risking their safety. As Douglas Coupland writes in *Generation X*, "Adventure Without Risk is Disneyland" (169). This fake desert has also been built over natural, "real" wilderness, the Wayne National Forest—the governor has destroyed the forest in order to make way for his desert (*Broom* 54). Umberto Eco's comments on Disneyland can be applied to this. He writes: "Disneyland tells us that technology can give us more reality than nature can" (*Faith* 44). The Wayne National Forest is not deemed a sufficient expanse of wilderness to be "a point of savage reference." The desert has been tailor-made to distill the nature experience of the real wilderness, to "enhance the blastedness aspect" and to capture the "size, desolation, grandeur" of a real desert (*Broom* 56). While the Wayne National Forest, as with other parks in the American National Park System (NPS), is nature presented in a managed form, it exists to protect "natural processes and endangered species while providing baselines for measuring environmental change" (Dilsaver 269). So while the Wayne National Forest stands for preservation, the G.O.D. represents a managed wilderness that is destructive in its nature, a man-made landscape that dominates everything else.

desert as labyrinth ... to another in search of escape

cf. Calvino - one labyrinth

Graham Foster

Douglas Coupland comments on the manufacturing of wilderness in his non-fiction book *Polaroids from the Dead*, in which he writes of the Nitobe Japanese Gardens at the University of British Columbia, "it is a manufactured version of wilderness, like a seventeenth-century Disneyland" (81). The pastoral, in the writings of Thoreau and Hawthorne, has an Edenic quality. The garden brings a spiritual redemption for the writers, but as N. Katherine Hayles writes, "wilderness loses its power to authenticate our lives as soon as we try to take advantage of its redemptive potential" (375). The power of the G.O.D. is negated by its commercial foundation.

However, as useful as this comparison to Disneyland is, it breaks down eventually. Baudrillard writes that "Disneyland is presented as imaginary in order to make us believe that the rest is real" (*Simulacra* 12). The G.O.D. on the other hand is presented as real. The characters believe that it is a real wilderness, has real desolation and represents the traditional American image of the desert as a place of self-reflection and escape. Lang says of the desert, "people don't go to a place like that to look for other people. That's the opposite of the whole concept that's behind the thing" (*Broom* 414) and becomes annoyed later when he sees that it has become "too goddamn commercialized" (it always has been a commercial endeavor, but the noticing of it reveals the simulation). The desert is a place for characters to experience "reality," not to experience the imaginary, and when that "reality" is punctured by commercialization or crowds it ceases to live up to its "concept." Paul Giles writes that Wallace describes "a landscape where objects have become commodified and commercially overdetermined, as if refracted through the prism of television advertising" (334). Indeed, when Lang and Obstat are spying on Rick and Lenore from the rowing boat, Obstat begins eating Pop Tarts, and throws the wrapper into the lake (*Broom* 433). This is a brief piece of action, easily overlooked perhaps, but it depicts the link between the desert and the consumer world. The use of the brand name is deliberate, artificial food being consumed in an artificial desert.

While the desert cannot be talked about in terms of the pastoral tradition, there are links between pastoral literature and the literature of the frontier or the desert. As Jonathan Raban writes, "On the bestseller lists between 1901 and 1910, two sorts of generic fiction

40

stand out—and they represent the masculine and feminine sides of rural nostalgia. The masculine ones romanticize life in the wild, on the frontier or the open range" (35). Naomi Klein notices that, in American culture, there is "a deep craving for metaphorical space: release, escape, some kind of open-ended freedom" (64). Similarly, there is the romantic idea that the desert "resists commerce and human intervention but promotes imaginative endeavor," much like Thoreau's Walden Pond (Tate 125). So, while the desert cannot support traditional pastoral descriptions, such as the fresh, green landscapes and the cultivation of farmland, it embodies similar sentimental ideals. The link between the pastoral and the idealized desert has been noticed by other critics, notably Lawrence Buell in his essay "American Pastoral Ideology Reappraised." In defining the terms of his study, he writes:

> "Pastoral" is used in an extended sense, familiar to Americanists, to refer not to the specific set of obsolescent conventions of the eclogue tradition, but to all literature—poetry or prose, fiction or nonfiction—that celebrates the ethos of nature/rurality over against the ethos of the town or city. This domain includes for present purposes all degrees of rusticity from farm to wilderness. (n. 1)

A traditional theme in the pastoral literature of America is the intrusion of man and industry into the romanticized natural realm. A good example of this is Thoreau's *Walden*, where his solitude and reflection are dotted with the intrusion of the railroad. He writes:

> That devilish Iron Horse, whose ear-rending neigh is heard throughout the town, has muddied the Boiling Spring with his foot, and he it is that has browsed off all the woods on Walden shore. (1869)

Similarly, Nathaniel Hawthorne declares that industry, specifically the railroad, "brings the noisy world into our slumberous peace" (Marx 13). However, in Wallace's vision of America in *The Broom of the System* it is the idea of the restorative power of the wilderness itself that has mutated and become destructive. The members of the Ohio government desire the iconic and seek to overtake the natural with the exaggerated unreality of the pastoral.

This is a literal depiction of what Marx describes as "nature being represented by an idealized image of landscape" (25). In this case, the governor wants an idealized version of the desolation a real desert has to offer, down to the flora and fauna, as a counterpoint to the privileged, soft lives his public live. Wallace, as Paul Giles writes, is reconvening "traditional forms of American cultural idealism in a radically alien technological environment" (332).

The G.O.D. serves an ironic purpose. The traditional view is of "the felicity represented by an image of a natural landscape" and that the attraction of such a landscape "also may be understood as movement away from an "artificial" world" (Marx 9). The artificial in Wallace's world is so pervasive that even the landscape is marked by it, and the characters display no "felicity" when entering into it. As Umberto Eco says, "the American imagination demands the real thing and, to attain it, must fabricate the absolute fake" (*Faith* 8). This can be seen throughout *The Broom of the System*: The Reverend Hart Lee Sykes fabricates religious meaning from the confused echolalia of Lenore's parrot; Mr Bloemker"'s relationship with Brenda, the inflatable doll; the Spaniard family's theatrical recitals in front of an "audience-disc" (*Broom* 166). Don DeLillo's novel *White Noise* also concerns itself with the American landscape being commercialized and artificial, and "the Postmodern logic of endless reproduction" (Bilton 44). The narrator is taken by Murray, one of his academic colleagues, to see "the most photographed barn in America" (DeLillo 12). It is a place dedicated to the reproduction of the American pastoral ideal, a landscape that has been defined by advertising signs and the perceived image of perfect rurality. Murray comments that "once you've seen the signs about the barn, it's impossible to see the barn." As with Wallace's desert, the characters go to the barn to experience the idealised image of nature, not nature itself. It is the marketed implication of what the landscape means that draws in the crowds, just as people pay for a Wander Pass in the G.O.D. As Murray says, "We're not here to capture an image, we're here to maintain one" (12). Wallace himself comments on DeLillo's scene in "E Unibus Pluram," saying that Murray is trying to "figure out the hows and whys of giving in to collective visions of mass images that have themselves become mass images only because they've been made the objects of collective vision" (*Supposedly* 49).

Although Wallace, in this particular essay, is primarily writing about the role of television and the watcher in contemporary American society, this quotation is relevant because he depicts landscapes as "objects of collective vision" in his novels (i.e. the constructed ideal of the desert, based on the collective vision of what the desert *should* stand for, in *The Broom of the System*). N. Katherine Hayles goes further, saying that "viewpoint turn-offs and photo-ops" are "activities which construct wilderness as a category of visual experience and leisure consumption rather than an everyday part of life and the occasion for hard physical labor" (677).

In *Infinite Jest*, Wallace again uses man-made landscape to illustrate his central themes. Unlike *The Broom of the System*, the landscape has not been designed by man, but mutated by a reconfiguring of the map and the intensive dumping of waste. The Great Concavity/Convexity is a wilderness that has developed over a previously inhabitable area of New England and Quebec as a result of the U.S.A. dumping its waste—it is a literal wasteland, albeit one that changes from a wilderness "so fertilely lush it's practically unliveable" to a "barren Eliotical" wasteland several times over the course of a day (*Jest* 573-574). It is a nightmare vision of a man-made landscape, a ever changing space that has to be controlled by catapulting waste over the dividing wall which, because of "a fusion that feeds on the poisons" that is "so greedily efficient that it sucks out every last toxin," results in uninhibited organic growth with "rapacial feral hamsters and insects of Volkswagen size" running amok (572-573). While this is a comic and grotesque description, it depicts the characters" fear of the unknown interior of the Concavity and this perceived perversion of nature, while sensational and ludicrous, helps further Wallace's criticism of a society that is in terminal decline.

As with the G.O.D. Wallace is describing a landscape of the hyper-real, the enhanced image of nature that can only come about with man's interference. Both the man-made landscapes are a product of waste; the G.O.D. is a product of cultural waste (i.e. the governor's desire for the perfect, marketed desert), while the Great Concavity is a product of the literal waste of the American lifestyle.

However, the role of the Great Concavity is not that simple. The protagonists are drawn to the wilderness, but not to escape their culture.

Unlike the characters that seek escape and meaning in the G.O.D.
(regardless of the fact that this escape is impossible in a landscape
constructed out of the culture), Hal and Don Gately are reported to
have entered the Concavity to seek the ultimate piece of contemporary
culture, The Entertainment. While there is some ambiguity in the
reason Don and Hal are digging up Hal's father's head, there can be
some logical deduction. It is stated early on, by Himself in disguise as
Hal's therapist, that he has a "gyroscopic balance sensor and *mise-en-scène*
appropriation card and priapistic-entertainment cartridge" implanted
into his "anaplastic cerebrum" (*Jest* 31). It can be concluded that Hal
and Don are seeking equipment to be able to safely view the cartridge,
the filmmaking implants, or the cartridge itself. The Concavity is also the
brainchild of a cultural icon, Johnny Gentle, the former Las Vegas
lounge singer and "the first U.S. President ever to swing his microphone
around by the cord during his Inauguration speech" (382).

The Concavity fits with the traditional themes of the American
wilderness being spoiled by progress, such as in the writings of
Thoreau and Hawthorne. However, the Concavity not only destroyed
rural settings (large parts of rural New England are located within its
borders, if the geographical information in the novel is correct), but
also some inhabited, built areas, such as: Montpelier, Vermont;
Presque Isle, Maine; and L'Islet County, Quebec (*Jest* 571). The fact
that the American government is destroying not only the natural
landscape, but also the populated, human landscape, emphasizes
Wallace's preoccupation with the decline and decay of American
civilization, something that has more in common with literature of the
fin de siècle than that of the frontier and the pastoral.

In *Infinite Jest*, Wallace breaks down the barriers between man
and the natural landscape, highlighting the paradoxical nature of the
idea of redemptive wilderness (i.e. "the place where we are is the place
nature is not" (Cronon 80)) and the "American experience of a frontier
that was no sooner proclaimed than it began disappearing" (Hayles
676). Man is ever-present in the depictions of landscape in *Infinite Jest*,
from the man-made wilderness of the Concavity, to the architectural
structures of the cityscape. The introduction of Remy Marathe shows
him to be dominating the landscape with his shadow that is "enlarged
and distended [...] far out overland, so that the spokes of his chair's

rear wheels cast over two whole counties below gigantic asterisk-shadows […] and his head's shadow brought much of the suburb West Tucson a premature dusk" (*Jest* 88). Marathe, a figure who represents the threat of annihilation of the U.S.A.'s culture, dominates the wilderness area and encroaches gradually on the city limits of Tucson. Metropolitan Boston is presented as an urban location built around the brain-shaped M.I.T. students" union building and the heart-shaped Enfield Tennis Academy which also constructs a temporary shelter for the courts that is nicknamed "The Lung". Also, the word "map" is used as slang for a human corporeal body, linking the very existence of human beings to the territory they occupy.

The fact that the characters are so entwined with the idea of American landscape also ties together the ideas of ecological decline in The Great Concavity and social decline. The creation of O.N.A.N. has brought about a desire for Quebecois terrorists to destroy the American way of life, while they suffer because of the toxic waste being dumped in their homeland. However, the dissemination of the Entertainment will not just destroy the American way of life, but any person who watches it—it is an uncontrollable culture, much like the increasingly unstable wilderness-to-wasteland annular cycle in the Concavity. The very acronym for the reconfigured North America foreshadows this socio-ecological destruction. O.N.A.N. brings to mind the biblical story, the acronym implying an apocalypse, a termination of the line brought about by man's interference with the cartographical landscape and his befouling of nature. N. Katherine Hayles says that "civilization and wilderness copruduce each other" (676), but Wallace shows their codestruction.

The apocalyptical thought that is indicative of *fin de siècle* art is evident in Wallace's novel, particularly in his depictions of The Concavity. The apocalyptic voice "mixes horror and hope, nightmare and dream, destruction and creation, dystopia and utopia" (Stewart & Harding 286). The Concavity's annular cycle is one of destruction and creation, but accelerated to an ever-shifting landscape of growth and decline. The dystopia of the "barren Eliotical wasteland" is contrasted with a natural, "fertilely lush" landscape that would be viewed as a utopia if not for the destructive mutation of the growth. This use of the landscape reinforces Wallace's preoccupations with an apocalyptic

45

fin de siècle. Despite its size, the novel is telling the end of a larger story. It is the last year of subsidized time, and O.N.A.N. is threatened both from terrorism and the policies of its own government. The novel's characters exist in a state between "horror and hope": for example Gately hoping for redemption in a life with Joelle while battling his cravings for painkillers in his hospital bed, and Hal's desire for a substance-free existence and a chance at "The Show" is undercut with his uncontrollable "howling fantods."

While the landscape in *Infinite Jest* evades description in pastoral terms, it is still linked to the tragic careers of the characters. This idea is distilled in the Eschaton sequence. The map is man-made, constructed for a specific purpose and is the catalyst for a destructive brawl that endangers the tennis careers of those involves. The fight is over what is part of the map and what is part of the territory, and whether the territory is "the real world, quote unquote" (*Jest* 334). This develops into an argument about whether the players are part of the territory or the map. As Pemulis debates, "Players themselves can't be valid targets. Players aren't inside the goddamn game. Players are part of the *apparatus* of the game. They're part of the map" (338 [emphasis in original]). Stephen Burn writes, "A map, as Pemulis realizes, is subject to all kinds of distortions and local disturbances that may have no relation to the complex topographies of the territory" (24). While this may be true when talking about the game, it is not necessarily so in the novel as a whole. It is the distorting of the map of the United States that changes the landscape and brings into being The Great Concavity, the catalyst for the decline in the ecological and the social world of the novel. The Eschaton players attempt to alter the boundaries of the map and the territory, and the "elegant complexity" is lost to chaos and violence. The eschatological theme of the game bleeds into the reality, just as the boundaries of the map are blurred, causing not only devastating injury and punitive measures for the players, but also setting in motion many of the climactic events of the novel (particularly the linking of Gately's world with that of Hal through the injured Lord).

The landscape in both *Infinite Jest* and *The Broom of the System* is tied to the idea of social and ecological decline through the dominance of the human world over that of the natural, but it also helps structure "apocalyptic-millennial vacillations between utopian and dystopian visions in which anti-modern nostalgia for origins and simpler times meets dreams of enlightenment and progress" (Stewart & Harding 291). While Wallace does not display any nostalgia, he shows its effects, specifically in the governor of Ohio's reasons for building the G.O.D. The governor shows "vacillations" between this nostalgia and his "dreams of enlightenment and progress." The desert is to encourage "hewing," to motivate people out of their perceived complacency.

In both novels, Wallace depicts the landscape as an intensely culturalized and commercial space that negates any historical or nostalgic importance, and promotes Wallace's critique of "American cultural solipsism" (Jacobs, "Brothers Incandenza" 268). While Wallace writes about an American landscape that has been overtaken by commercial interests and the artifice of contemporary American culture, his peers write about the American landscape in terms of it being a redemptive space, a place that "renders visible the superficiality of American culture and the triumph of the transparency of form over the depth of substance" (Ulrich & Harris 15). Douglas Coupland, for example, writes about the desert as a space that fosters imaginative thought while also providing an escape from the superficial elements of modern life in his characters" Walden-esque existence in the Californian desert. Similarly, Bret Easton Ellis writes about the desert in *Less Than Zero* in nostalgic terms, the narrator memories of how he would "take his father's car and put the top down and drive through the desert listening to The Eagles or Fleetwood Mac, the hot wind blowing through my hair" (179). The American cultural imagery of the convertible car ties in with the nostalgic image of the desert to create a scene of escape in a novel that deals with the superficial live of the young characters.

Wallace, however, uses the American landscape to reflect millennial angst and the threat of decline, through the prevalence of consumerism, commercialization and the American lust for entertainment. The environmental landscape is reflective of the cultural landscape, and Wallace depicts a land where escape from "a corrupt and mercantile civilization" is impossible, a land where there is nothing beyond this commodification. The G.O.D. has crowds and overpriced entry fees, while everything from the cartographical landscape to the temporal landscape in *Infinite Jest* has been reconfigured because of the commercial interests of the consumer culture. There is an implication in both novels that the inevitability of this is unavoidable, and that the characters are trapped. David Foster Wallace may not have been the first to depict this kind of marketed America, but his influence lives on. Chris Bachelder, arguably the closest we currently have to Wallace's heir, writes:

Tell us about the American Landscape.

Pavement, Cancer, Food Marts, Wires & Cables, Bumper Stickers, Billboards, Weather. Some of it's pretty still. (148)

David Foster Wallace: Westward with Fredric Jameson

Connie Luther

In his interview with David Foster Wallace in 1993, Larry McCaffery suggests that Wallace's novella, "Westward the Course of Empire Takes its Way," published in the story collection *Girl with Curious Hair*, conveys the implication that "metafiction is a game that can only reveal itself, or that can't share its valence with anything outside itself—like the daily world" (142). Wallace agrees, but then points out the necessity of the metafictional perspective, because it "helps reveal fiction as a mediated experience. Plus it reminds us that there's always a recursive component to utterance" (142). However, Wallace argues, focusing on language's recursivity gets "empty and solipsistic real fast [. . .] By the eighties it'd become a godawful trap" (142). Wallace explains that in "Westward" he wanted to expose metafiction as itself a discourse trapped in the same discursivity it critiques in other discourses, but in the process he became entrapped himself in the "recursive loop" that occurs when we try to rise above language in claiming metanarrative status, because we cannot do so without language. For this reason, Wallace concludes, the only value of his novella is "showing the kind of pretentious loops you fall into now if you fuck around with recursion" (142, emphasis mine).

The little word "now" in the above quotation reveals much. Wallace believes that the literary heritage of postmodernism has culminated in this recursive dead end, a philosophical cul-de-sac from which he struggles to emerge. But in "Westward," which he wrote at the age of twenty-five (142), he thinks he can explode what he perceives as the hypocritical myth of metafictional privilege, by writing a satirical metafictional send-up of earlier metafiction, specifically John Barth's *Lost in the Funhouse*. In the process of writing his story, however, Wallace apparently discovers that he can't really expose metafictional recursion as bogus and empty, because it has real power, and Wallace ends by feeling entrapped in it even while he tries to debunk it as a mediated myth. Although he makes it sound in the interview as though he only discovered this power in writing the story, I suggest that when we examine the imagery in this story, Wallace knows all along that he is dealing with something real and impossible to overcome, even if he fights it. In "Westward," Wallace identifies a postmodernism that is more far-reaching than a mere literary movement limited to a select social segment of elite artists and academics, portraying rather an all-pervasive cultural phenomenon. He conveys this idea through an elaborate allegorical system which spreads its roots everywhere in the narrative. This paper will examine two aspects of this representation of postmodernism in "Westward"—the Illinois Funhouse setting, and the character development of Drew-Lynn Eberhardt, or D.L., the character most openly identified in the story with a postmodern theoretical position. I will argue also that Wallace's vision of postmodernism, with its bizarrely funny yet disturbing qualities, and its ubiquity throughout the entire fabric of "Westward," remarkably resembles the features that theorist Fredric Jameson, who decries the negative impact of postmodern philosophy on contemporary society and mentality, also identifies as a new state of cultural being. Both Wallace and Jameson think that this new cultural status quo has damaging qualities.

During the McCaffery interview, McCaffery brings up the subject of Jameson's theoretical view of culture, and Wallace responds by saying only, "I don't know much about Jameson," before resuming his discussion of rap music (146). This casual dismissal perhaps indicates the level of Wallace's earlier acquaintance with Jameson, because we know, from a footnote in Wallace's later essay, "Authority and American Usage," that as a graduate student and teacher he had read Jameson, or was at least scornfully aware of his notoriously complex grammatical syntax (*Lobster* 115). From the evidence, it would appear that Wallace has little use for Jameson's work, yet intriguingly, Wallace's vision of postmodernity in "Westward" exhibits the same qualities that Jameson attributes to this cultural phenomenon: ahistorical, flat, directionless, and representing the end-point of a linear historical progression. Wallace also seems to agree with Jameson that this place/state-of-mind has its origin, or at least has been fuelled by, the overwhelming materialism fostered by late-stage capitalism.

Most importantly, Jameson and Wallace agree that this cultural dominant of postmodernity has changed perceptions of what it means to be human, and both writers demonstrate unease with this perceived deep-level change. Jameson characterizes postmodern mentality as distinctly unhealthy, "described in the negative terms of anxiety and loss of reality, but which one could just as well imagine in the positive terms of euphoria, a high, an intoxicatory or hallucinogenic intensity" (*Postmodernism* 28-29). Wallace also thinks that contemporary culture has a negative impact on the way we function: "If you operate, which most of us do, from the premise that there are things about the contemporary U.S. that make it distinctively hard to be a real human being, then maybe half of fiction's job is to dramatize what it is that makes it tough" (Interview, McCaffery 131). Both artist and critic share not only the same unease with a society they consider unhealthy, but also seem to have diagnosed the same disease.

Wallace's narrative flatly states that "Central Illinois is, by no imaginer's stretch, a Funhouse" (*Curious* 242). This Funhouse is an elaborate allegory, and throughout "Westward" we collect strange details describing this place and its inhabitants. To begin with, the amazing fertility of the Funhouse, indicated by its ubiquitous corn crop, is abnormal and disturbing to many of the characters, even to J.D. Steelritter, who lives in it (242). But this fertility is paradoxically sterile. Ironically, the sheer output of the rich soil here renders its huge corn crop practically worthless because of overabundance (299-300, 349). D.L. thinks that the ubiquitous corn-crop of the area is "disorienting, wind-blown, verdant, tall, total, *menacingly* fertile. This entire area is creepy" (275, italics mine). Tom Sternberg's mother, who once brought young Tom to Illinois in the summer for commercial auditions, "still has nightmares about all the corn. She wakes up, sometimes" (254). These descriptions suggest an unhealthy, unnatural quality to production in the Funhouse. This astonishingly abundant but ultimately worthless overgrowth in Wallace's story relates to Fredric Jameson's contention that postmodernity features an enormous expansion of the cultural sphere, and that its production is artistically worthless. Jameson argues that, contrary to what some theorists have suggested, postmodernity has not eliminated cultural restraints by deconstructing its discourses and categories, but rather has hugely expanded it: "[T]he dissolution of an autonomous sphere of culture is rather to be imagined in terms of an explosion: a prodigious expansion of culture throughout the social realm" (*Postmodernism* 48). That Jameson considers this burgeoning growth paradoxically sterile and worthless is abundantly evident in his carefully qualified but ultimately scornful description of this expansion as a "'degraded' landscape of schlock and kitsch, of TV series and Reader's Digest culture, of advertising and motels, of the late show and the grade-B Hollywood film, of so-called paraliterature, with its airport paperback categories of the gothic and the romance, the popular biography, the murder mystery, and the science fiction or fantasy novel" (3). Jameson contends that postmodernism has precipitated the collapse of the division between "low" and "high" art, and it is obvious that he disapproves. Wallace, in his interview with McCaffery, bluntly states that much "bad" writing exists in the contemporary scene, but for him, it is postmodern, avant-garde literature that is bad, and this low quality reflects a world that is "hopelessly shitty, insipid, materialistic, emotionally retarded, sadomasochistic and stupid" (131). Wallace's note of outrage is considerably less nuanced than Jameson's attempts to be objective, but Jameson's overall assessment of postmodernity is no less negative on close examination.

Postmodern cultural expansion is reflected, not only in the huge but worthless yields of corn in Wallace's Funhouse, but also in its geographical features. It is not enclosed and restricted, like Ambrose's original carnival Funhouse, but a terrifyingly wide-open place: "[T]here's nothing to hold your eye, you have to pan back and forth, like a big No, your eyes so relaxed and without object they almost roll. It can be scary" (*Curious* 244). We see here again an image of immense cultural expansion, and that it is not only worthless but disorienting. When you face East in Wallace's Illinois Funhouse, you feel overwhelmed by the flatness and openness, but to the West we can see the reassuring "skyline of Collision's silos and arches and neon" (244). Collision, the town at the heart of the Illinois Funhouse, lies to the West of the regional airport where the characters arrive, even though the terminal itself, significantly, has no windows facing West. Looking to the West has been an ubiquitous symbol of hope and progress throughout American literary history, and Wallace also uses it in this

way. East represents looking back at the past, a flat, featureless and
frightening place, stripped in postmodernity of its historical content.
Jameson's contention that postmodernity is characterized by a
suspension of history is well known: he deplores the "historical
deafness" of postmodernity (*Postmodernism* xi), and his rallying cry is
"Always historicize!" (*Political Unconscious* 1).

In "Westward" the characters must travel West to get to the
Reunion, but they end up approaching their destination from the
North (314). If East is the past, and West is the future, perhaps the
North represents a suspension of time here, making the trip West
interminable because you cannot logically move West by going North.
The future is not too hopeful either; after all the storm that stops the
West-bound travelers in their tracks comes out of the West. DeHaven
Steelritter eventually defines the travelers' orientation as approaching
Collision from the Northeast (314). This indirect approach again
proffers an invitation to find allegorical parallels: in Wallace's Illinois
Funhouse, as in Barth's carnival Funhouse, it is easy to lose your way,
because your logic is confused by the features (or featurelessness in this
case) of the place. Jameson contends that postmodernity is spatially
rather than historically organized, and that this space is directionless
and disorienting: "[D]istance in general (including 'critical distance' in
particular) has very precisely been abolished in the new space of
postmodernism [. . .] our now postmodern bodies are bereft of spatial
coordinates and practically (let alone theoretically) incapable of
distantiation" (*Postmodernism* 48-49). Jameson concludes that "it is this
whole extraordinarily demoralizing and depressing original new global
space which is the 'moment of truth' of postmodernism" (49), and that
any effort to leave it results in immediate reabsorption, since no one
can distance themselves from it (49). This spatiality is more like a
suspension, and there are no directions in it because it contains no
distinguishable features to mark any one position. This inescapability is
mirrored in the endless and frustrating attempts of Wallace's
characters to arrive at Collision, the town in the West.

Collision, in the heart of the Illinois Funhouse, functions
symbolically as the apocalyptic birthplace of postmodernism, resulting
in the death of human endeavor, and the beginning of a timeless,
directionless space. In the story, the town is founded when a wealthy

woman driving through the area accidentally kills Ray Kroc Sr., a local farmer, with her car. The woman decides to stay put, literally, living in her car and eventually marrying a peddler named Steelritter, one of many entrepreneurs attracted to the place by the woman's patronage. The peddler and the woman then become the commercial heart of a new community. Most importantly, the younger Ray Kroc (the name of the actual founder of McDonald's), establishes in Collision the first McDonald's restaurant, which is then nurtured into a mega-corporation by advertising genius J.D. Steelritter, the son of the peddler and the wealthy woman. The birthing of postmodernity in late capitalism, the central argument of Jameson's theory, is clearly suggested here. He argues that postmodern suspicion of all cultural truth as mere elaborations of ideology makes it a perfect partner for capitalism (*Postmodernism* xxi), and in making Collision the birthplace of McDonald's, long the icon of multinational capitalism, Wallace evidently agrees with this position.

Finally, Collision is also the location of the McDonald's Reunion which, as J.D. Steelritter the ultimate adman foresees, is the event that will achieve what commercial culture has been building toward—the complete satisfaction of desire. J.D. anticipates this outcome: "He will watch desire build to that red-and-gold pitch, that split-second shudder and sneeze of thirty years' consumers, *succumbing*, as *one* [. . .] the alumni will give in, reveling, utterly" (310). This orgiastic, literally blood-spurting moment, will suspend all action or change:

> And that, as they say, will be that. No one will ever leave the rose farm's Reunion. The revelation of What They Want will be on them; and, in that revelation of Desire, they will Possess. They will all Pay The Price—without persuasion. It's J.D.'s swan song. No more need for J.D. Steelritter Advertising or its helmsman genius. Life, the truth, will be its own commercial. Advertising will have finally arrived at the death that's been its object all along. And in Death, it will of course become Life. The last commercial. Popular culture, the U.S. of A.'s great lalated lullaby, the big remind-a-ad on the refrigerator of belief, will, forever unsponsored, tumble into carefully salted soil. The public, one great need, will not miss being reminded of what they believe. They'll doubt what they fear, believe what they

wish; and, united, as Reunion, their wishes will make it so. Their wishes will, yes, come true. Fact will be fiction will be fact. Ambrose and his academic heirs will rule, without rules. *Meatfiction.* (310)

In this passage we can see clear parallels with Jameson's contention that postmodernity is a perception of epiphany followed by Utopian stasis, of the suspension of time inherent in reaching a goal, the result of a mentality in which time is suspended, and replaced with a spatial conception of society and culture (*Postmodernism* 48-9). The "carefully salted soil" of postmodernity in this passage ensures that nothing further will grow. This new state of being is permanently sterile, having no need to produce anything new, because the goal of human existence has been reached—not the ultimate understanding or realization of truth or goodness, but the ultimate satiety of desire. But the image is disturbing, suggesting a deadly outcome. The signal for the achievement of this state is a rush of blood, hauled in by the truckload and spurting out of myriad orifices constructed in the golden arches and altar in Collision. This detail suggests sacrifice (or rape), and Wallace's wry pun on metafiction makes this point still more apparent. In this moment of orgiastic completion (or death, or violation?) the sacrifice is individuality, thought, dissent—the paralysis of all minds in a timeless suspension of perfect emotional and physical satisfaction.

Unlike the featureless Illinois Funhouse, Collision, with its comforting marker of the familiar golden arches and its promise of ultimate satisfaction, is a specific place, the final destination for human desire, the fulfillment of which is unceasingly promised in commercial culture, and which postmodern society has come to believe is not only more important than pursuing truth or justice, or anything outside self-gratification, but also is the only realizable goal of all individuals. The factor which will fulfill all desire is the paradoxical unity provided by simultaneous satisfaction of all difference. In other words, everyone will be brought to desire the same thing, and will become convinced that they have all achieved it, at the same moment, in the moment of cascading blood that signals the death of individuality. Like Wallace, Jameson acknowledges the power of postmodernity to create an illusion of utopia, but he deplores its consequences for human freedom as Wallace does. Jameson questions the self-congratulatory tone of theorists who celebrate postmodernity as a form of utopian achievement, in which all restrictive cultural myths are rejected, and all individuals may choose their own identities and destinies in the ultimate marketplace. For both Wallace and Jameson, this wide-open freedom of choice has mutated into a crushing of all difference, a tragic irony.

The citizens of Wallace's Illinois Funhouse also invite comparison to Jameson's theory of postmodernity. On one level, they remind us of Barth's laughing mechanical Fat Lady, which is ruined along with the rest of Ambrose's Funhouse in Wallace's narrative, deformed by the heat of fire (*Curious* 243). Some of the characters of the Illinois Funhouse, like Fat May, are outsized and mechanical: we have a "big-armed woman," watching the storm approaching from her front porch. She waves at the carload heading for the Reunion, and her wave is machinelike, "deliberate and even, like a windshield wiper" (325). But the most important quality of these Funhouse characters is their helplessness. A pesticide salesman, who has tried to pick up Magda at the airport, is a good example of how these characters are sterilized by their environment. This unfortunate man has to deal with the bizarre fact that the vermin of Funhouse Illinois actually *like* his company's pesticide (289), and find the Funhouse's product (corn) unpalatable. Also, the little gnats that are everywhere in the Funhouse are "odd" and weird. They have wings, but they "seem not to fly, but just sit there, all over the windows' insides, inviting squashing, and when squashed, smell" (301-302). J.D. notes that these insects "are creepy. Lemming-like. Nihilistic. Plus dull" (321-22). Again, we see a bizarrely funny, yet ultimately disturbing, image here of unnatural function. The empty fertility of this place is reflected in these insects, which are inert, crave what is meant to destroy them, and in consuming it mutate into "lemming-like" creatures that smell bad. Again, we have the sense that this state is deathlike.

Perhaps the outsized farmers who live and work in the Funhouse provide the best example of this paralysis. We first meet one of these characters at the car rental counter at the regional airport, and he is so big that "he unconsciously treats the counter like a footstool, has his boot on the counter and his elbow on his knee" (267). This farmer, in spite of his "thousand-bushel crop of prime Illinois feed corn" (267) cannot rent a luxury car for his son. Another giant farmer also appears later, hitchhiking along the road to Collision after his old harvester breaks down, and his great thumb casts a giant shadow (311) as DeHaven Steelritter's car goes by. In the end, another enormous farmer, with his outsized horse and outsized chain, comes to rescue DeHaven's car, hopelessly mired down in mud after the storm, but in spite of his great size and his great horse, this giant is unable to free the car. These outsized Funhouse inhabitants represent the importance of postmodern individuality, which is supposedly the center of postmodern/consumer culture, in which individual choice is everything. Yet, these characters are powerless, suggesting again the numbing de-individualization that ironically results from a culture that focuses on individual fulfillment of desire. That these farmers have no distinguishing individual features further underlines this point.

The landscape, the people, and even the vermin of Wallace's Funhouse are deformed and unnatural. But in addition to this elaborate landscape or background allegory, we can also trace the theme of postmodernity's deforming function in the character development of Drew-Lynn Eberhardt, or D.L. She is the most important example in the story of what Wallace thinks can happen to an individual who embraces postmodern thinking. D.L. exhibits qualities that are the same as those of the Funhouse inhabitants, and this resemblance reinforces the idea that the Illinois Funhouse is a representation of postmodernism. Even more disturbing is the notion that a "real" character, as opposed to the static background of the Funhouse, can also be appropriated by this paralyzing mentality. Jameson argues that postmodernism can be seen as "an enculturation of the real" (*Postmodernism* x), and Wallace illustrates this in his development of the "realistic" characters in his narrative.

D.L. is initially a member of the writing class presided over by Professor Ambrose, the central character in Barth's story, and now famous, in "Westward…", as the foremost writer of postmodern metafiction. D. L. has proclaimed herself a postmodernist, something, the narrator states, emphatically, that you should never do: "No matter where you are, you Don't Do This" (234). This remark suggests an understanding of the idea, also outlined by Jameson, that postmodernism is auto-referential and self-understood because of its ubiquity, and therefore meaningless as an actually defined position, distinguishable from everything else (*Postmodernism* xii, xx). In "Westward" D.L. naïvely attempts to distinguish herself as a "real struggling artist. A postmodernist [. . .] [s]pecializing in language poetry and the apocalyptically cryptic Literature of Last Things, in exhaustion in general, and metafiction" (328). "Westward" opens with a thoroughly derogatory description of D.L.'s unpleasant personality and physical appearance, neither of which has any outward redeeming qualities. D.L. has completely embraced "postmodernism" as a sort of life philosophy, and this is absurd to the narrator, who notes that "[b]y convention it's seen as pompous and dumb" (234). D.L. literally and unsubtly transforms what the narrator seems to think of as the non-principles of postmodernism into a formula that she applies not only to her writing, which is so obscure that her major work has become a twenty-page poem consisting entirely of punctuation (251), but also to her very sense of self. After she panics during takeoff, she says to Mark, "I'm bad at will, I've decided. Postmodernism doesn't stress the efficacy of will, as you know" (249). This remark, amusing and ironic as it is, underlines Wallace's opinion of pretentious avant-garde literary production (Interview, McCaffery 131), which is clearly linked in the story to postmodernism, through D.L.'s self-proclaimed identification with it.

Yet D.L. also functions as an ingénue, despite her self-described adherence to a jaded, pessimistic philosophical perspective and her thoroughly repugnant persona. Her sincere commitment to live by postmodern "principles" is admirable and absurd at the same time. D.L. has been deformed by postmodernism, and we ultimately sympathize with her as a victim. We see this alteration in her character developing in her correspondence with Tom Sternberg, which "started out so lilting, warm, putting-the-reader-at-ease," but then "the poems and stories she later sent were less so; they seemed cold, coy for coyness's sake, he never forgot he was sitting in a chair in his parents' living room, reading print on paper" (281-82). Tom also notes that D.L.'s appearance has altered in a way that he finds "frightening" (282). As a young girl, she had been attractive and well-grown, as J.D. Steelritter remembers as he recalls his decision to cast her in a commercial. At that same time, Tom had found her alluring too, so that she "kick-started" his late-developing puberty (281). Yet now, she's repulsive to him, smelling "weird—orangy on top and then a whiff of something dead and preserved underneath. Let's face it. She looks like her vagina would smell bad" (282). Here we see a parallel with the scent of death that seems to hang over the Illinois Funhouse, especially Collision, and its occupants.

D.L.'s deformation is clearly connected to the influence of her father, a Vietnam war veteran who, although he tells D.L. that "she is loved," has warped her sensibilities: "Took her exclusively to ruined amusements [. . .] Read her *Moby-Dick* at ten. One sitting. Whale trivia and all" (319). Significantly, the Vietnam War was both the cause célèbre and the rock that broke the spirit of renewal in the sixties that both Jameson and Wallace think produced the last great wave of literature (*Postmodernism* xx, McCaffery 132). Additionally, D.L. as a child feels affinity with Barth's animated Fat Lady, which is in this story has been grotesquely deformed by fire. D.L. sees the Fat Lady when her father takes her to the amusement park after it's been destroyed. At that time, J.D. had observed "the *way* she [D.L] touched the melted lurid shell of the ruined Funhouse's Fat May, palm to its big sagged forehead, a tiny mother with a giant fevered child" , thinking that "here is a child who is most at home with the luridly disclosed" (313, emphasis original), a reference to the prime directive of postmodernism, which is to relentlessly expose the metanarrative of any cultural assumption. We can see here that D.L. is the ingénue who has been deformed by postmodernity, the fallout cultural heritage of the ultimately failed rebellion of the sixties. As the "tiny mother" of a "giant fevered child" D. L. she unwittingly, but understandably, embraces her postmodern literary heritage. We can see, again, that D.L. shares the abnormal, deformed qualities of the Illinois Funhouse and its inhabitants, and we can also see (again) the ominous real power of postmodernity's mentality.

From this negative characterization alone it would seem clear that Wallace's text creates a nightmare image of postmodernism as a cultural phenomenon. But the figure of Ambrose in the story also provides a strong indictment of what Wallace sees as an artistic abandonment of social responsibility in postmodernism. Ambrose has "sold out" his literary concept of the Funhouse to J.D. Steelritter for lucrative commercial development, illustrating the frank complicity of postmodern production with the materialism and greed that Wallace finds so repugnant in American capitalist society. But Ambrose also represents the cold isolation and selfish disconnect in postmodernity that Wallace finds so disturbing. Ambrose has not responded warmly to D.L.'s work, even though it is only a naïve application of what postmodernism dictates, taken literally. D.L. eventually leaves Ambrose's seminar in tears, after scrawling a limerick on the blackboard of the classroom. This limerick, while wincingly bad, contains the central question of this story. John Barth opens his famous story by asking, "For whom is the Funhouse fun?" But in her limerick D.L. asks, "Who LIVES in the Funhouse?" She thought she did, only to be rejected by Ambrose, the builder of the place. The clear indication here is that the Funhouse in Wallace's story is postmodernism, and that it is not only inhospitable, but uninhabitable, and that postmodern artists and intellectuals bear responsibility for a betrayal of the generation to whom they initially held out hope.

If anything, Wallace's vision of postmodernity is even more pessimistic than Jameson's theoretical description, considering the harshness of his remarks on contemporary society in the McCaffery interview. But, like Jameson, Wallace refuses to abandon what he sees as his artistic and critical responsibility to make the world a better place, despite the daunting power of postmodern cultural reality which negates this possibility. Wallace acknowledges that in writing "Westward," he is attempting to debunk postmodernism's foreclosure of real meaning, in language or anywhere. He remarks,

> Look man, we'd probably most of us agree that these are dark times, and stupid ones, but do we need fiction that does nothing but dramatize how dark and stupid everything is? In dark times, the definition of good art would seem to be art that locates and applies CPR to those elements of what's human and magical that still live and glow despite the times' darkness. Really good fiction could have as dark a worldview as it wished, but it'd find a way both to depict this dark world and to illuminate the possibilities for being alive and human in it. (Interview, McCaffery 131)

It is evident from Wallace's later work, especially *Everything and More: A Compact History of* ∞, that Wallace's knowledge of modal logic and mathematics has shaped his philosophy, and his theories of language and art. Wallace knows that higher mathematics are not built on certainties but on theory, and that such theory is often built on illogical assumptions such as dividing by 0. But this imaginative approach to math has been validated by its successful application to the material world. Wallace understands that absolute confidence in knowing what's true and real seems disproved by the very disciplines that have always been relied on to provide such stability: "[T]he abstract math that's banished superstition and ignorance and unreason and birthed the modern world is also the abstract math that is shot through with unreason and paradox and conundrum. . ." (*Everything* 30). This realization, one of the knowledge foundations on which postmodern philosophy is built, he honestly acknowledges. But, Wallace immediately rejects both despair and any giddy abdication of responsibility, the respective stereotypical modern and postmodern reactions to such uncertainty, if it is taken as implacable. Wallace instinctively turns instead to an essentially moral position of compassion, prioritizing encouragement and hope, the same goal that Jameson is relentlessly pursuing in his search for potential utopias in the future. Courageously, Wallace devoted the rest of his literary efforts to finding a way to do this, fighting a cold current of logic with artistic innovation that acknowledges the philosophical instability and lurking despair that is his modernist heritage, yet rejecting any postmodern celebration or embrace of this instability as an excuse to abandon social responsibility. We are left to analyze his success in addressing this daunting problem.

Consider Berkeley & Co.: Reading "Westward the Course of Empire Takes its Way"

Philip Coleman

> "Their wishes will, yes, come true. Fact will be fiction will be fact."
> (*Girl With Curious Hair* 310)

> "Is it an account that I entitle? asks the title in entitling."
> (Derrida, "The Law Of Genre" 73)

This essay is informed by a fairly obvious claim in relation to literary critical practice, which is that everything matters in a work of literature: nothing is accidental, everything is strategic. Critics of fiction, unlike the best critics of lyric poetry—people like Helen Vendler and Charles Altieri, for example, despite their espousal of radically different critical ideologies—are often unable to pay attention to every detail in a text simply because novels tend to be much longer than (most) poems. Exhaustive critical commentary quickly tends towards annotation, which in turn tends ultimately towards a kind of Borgesian replication of the text in itself. Leaving such absurdities aside, however, it is clearly the case that important things are often (perhaps unwittingly) overlooked in critical studies of prose fiction simply because critics do not always pay sufficient attention to detail. In relation to Wallace, it is perhaps hard to imagine how a reader of *Infinite Jest* might respond—or be expected to respond—to every single detail of that text, but Greg Carlisle has shown how valuable and viable close reading can be in his study of that work, *Elegant Complexity*. The kind of close reading I have in mind is slightly different because it treats textual details of a given work not only as particulars that need to be explicated in relation to the rest of that work, but I see things like titles, epigraphs, and references as (inter)textual signposts, pointers not just to other texts but also to other contexts within which we are invited to read and interpret the work under consideration.

This approach to reading is probably so commonplace and obvious that there is no need for it to be (re)stated here. Jacques Derrida, that closest of close readers, has shown again and again just how productive, and provocative, attention to such textual markers can be. I want to begin in this deliberately self-conscious way, however, because the analysis of Wallace's "Westward the Course of Empire Takes its Way" offered below proceeds through a consideration of the initial signposts one encounters when reading that text—its title and epigraphs—and a description of some of the places where they appear to send or direct us. I am not interested in pursuing a Derridaen reading of the text here, but considering these details with regard to "Westward," I argue, opens up areas of interpretative possibility that have been somewhat overlooked (if not altogether underappreciated) in Wallace criticism to date. Moreover, the strategic significance of these details, as I read them, challenges the assumption that "Westward" is little more than a parodic, and self-parodying, reflection on John Barth's *Lost in the Funhouse* and other canonical works of postmodern metafiction. Behind all the comic absurdity of the text—all of its metafictional grandstanding—lies a work that is as serious, ultimately, as anything else Wallace wrote in his desire to get us to think about the relation between literature and the world in which we read it. Despite or, perhaps, in spite of Barth's suggestion that epigraphs *"should be avoided"* in *The Friday Book*, as well as his detailed discussion of the necessity for "straightforward" titles in that work (Barth xix, ix; emphasis in original), the title and epigraphs to "Westward" signal a nexus of intertextual routes over a range of contextual domains that reveal interesting possibilities for interpreting Wallace's work.

Wallace sanctions such a careful consideration of a text's title and epigraphs in his fascinating and insightful uncollected essay "The Empty Plenum: David Markson's *Wittgenstein's Mistress*," which he begins by claiming that "[c]ertain novels not only cry out for critical interpretations but actually try to direct them." (217) In that essay he goes on to describe the role and importance of titles and epigraphs in what he calls "INTERPRET-ME fiction" (218). My argument here, then, is that "Westward the Course of Empire Takes its Way" is also an "INTERPRET-ME fiction" and some of the most significant "directions" in it are given in its title and epigraphs. In what follows I show that these are drawn from an intriguingly diverse and richly suggestive range of sources, but I am not only interested in identifying those "sources" here: I also want to explore and describe some of the interpretative routes along which they lead us—"Westward" or not—as the text "takes its way" towards an elaboration of Wallace's unmistakably original, and increasingly valuable, worldview.

In an "IYI" "factoid" (as opposed to an ordinary bibliographical/informational footnote—even if these things are rarely "ordinary" where Wallace is concerned) in his discussion of the Newtonian understanding of "infinitesimal quantities" in *Everything and More* Wallace refers to the Irish philosopher George Berkeley, whom he describes as a "major empiricist philosopher and Christian apologist (and a world-class pleonast)" (*Everything* 138). A pleonast, according to the OED, is "one who uses pleonasm" which, in turn, is defined in the first instance as "the use of more words in a sentence or clause than are necessary to express the meaning; redundancy of expression either as a fault of style, or as a rhetorical figure used for emphasis or clarity." Wallace's nod to Berkeley as a fellow pleonast reveals an interesting non-literary source for his work's frequently expansive syntactical structures, and on this occasion he refers in particular to what he calls Berkeley's "famous critique of classical calc [...] in an eighteenth-century tract whose 64- (yes, 64) word title starts with "The Analyst...."" He goes on:

> Berkeley's broadside is in some ways Christianity's return-raspberry to Galileo and modern science (and it's actually great cranky fun to read, though that's neither here nor there). Its overall point is that eighteenth-century math, despite its deductive pretensions, really rests on faith no less than religion does, i.e. that "[H]e who can digest a second or third fluxion, a second or third [derivative], need not, methinks, be squeamish about any point in divinity." (138)

Wallace's "factoid" does more than throw light on Berkeley's understanding of "classical calc." It seems to me that it also provides a key to understanding other areas of Wallace's work, from his engagements with philosophical ideas and styles—how those ideas are articulated—to his understanding of what might be called the metaphysics of the American self.

Wallace also invokes Berkeley in his 1993 essay "Getting Away From Already Pretty Much Being Away From It All," in which he describes a "child's radical delusive self-centerdness" in terms of what he calls the "regally innocent solipsism of like Bishop Berkeley's God" (*Supposedly* 89). To think of Wallace's invocations of Berkeley in terms of his considerations of American selfhood, then, is not as incongruous as it might seem. Considering "Westward the Course of Empire Takes its Way," in fact, necessarily invokes the philosopher whose "Verses on the Prospect of Planting Arts and Learning in America"—his "only known serious poem" according to A.A. Luce (Berkeley 373)—contains the phrase chosen by Wallace as the title for his text. The poem is worth quoting in its entirety:

The Muse, disgusted at an age and clime
Barren of every glorious theme,
In distant lands now waits a better time,
Producing subjects worthy fame;

In happy climes, where from the genial sun
And virgin earth such scenes ensue,
The force of art by nature seems outdone,
And fancied beauties by the true;

In happy climes, the seat of innocence,
Where nature guides and virtue rules,
Where men shall not impose, for truth and sense,
The pedantry of courts and schools:

There shall be sung another golden age,
The rise of empire and of arts,
The good and great inspiring epic rage,
The wisest heads and noblest hearts.

Not such as Europe breeds in her decay;
Such as she bred when fresh and young,
When heavenly flame did animate her clay,
By future poets shall be sung.

Westward the course of empire takes its way:
The first four acts already past,
A fifth shall close the drama with the day:
Time's noblest offspring is the last.
(Berkeley 373)

The phrase from the final quatrain is perhaps more commonly known as the title of Emanuel Gottlieb Leutze's 1861 painting, which can be seen on the wall of the Capitol Building in Washington, DC, and which Wallace's text may in some respects to said to parody. Berkeley's poem signals the larger historical backdrop against which the novella is sketched, however, which involves a context of ideas about the meaning of "America" and "Americanness" that precedes the representations of the nineteenth-century notion of "Manifest Destiny" in Leutze's mural and includes much earlier projections of the American self and its possibilities for future development (if not its demise).

It is curious that neither Berkeley nor Leutze are mentioned in Marshall Boswell's *Understanding David Foster Wallace*, where "Westward" is described as "a short story that goes on too long" and "an engaging piece of pretentious juvenilia" as well as "a fascinating programmatic declaration of intent" in relation to *Infinite Jest* (102). Perhaps Boswell was taking his lead here from Wallace himself, who more or less dismissed "Westward" in his interview with Larry McCaffery where he said:

> Maybe "Westward"'s only real value'll be showing the kind of pretentious loops you fall into if you fuck around with recursion. My idea in "Westward" was to do with metafiction what Moore's poetry or like DeLillo's *Libra* had done with other mediated myths. I wanted to get the Armageddon-like explosion, the goal metafiction's always been about, I wanted to get it over with, and then out of the rubble reaffirm the idea of art being a living transaction between humans, whether the transaction was erotic or altruistic or sadistic. God, even talking about it makes me want to puke. The *pretension*. Twenty-five-year-olds should be locked away and denied ink and paper. Everything I wanted to do came out in the story, but it came out

as just what it was: crude and naive and pretentious. (142; emphasis in original)

Reading this I am reminded of T.S. Eliot's description of *The Waste Land* as "just a piece of rhythmical grumbling" (Eliot 112)—not because I believe "Westward" has as important a place in Wallace's oeuvre as The Waste Land has in Eliot's, but despite Wallace's protestations, "Westward" is important in terms of the development of his writing for a number of reasons in addition to the bibliographical/biographical ones suggested by Boswell. Boswell's developmental view of "Westward" in *Understanding David Foster Wallace* continues to inform the text's popular and scholarly reception as, for example, Scott Esposito's recent online discussion of the text shows, where it is described as "probably the best fictional text of Wallace's to prepare you for his masterpiece."

In a recent reappraisal of Wallace's work in relation to "Westward" for the *Sonora Review* feature on the writer, Boswell writes:

John Barth's anthology staple ["Lost in the Funhouse"] also serves as the scaffolding upon which Wallace builds the collection's [...] major, but largely forgotten, piece, the novella "Westward the Course of Empire Takes its Way." As evidenced by the title—itself a perhaps too clever allusion to Emanuel Leutze's 1861 painting celebrating American Manifest Destiny—the novella announces itself right from the start as ancillary to something yet to come, an assumption confirmed by the story's plot.... ("Heading Westward" 30)

Boswell may himself have contributed to the temporary forgetting of "Westward" among readers of Wallace's work by dismissing it so enthusiastically in his 2003 study, but his recovery of the text here is also marked by a deeper hermeneutic forgetfulness, claiming as it does Leutze as the source of its title rather than Berkeley. Nothing was "too clever" for Wallace, and the fact that he may have considered using Berkeley's line not just as the title of his novella but for the book that became *Girl With Curious Hair* indicates just how resonant he believed it was for readings of his work. The author note he used to accompany his story "Solomon Silverfish" when it first appeared in the *Sonora Review* in 1987, indeed, stated that a "collection of short stories and a novella, *Westward the Course of Empire Takes its Way*, will be published by Viking in 1988." ("Solomon Silverfish" 96) The note is ambiguous, but the italicization of "Westward"—particularly for Wallace, who paid scrupulous attention to such formatting/ typographical/editorial details—suggests it is the title Wallace was considering using for the (or a) whole book, and not just the novella of the same title. Archival evidence may in time be able to reveal the extent to which Wallace toyed with and thought about Berkeley's phrase in the making of both the novella that uses it as a title and the book in which it first appeared. Recognizing Berkeley's poem as an important starting place for a reading of the text, however, does more than expose another source for the title: it also helps to situate it within a discourse on Americanness that extends back at least a century more than that suggested by Leutze's mural and which involves earlier projections and imaginations of the American self and project.

Boswell is absolutely right to argue that "Westward" represents a detailed and complex engagement with the work of Barth, then, and it may be said to embody an important critique of the metafictional devices and techniques used by him and others such as Donald Barthelme and Robert Coover. Bound up with the ways that he thinks about metafiction in "Westward," however, is an analysis of the relationship between fiction-making, the formation of cultural identity, and self-construction in the American context that raises the stakes of Wallace's text beyond the formally playful to include a consideration of questions that are, ultimately, of broader historical and cultural/ political or ideological import. These are perhaps large claims to make for a text the author himself dismissed so thoroughly, but the fact that Wallace explored these ideas more comprehensively and, perhaps, convincingly, in *Infinite Jest* and his other writings should not preclude a critical consideration of their importance in the earlier novella. "Westward the Course of Empire Takes its Way" presents some interesting problems, beginning with the question of the title, which signals a history of thinking about the American project from the eighteenth century, if not earlier, to the present. Given his intimate knowledge with Berkeley's works on "classical calc"—works that are perhaps even less widely read today than the bishop's poems—it is fair to assume that Wallace had the poem in mind also when he chose the title for his novella. Indeed, certain lines in the poem chime with themes that are explored in the course of Wallace's text (and elsewhere in his work, such as the important essay mentioned above), from the speaker's invocation of a Muse that is "disgusted at an age and clime / Barren of every glorious theme" to the projection of a place "Where men shall not impose, for truth and sense, / The pedantry of courts and schools." Wallace may well have appreciated the idealist strain in Berkeley's thought: when he talks in *This Is Water* about "the real value of a real education [as having] nothing to do with grades or degrees and everything to do with simple awareness—awareness of what is so real and essential, so hidden in plain sight all around us" (131), he also rebukes Dr Johnson's claim that Berkeley's theories can be disproven simply by kicking a stone, which shows just how real and solid the world actually is. Quite apart from the extent to which Wallace considers Berkeley's philosophical theories in his work, however, "Westward the Course of Empire Takes its Way" engages most centrally with ideas about America and their historical development that are summarized in the poem of that title written nearly three hundred years ago (Berkeley wrote it in 1726) and explored in elaborate if at times hilarious ways in his novella.

In choosing "Westward the Course of Empire Takes its Way" as the title for his work, in other words, Wallace signals Berkeley's poem about the American project in a way that places his text, also, within a discourse on Americanness that centers on the pursuit of what Sacvan Bercovitch has called the idea of a "representative American self" which, "for well over two centuries [has] subsumed the facts of social pluralism (ethnic, economic, religious, even personal) in a comprehensive ideal." (Puritan Origins 186) That "ideal" is represented in a number of ways in Wallace's novella, from Mark Nechtr and Drew-Lynn Eberhardt's pursuit of the ideal narrative (literary) form to J.D. Steelritter's desire to create a television commercial that will end the need for advertisement forever. In their different ways all of the main characters in "Westward" are on quests that involve the pursuit of some ideal or other, ideals that are aimed or projected towards the "Funhouse" that "Professor Ambrose" has designed and Steelritter has constructed in Collision, Illinois. No such town exists in reality, but "Collision" gives the story a spatial focus for

Wallace's projections of disparate aspects of the American pursuit of happiness that is analogous to the space more generally represented in narratives of the New World as "the new end-time Eden" as Bercovitch calls it (Transformations 157), the space that will be radically reconfigured and represented by Wallace as "ONAN" or the "Organization of North American Nations" in *Infinite Jest*.

The "Edenic" ideal has of course persisted in the Western (European and American) imagination for centuries, and it is present in Anglophone American writing from the sermons of seventeenth- and eighteenth-century Colonial ministers such as William Hubbard and Jonathan Edwards down to the writings of Ralph Waldo Emerson in the nineteenth-century, for whom, as Bercovitch notes, "America is a garden of plenty [...] a magazine of power." (Rites 63) Edwards described the Colonial settlements of the seventeenth century in terms of "the rising of a New Heaven and a New Earth in the New World"(qtd. in Rites 157), and in "Westward the Course of Empire Takes its Way" Wallace plays all of these ideas of American "newness" against each other—and then some. In addition to providing a critique of the social and cultural processes of capitalism he also calls into question the idea of cultural innovation-as-exception that extends to the text's explicit interrogations of the very metafictional techniques it seems, on the surface, to celebrate. "America" itself, however we perceive it, is presented not just as a fiction then but it is the great metafiction—or "Meatfiction" as the narrator puts it at one point (Curious 310): it represents pure recursion not just because it is haunted by an idea of itself that recurs throughout the nation's history but because it resists being defined except on (and in) its own terms. (Recursive formulae or formulations are always functions of themselves, in cultural and literary narratives as much as mathematics or computer science.)

Bercovitch's description of the American project as the pursuit of what he calls "the new end-time Eden" is useful then in understanding the ways that Wallace's text—after Berkeley—engages with notions of Americanness. It is also worth keeping in mind when considering the second (inter)textual signpost provided by Wallace in "Westward the Course of Empire Takes its Way." The first of two epigraphs—"As we are all solipsists, and all die, the world dies with us.

Only very minor literature aims at apocalypse." (232)—is taken from an essay by Anthony Burgess called "Endtime," a mixed review of historian and future studies scholar W. Warren Wagar's book Terminal Visions: the Literature of Last Things, first published in 1982. Interestingly, Wallace does not quote Burgess directly but brings two sentences together without indicating that they are quite separate in the original essay—they are from the first and last paragraphs in fact—but the epigraph indicates an interest in larger questions of self and world that, for all of the text's comic absurdity, are subsumed beneath the layers of metafictional playfulness that might be said to have distracted many critics and readers. Considering "Westward the Course of Empire Takes its Way," however, necessarily involves a consideration of all of those other texts that were drawn on by Wallace in making it, from Berkeley to Burgess to Barth and beyond, texts that ultimately enlarge the frame of reference for reading the novella beyond its purely biographical or primary bibliographical contexts. In an essay on *The Waste Land*, Harriet Davidson has described the function of allusion in Eliot's poem as "a metaphoric device [...] and a dispersive figure, multiplying contexts [...] and suggesting a cultural, historical dimension of difference." (Davidson 128) By alluding (indeed, referring) to Berkeley's poem in the title of his novella, Wallace invites us to consider the similarities and differences between the projections of America provided in both texts, despite their radically dissimilar generic and cultural backgrounds. In the epigraphs from Burgess and Barth he also indicates horizons of hermeneutic expectation—areas of interpretative possibility we are intended to explore—that are easy to miss in cursory readings that take for granted Wallace's subsequent dismissal of "Westward" and the assumption that his principle purpose in writing it was to examine the limits of metafictional technique.

Following the route suggested by the quotation from Burgess, however, brings us ultimately to a consideration of ideas about the value of literature in a text that seems, in its formal eccentricity, to resist such notions as those indicated by Wallace when he said that "wanted to [...] reaffirm the idea of art being a living transaction between humans" in the novella, a reaffirmation he believed he had failed to achieve. In "Endtime" Burgess asserts that:

Fiction is not about what happens to the world but what happens to a select group of human souls, with crisis or catastrophe as mere pretext for an exquisitely painful probing, as in James, of personal agonies and elations. If books have to be written about the end of the world, they should be speculative as science and not as subliterary criticism. (Burgess 16)

This is Burgess at his bitchiest, and it follows an earlier point where he says that "[t]he virtue of Professor Wagar's book on endtime is that he has read so much rubbish." (14) What he says here about Wagar's book is relevant to our understanding of Wallace's novella, however, and to our sense of his project as a writer: after all, Wallace himself stated that: "Fiction's about what it is to be a fucking human being." (Interview, McCaffery 131). The turn in "Westward the Course of Empire Makes its Way" towards Mark's discovery of himself as "Dave" in a story that marks a return to so-called traditional modes of narrative might be regarded as an example of such fiction but it is framed by Wallace within the larger American "story" in the novella, just as his comment about the nature of fiction and what it means to be human is followed by a culturally specific clarification:

If you operate, which most of us do, from the premise that there are things about the contemporary U.S. that make it distinctively hard to be a real human being, then maybe half of fiction's job is to dramatize what it is that makes it tough. The other half is to dramatize the fact that we still "are" human beings, now. Or can be. This isn't that it's fiction's duty to edify or teach, or to make us good little Christians or Republicans; I'm not trying to line up behind Tolstoy or Gardner. I just think that fiction that isn't exploring what it means to be human today isn't art. (131)

What Wallace doesn't say here is that there are things about the contemporary United States that make it distinctively hard, also, to be a writer, and the fascination of this particular difficulty in all of its human hilarity was one of the things he sought to examine in "Westward the Course of Empire Takes its Way," a text whose central theme in this reading of it is not the insufficiencies of metafiction in general but the American writer's failure to find a style that actually describes the mysterious "Way" signposted by Berkeley's poem.

"Westward the Course of Empire Takes its Way," like so much of what Wallace wrote, is far greater than the sum of its parts. Reading it without thinking too much about the work that comes later—without seeing it merely as a developmental milestone in Wallace's development towards *Infinite Jest*, as Boswell and others have suggested—repays careful consideration in itself, not least because of the way that it reveals the complex relation between truth and fiction in constructions of the American self. A belief in the idea that there is something unique or exceptional about the American project pervades American literature and American cultural production generally, but Wallace's novella, in its careful deployment of texts by Berkeley, Burgess, and others, also shows that the American story in itself—how it has been written in the past and how it might be told in the future—needs to be reconfigured to account for the lives of ordinary human beings without whom the notion of American identity would not need to exist. As he puts it in "Westward"'s concluding sequence, in a closing gesture that seems to affirm the profound humanism of Wallace's vision:

> See this thing. See inside what spins without purchase. Close your eye. Absolutely no salesman will call. Relax. Lie back. I want nothing from you. Lie back. Relax. Quality soil washes right out. Lie back. Open. Face directions. Look. Listen. Use ears I"d be proud to call our own. Listen to the silence behind the engines" noise. Jesus, Sweets, listen. Hear it? It's a love song.

> For whom?

> You are loved. (373)

Paul Giles has described Wallace as a "posthumanist" writer, but this passage seems to me to affirm his belief in the human capacity for love that persists beyond the delusions and deceptions of ideology and commerce. "Absolutely no salesman will call" he writes, signaling his desire to create a cultural space that might ultimately be free from the demands of politics and the marketplace. Until such a space can be found, it is up to the reader to decide how to read and negotiate the various texts that make her or his world, but Wallace insists on the matter of choice, implicitly in "Westward the Course of Empire Takes its Way" and explicitly in *This Is Water*, where he describes the pursuit of the kind of consciousness that "means being conscious and aware enough to *choose* what you pay attention to": "Because if you cannot or will not exercise this kind of choice in adult life," he continues, "you will be totally hosed" (54-55, emphasis original).

The Ideal Athlete: John Wayne in *Infinite Jest*

Gregory Phipps

In *Infinite Jest* Canada forms the paramount Other to America, a configuration which is, on the immediate level, highly satirical. Due to socioeconomic interconnections and a certain cultural colonialism, there is a light-hearted collective perception among Americans that Canada is a sort of "America Junior." At the same time, while much of the American national identity is grounded on idealistic and mythologized narratives of freedom, individualism, and the pursuit of the so-called American dream, such narratives—ranging from Paul Revere to the Founding Fathers—do not generally form part of a Canadian's education. Consequently, many Canadians find such narratives merely sentimental and self-servingly ideological. By positioning Canada as the primary antagonist to America, Wallace orients his representation of American idealism towards a dialectic in which Canada is oppositional merely through its general non-participation in the sentimentalized narratives of the American ethos. This dialectic is Hegelian insofar as its paramount ideal is freedom,[1] and, of course, the Quebecois A.F.R. insider Remy Marathe has many discussions with undercover agent Hugh Steeply about the possibility of social and political freedom. In the America of *Infinite Jest*, however, freedom is not, as in Hegel's philosophy, a continuously expanding manifestation of historical progress, but is rather a unidimensional extreme in an increasingly unstable dialectic movement. Freedom pushed to its self-contradictory nadir becomes a bizarre hybrid of solipsism and socially imposed constructions of empathy. Moreover,

---

1 In Hegel's worldview, the progression of human history is the continuous unfolding of Spirit, which is the movement towards an increasing consciousness of freedom. In *The Philosophy of History* Hegel states: "Freedom is the sole truth of Spirit" (17), because cultures are defined by the manifestation of freedom in both their ideals and, correspondingly, their political and social apparatuses. In *Infinite Jest* Steeply tells Marathe that the "crux of the educational system" in America is "To teach how to be free" (429).

the American dream itself is allied most closely to "The Show," a mechanistic industry which is known as a catalyst for addiction and self-destruction. What the America of *Infinite Jest* seems to need is not more freedom or a better use of freedom, but rather the negation of the very ideal of freedom—a role that the Quebecois anti-O.N.A.N. terrorists are willing to play.

Just as the word Canuck can refer to either a Canadian or, more specifically, a French Canadian, so too the boundaries between Canada and Quebec are slippery throughout *Infinite Jest*. In a long hilarious footnoted conversation, Orin Incandenza tries to work through the intentions of the Quebecois terrorists with his brother Hal. Of particular interest for Orin here is the "shift from anti-Canadian Quebecer nationalism to anti-O.N.A.N. Canadian nationalism" (1013), though Orin later states that this change might be part of a Quebecois nationalist attempt to "orchestrate the appearance of pan-*Canadian* anti-O.N.A.N.ism" (1020, emphasis original). This complex interweaving of Quebecois and Canadian identity is best exemplified through John Wayne, the top ranked tennis player at Enfield Academy. While his name is obviously Anglo, Wayne is from Montcerf, Quebec, "an asbestos-mining town ten clicks or so from the infamously rupture-prone Mercier Dam" (259). Prior to his arrival at Enfield he possessed both Canadian and Quebecois citizenship (262), but at the academy he is simply the "Canadian Wayne" (659)—something of a figurehead for all of Canada. For instance, when Kyle Coyle tells a joke "about what do Canadian girls put behind their ears to attract boys," the narrator focuses on Wayne's reaction, or rather lack thereof ("John Wayne gives him not a look" [633]); at another point, "John Wayne, as do most Canadians, lifts one leg slightly to fart, like the fart was some kind of task" (95). These rather vulgar examples form part of a more general trend in which Canadian identity is filtered through vague idiosyncrasies, including, among other things, "Canadianly inevitable checked-flannel shirts" (480); a "mammoth Canadian gut" (485); the "ethnic Canadian's horror of fluorescent light" (898); and various linguistic strains such as "Canadianese party-voices" (586) and "Nuck obscenities" (1015).

These examples of prototypical Canadian eccentricities are, for the most part, quite vacuous; for example, Coyle's misogynistic joke could involve potentially any nationality. The impression one gains from these "stereotypes" is that Canada is a blank entity to the American characters—an antagonist in which boorish habits stand in for a specific identity. Wayne himself is a personification of this projected vacuity, in part because he is not communicative. Teddy Schacht notes that Wayne is "as reserved as they come" (262-63), and Michael Pemulis verifies this view when he states that Wayne is "pretty much reserve in motion" (1073). Wayne's general manner is "less alive than undead" (263), and he always eats and studies alone, except when he is "seen with two or three expatriate E.T.A. Nucks" (263). Despite a fair number of appearances, Wayne ultimately seems to lack any sort of interiority, an impression strengthened by the numerous comparisons between him and machines. A "grim machine" (438) who is "Aimed like a fucking missile at the Show" (662), Wayne is a "pure force" (682) with "exactly one gear" (1010). He is not "fatiguable" (454), his "emotions emerge in terms of velocity" (263), and he is powered on the court by a "tungsten-steel will and resolve" (681). Whenever he plays against Wayne, Hal Incandenza "gets the creepy feeling that Wayne had control out there not just of his voluntary CNS but also of his heartrate and blood pressure, the diameter of his pupils" (1079).

While Wayne is undoubtedly a private person, his apparent lack of subjectivity is based largely on his inability to occupy the idealistic American narratives of athletics which would ostensibly humanize him. These narratives habitually center on validations of individual freedom and the actualization of the American dream. The ideal American athlete is one who displays tenacity in the face of hardship. Irrespective of his or her background and social circumstances, the athlete remains inexorably free to overcome any and all obstacles to "make it" as a star player. That is to say, the truly determined athlete does not let societal or economic restrictions bar the way to the American dream. Broadly speaking, there are two main subdivisions in this oft-repeated story: first, the athlete who overcomes injuries, and, second, the athlete who overcomes childhood poverty— and, as a result, is able to "rescue" his or her family. Wayne is the "best male player to appear at Enfield Academy in several years" (260) and fits squarely into the second category. His father is an asbestos miner in

Montcerf "who at forty-three is far and away the seniorest guy on his shift; he now wears triple-thick masks and is trying to hold on until John Wayne can start making serious $ and take him away from all this" (262).

Despite this classic story of deprivation, Wayne is not afforded the attendant sentimental and essentially one-size-fits-all story of struggle and potential victory. When the transvestite Hugh Steeply visits Enfield in the guise of Helen Steeply, a reporter for *Moment* magazine, Aubrey de Lint raises the issue of Wayne's place in the narrative of American athletics. Steeply is purportedly at Enfield to gather material for a story on Orin Incandenza, who left tennis to become an NFL punter; in actuality, Steeply is attempting to acquire information on a cartridge James Incandenza produced[2] which pulls its viewers into a state of infantile addiction—a cartridge the A.F.R. Quebecois terrorists plan to use as a weapon against O.N.A.N. While Steeply and de Lint converse as they watch the Enfield players practice on the Show Courts, Steeply works her hidden agenda by trying to gain access to Hal. De Lint chastises her for prying, remarking that Enfield is a "little slice of space and/or time that's been carved out to protect talented kids from exactly the kind of activities you guys come in here to do." De Lint proceeds to question the worth of pursuing a story on Orin:

> Why Orin anyway? The kid appears four times a game, never gets hit, doesn't even wear pads. A one-trick pony. Why not John Wayne? A more dramatic story, geopolitics, privation, exile, drama. A better player than Hal even. A more complete game. Aimed like a fucking missile at the Show, maybe the Top Five if he doesn't fuck up or burn down. Wayne's your ideal food group. Which is why we'll keep you off him as long as he's here.

> Steeply simply responds by looking around the Show Courts and asking: "Carved out of what, though, this place?" (662)

While the tunnels underneath Enfield are carved out of "sedimentary shale and ferrous granite and generic morphic

---

[2] The film entitled *Infinite Jest V*, though some "archival authorities" list it as *Infinite Jest IV* (993).

crud" (666), the covers over the courts are associated with snow. Teddy Schacht notes that the "E.T.A. Lung" (268) which covers the Center Courts resembles the "inflated shape of a distended igloo" (269), as though the protective bubble has been built from snow. Later, Hal recalls a blizzard which came "barrelling in southeast from Canada" and overloaded the covers of the courts: "The Lung's new bubble had had to be taken down and fixed when snow-weight stove it in on one side" (949). That the snowstorm originates in Canada is not merely realistic but an extension of a common American perception of the "Great White North." As Hal himself indicates, one of the problems that has arisen in Quebec because of the waste in the Concavity is the appearance of "grotesquely asymmetrical snow-crystals" (1017). So too the comparison between the Lung and an igloo might be partly Schacht's own association—at the time, he is preparing to play against a French Canadian from Port Washington whose face has "a kind of Eskimoid structure to it" (267). While the various stereotypes which cluster around Canadians in *Infinite Jest* are usually rather elastic, superficial American perceptions of Canada *do* often include mentions of snow, igloos, and the Inuit. If one potential answer to Steeply's question is "snow," de Lint's conception of Enfield as a time and place carved out to protect talented kids takes on another meaning. Instead of a story about Wayne's privation and exile, we get a protective cover which merely projects a series of stereotypes about Canada.

Why *can't* Wayne be the subject of a triumphant story about geopolitics and exile and drama? The facile response would be because he is Canadian, but, in actuality, the standard mawkish narrative of American athletics is very much open to non-Americans. In *Infinite Jest*, however, Wayne's background is too charged with the very socio-political issues de Lint thinks would make an interesting story—and Steeply probably knows it. In mainstream contemporary American sports the story of the "inner city youth" (almost always a term used in lieu of "African American youth") who overcomes poverty to make it as a star must always elide questions concerning the political and social causes behind the lack of opportunity and infrastructural development in the so-called inner city. In Wallace's satire, Wayne's entire story is taboo because he comes from a region of Quebec that is not only a hotbed for terrorist cells but is also known for birth defects ("kids the size of Volkswagens shlumpfing around with no skulls . . . infants born with just one eye in the middle of their forehead" [1017]) caused by waste management in the Concavity. It is therefore fitting that de Lint would raise the question of Wayne's story with Steeply; Helen Steeply the journalist might be willing to write a feel-good story about Wayne's steadily increasing chance of making it to "the Show," but Hugh Steeply the O.U.S. operative would be well aware of the potential firestorm (or snowstorm, as the case may be) a comprehensive profile of Wayne could release.

With no access to a conventional American tale of athletic hardship, alternate narrative threads cluster around the reticent Wayne. One of these threads is, as mentioned, composed largely of both fictive and familiar stereotypes about Canadians; another strand is supplied by Teddy Schacht. Schacht fits into the other category of the athlete who battles his or her way through adversity: he has fought to overcome both injuries (a knee injury at the age of sixteen) and illness (Crohn's disease). However, despite returning to the courts, Schacht does not occupy a standard narrative centered on the athlete's refusal to allow injuries to stand in the way of the American dream. Instead, Schacht has adopted the philosophy of indifference—an attitude that sports fans generally despise. Schacht even believes that his "tennis seems to have improved slightly in the two years since he stopped really caring," though he has to admit that "everybody else has been improving too, even faster" (266). The attitude of indifference that is so loathsome to fans has a counterpart in the business-oriented approach to the game, best demonstrated by the athlete who takes no measures to conceal the overarching importance of money and in fact even refers to the game as a "business." It is precisely this business-first approach that Schacht identifies with Wayne:

> The thing about Wayne is he's all business . . . It's wholly unclear to Schacht how Wayne feels about the U.S. or his citizenship-status. He figures Wayne figures it doesn't much matter: he is destined for the Show; he will be an all-business entertainer, citizen of the world, everywhere undead, endorsing juice drinks and liniment ointment. (262-263)

Here, Wayne's desire to make enough money to rescue his father from his dreadful job veers away from a story of tenacity towards a more cynical narrative. In the absence of the former storyline, Schacht is quite at his liberty to craft a harsh evaluation of Wayne's motivations. Needless to say, this evaluation is self-serving; Schacht even achieves some degree of imagined superiority over Wayne when he reflects that he would never "let an academy tell him what brand of stick to swing" (263).

While Schacht guesses that Wayne is indifferent to his citizenship status (both his Quebecois and Canadian citizenships were revoked when he came to Enfield), it is, in fact, precisely this status which leaves the door open for Schacht to build the all-business future-endorser version of Wayne. Of course, the point is that Schacht, like the other students at Enfield, does *not* know how Wayne feels. Wayne's consciousness is concealed throughout most of the novel, but different interpretations of his rather blank public identity gather around him—based on his status as a Canadian expatriate, his "all business" approach to tennis, and, in Hal's case, his machine-like efficiency on the court. Significantly, Wayne is first discovered by James Incandenza, who originally wanted to use Wayne in one of his avant-garde films. The film, entitled *Homo Duplex*, is a "Parody of Woititz and Shulgin's 'poststructural antidocumentaries'"[3] and contains "interviews with fourteen Americans who are named John Wayne but are not the legendary 20th-century film actor John Wayne" (988). The title refers to Emile Durkheim's theorization of duality, which maintains that the pursuit of individualistic desires is only restrained by strong social integration. In *Infinite Jest*, however, the duality of the individual operates through a fractious dialectic. American-style freedom is pushed to a destructive philosophic conclusion: the individual is inexorably free because she cannot traverse the boundaries of her own consciousness or experience another individual's subjectivity, and is thus not dependent on anyone or anything. This idea, which is

---

[3] The names Woititz and Shulgin probably allude to the writers Janet Woititz and Alexander Shulgin. Woititz wrote therapeutic books with titles such as *Adult Children of Alcoholics* and *Self-Sabotage Syndrome: Adult Children in the Workplace*. Shulgin wrote books about the uses of psychedelics to treat depression.

painfully common in philosophy, is perhaps best expressed by Wittgenstein in the *Tractatus*: "For what the solipsist *means* is quite correct; only it cannot be *said*, but makes itself manifest" (emphasis original, trans. Pears/McGuiness 68).

As critics such as Catherine Nichols, Mary K. Holland,[4] and Timothy Jacobs have indicated, one of the paramount thematic concerns in *Infinite Jest* is solipsism. In an article in which he draws parallels between *Infinite Jest* and *The Brothers Karamazov*, Jacobs writes: "Wallace's concern with belief is often yoked to his concern with American cultural solipsism; belief is essential, in his view, to considering something that is larger than the immediate subject, something that shifts the solitary perspective beyond the self-absorbed concerns of the contemporary individual" ("Brothers Incandenza" 268). Jacobs further reinforces the particularly American character of this "cultural solipsism" when he states that *Infinite Jest* deals with the "acute problems of millennial American (dis)belief: a jaded, ironic perspective and solipsistic pursuit of individual 'happiness'" (276). What Jacobs does not note is that it is only through a dialectical construction of specifically American mythological and historical ideals such as freedom, individualism (the pursuit of happiness), and the American dream that this collective solipsism can be conceived as uniquely *American*. There is, after all, no reason why such an assessment cannot apply to Canada, unless one implies that this hegemonic American solipsism infiltrates surrounding cultures. On the other hand, in the world of *Infinite Jest*, the focus on the dialectic movement of an American brand of freedom positions Canada as *the* Other—an antagonist to American ideology, and, by extension, an oppressed victim of American infrastructure. Interestingly, Wayne's "not-to-be-fucked-with papa" litigated his son's role out of *Homo Duplex* because "the film had the word *Homo* in the title" (*Jest* 260). John Wayne the actor was himself a classic American personage; straddling the divide between law enforcement and a rugged individualistic frontier spirit, he personified the mythic (and paradoxical) connection between

---

[4] See Catherine Nichols's "Dialogizing Postmodern Carnival: David Foster Wallace's *Infinite Jest*," especially page 10, and Mary K. Holland's "The Art's Heart's Purpose: Braving the Narcissistic Loop of David Foster Wallace's *Infinite Jest*."

frontier life and the development of institutional democracy in America. Not surprisingly, Wayne's father does not appear to have any interest in this American figurehead, but because of his homophobia the film becomes a collection of interviews with fourteen *Americans*—a development which buttresses Hal's view that "Himself's work was all very self-consciously American" (1011).

At first glance, the contradiction at the core of the dialectically one-sided solipsistic incarnation of idealized American freedom is the array of socially entrenched imperatives which enforce this purported liberty. While the American government and military are already well known for "defending freedom" overseas and at home, the command to live freely or enjoy your freedom is also one of many subtle cultural "suggestions" which displace the very ontological state they supposedly try to foster. The ineffectual backlash against solipsism operates in much the same way in *Infinite Jest*, as the need for greater empathy and stronger bonds between people are institutionalized as commands—witness Hal's hilarious encounter with Kevin Bain at what he thinks is a Narcotics Anonymous meeting. Meanwhile, the Canadian John Wayne seems to stand entirely on the outside of this dialectic. His consciousness is hidden throughout most of the novel, but this concealment is precisely what makes Wayne something of a cipher. He is not a personification of solipsism, because he does not appear to have any thoughts or feelings at all; consequently, characters are able to impose *their* thoughts and feelings onto him to construct his narrative identity. Moreover, Wayne never gives any indication that he is in need of empathy or a confidante.

Wayne is nonetheless assuredly carrying a lot of baggage, notwithstanding his apparent vacuity. For one thing, Wayne is related in some undefined way to Bernard Wayne, the most reviled player in the history of the bizarre and deadly *le Jeu du Pochain Train*. This game forms the central trial of courage in a "Suicidal Nuck cult" known as *La Culte du Pochain Train*. Played among the "male offspring of asbestos, nickel, and zinc miners in the desolate Papineau region of what was then extreme southwest Quebec" (1058), the game involves "jumping in front of trains and seeing which Nuck could come the closest to the train's front without getting demapped" (560). Marathe's own terrorist organization (the A.F.R.—*Les Assassins des Fauteuils Rollents*, or the

"Wheelchair Assassins") is supposedly composed of "veteran devotees and practitioners of this savage, nihilistic, and mettle testing *jeu poure-meme*" (1058, italics original). Bernard Wayne was the only "miner's son" (1060) in the history of the game to refrain from jumping before the train passed. He was subsequently held in contempt and later drowned in the Baskatong Reservoir (1060). While the connection between Bernard Wayne and John Wayne is unclear, they are almost certainly relatives of some sort.[5] To say the least, John Wayne must have many emotional and even traumatic memories of growing up in Quebec. For one, he is linked in some way to the Quebecois terrorists, and, for another, he almost certainly suffered from the stigma attached to Bernard Wayne, not to mention the pain of the latter's death, which, after all, may not have been accidental.

In a related vein, Wayne's affair with Avril Incandenza has undoubtedly brought its own share of emotional turmoil. The relationship between Enfield's top tennis player and the matriarch of the Incandenza family is grounded partially or perhaps even largely on nationality. Avril is from L'Islet county and becomes aggravated at any mention of 1759, the year the Battle of Quebec was fought; moreover, according to Steeply's information, she has a penchant for having sex with "everything with a pulse . . . Particularly a Canadian pulse" (92). At the same time, Avril uses Wayne to enact an Oedipal fantasy. When Michael Pemulis walks into Avril's office he finds her wearing a "cheerleader's outfit" while Wayne crouches in a three point stance wearing a "football helmet and light shoulderpads and a Russell athletic supporter and socks and shoes and nothing else." Wayne is making the "classic low-register growling sounds of U.S. football" while Avril does "near splits"[6] and blows on a whistle "which appeared to be minus the little inside pellet because no whistling sound resulted" (552-553). The two have obviously crafted the tableau with

---

[5] Stephen Burn speculates that Bernard Wayne is John Wayne's father, in which case the A.F.R. might have forced Wayne to watch the *Infinite Jest IV/V* cartridge to punish the "son for the sins of his father" (38). This cannot be the case, though, because John Wayne's father is still alive.

[6] Incidentally, "Orin was the only male anybody at E.T.A.'d ever heard of who could do a fully splayed cheerleader-type split" (101).

Orin in mind, though there are many notable dissimilarities between Wayne's role-playing and Orin's task as an NFL punter. For one thing, a punter never gets into a three point stance (in fact, Orin's stance while awaiting a snap is "not unlike a diver's" [299]) and, for another, the "light shoulderpads" Wayne wears oppose the "padless uniform" (294) Orin wears when he is first starting out as the punter at Boston University, a contrast which is reinforced when de Lint tells Steeply she should forget about a football player who "never gets hit [and] doesn't even wear pads" (662) and concentrate on someone more like Wayne.

The crux of these connections between Wayne and his home country are elusive and ambivalent. Avril is linked to the ruthless Luria Perec, who works for the A.F.R. and seduces Orin in order to gain information about the location of James Incandenza's cartridge. Like Avril, Luria is from L'Islet county, and that their names are almost anagrams suggests that they may even be the same person. Is Wayne therefore an A.F.R. insider working with an Avril-Luria hybrid? The A.F.R. is able to make plans to infiltrate Enfield by replacing the provincial Quebec tennis team in part because there is a "Canadian instructor and student already inside" (726). Wayne very well could be the insider, because he obviously has some connection to the A.F.R. through Bernard Wayne. On the other hand, the latter was such an abhorrent figure to *La Culte du Pochain Train* that Wayne himself might have suffered some form of exile from the group. The various descriptions of Wayne as a machine link him symbolically to the train, as does de Lint's assessment that Wayne is, like Ortho Stice, a "straight-out killer" (659) on the court. Does this connection imply that Wayne is akin to a destructive force to the Quebecois terrorists? According to a *Wild Conceits* article James Albrecht Lockley Struck Jr. plagiarizes for an assignment, "*Les Assassins*' confinement to their epithetic wheelchairs can be traced to rural southwestern pre-Experialist Quebec's infamous '*Le Jeu du Prochain Train*,'" (1058) though the article also states that Quebec infants suffering from birth defects because of waste in the Concavity are "essentially passive icons of the Experialist gestalt" (1056). In other words, the train stands in as an O.N.A.N. sponsored excuse for disabilities in Quebec. Similarly, Wayne could be a token representative of Quebecois success within the hegemony of O.N.A.N. After all, if *he* can be such an absurdly fit and successful athlete, then perhaps the health problems in the Concavity are exaggerated.

Despite these ambiguities, Wayne does ultimately provide a version of what the A.F.R. terrorists are trying to accomplish: a spectacular negation of self-contradictory solipsistic American freedom which moves beyond the culture of enforced empathy and openness. For all his reticence, Wayne has an abundance of thoughts and feelings about Enfield and his peers and teachers,[7] and, with some inadvertent help from Pemulis's Tenuates, he seizes control of the WETA broadcast and begins "insanely holding forth innermost thoughts for public ears" (1072). There is a prevailing fear at Enfield that athletic success brings self-destruction, particularly when "the Show" emerges as a definite possibility for a player. For instance, Ivan Lendl "suicided well before the advent of Subsidized Time" (259), and a star player from Fresno, California drank Quik laced with cyanide after winning the Pacific Coast Hardcourt Boys 18's, an event that prompted tennis academies to staff a counselor to "screen student athletes for their possibly lethal reactions to ever actually reaching the level they've been pointed at for years" (437). At Enfield the counselor is a (ultimately useless) response to the perception that "there are certain very talented players who just cannot keep the lip stiff and fires stoked if they ever finally do achieve a top ranking or win some important events" (436). De Lint, of course, mentions the possibility that Wayne—who *is* the top ranked player at Enfield—might "fuck up or burn down." If Wayne is "Aimed like a fucking missile at the Show," one would expect a detonation at the point of impact. Explosions are tied to athletic success (Hal's turnaround on the court is referred to as a "competitive explosion" [635] and an "erumpent explosion up the rankings" [270]), and Wayne himself is also linked to explosions: he runs into the tarp in a match against a Port Washington player with a "boom that resounds" (261), and later in the same match he hits a backhand so hard "a little mushroom cloud of green fuzz hangs in the air" (269). At

---

[7] If he is the A.F.R. insider then he has in fact been systematically collecting information about them as part of his "surveillance" (726).

the same time, explosions invoke self-destruction, most notably James Incandenza's horrific death.

The explosion of the senior Incandenza's head in a microwave is linked to Wayne's on-air meltdown. While Incandenza's self-destruction is a physical and grotesque eruption of interiority into the external world (what remains of his head is afterwards plastered on "the kitchen walls" [253]), Wayne's mind explodes in a more symbolic manner. After apparently not speaking to any of his peers at Enfield during his duration at the academy, he launches into a drug-induced diatribe against numerous students and teachers over WETA. Among other things, he imitates Charles Tavis, Avril's lover and the head of the academy; but the imitation actually involves one of Orin's patented seduction techniques. He also states that Hal is "by all appearances addicted to everything that is not tied down, cannot outrun him, and is fittable in the mouth" and also targets students Francis Unwin and Bernadette Longley, and a number of faculty members including James Incandenza himself, who, according to Wayne, was "so full of himself he could have shit limbs" (1074). This abrupt externalization of Wayne's private thoughts and feelings supplants the narratives that others have constructed on his behalf. His rant also depicts the detonation of an ideal of freedom that has spiraled towards an increasingly paradoxical telos of solipsism. Wayne is something of a blank slate before his eruption, but over WETA he amply demonstrates that he has not only thoughts and emotions but bitter grievances. However, on the narrative level, the solipsistic interpretation of consciousness is entirely sublated here, as Wayne goes from having no subjectivity to expressing all of his innermost thoughts in a single bound. The Canadian Wayne thus provides a dramatic negation of American "free solipsism": at one point his consciousness is so private that it is basically non-existent, and at the next moment it is bursting forth into the public sphere.

The implication of the Wayne episode is that while consciousness may appear to be private and wholly "mine" it is, in actuality, always on the cusp of erupting into the exoteric environment. Yet, Wayne's self-detonation is not an argument against solipsism but simply a negation. It is, in fact, Hal who provides a measured opposition to solipsism. In one of the more famous passages in the novel, Hal runs through a series of associative thoughts: "The bad ankle hasn't ached once this whole year. I think of John N.R. Wayne, who would have won this year's WhataBurger, standing watch in a mask as Donald Gately and I dig up my father's head. There's very little doubt that Wayne would have won" (16-17). The chain of association begins with Hal's ankle and proceeds to Wayne, a sequence which looks back in time and forward in the narrative to a pep talk Coach Schtitt gives his players: "Use a head. You are not arms. Arm in the real tennis is like wheels of vehicles. Not engine. Legs: not either. Where is where you apply for citizenship in second world Mr. *consciousness of ankle* Incandenza, our revenant?" (461, italics mine). Here, Schtitt implies that Hal is in second place ("in second world") to Wayne at Enfield because he is worrying too much about an injury. Hal replies drolly: "The human head, sir, if I got your thrust. Where I'm going to occur as a player. The game's two heads' one world. One world, sir" (461).

Hal construes Schtitt's words philosophically; there are not two worlds, but instead two heads which belong to "the game." Furthermore, there is one world which belongs to the two heads. In other words, while there may be an ontological division between one's own consciousness and the consciousness of one's opponent, both minds not only occupy one world but also contribute to the making of the world. The attempt to recover James Incandenza's head, then, is not based on the desire to recover an inaccessible private consciousness but is rather an attempt to locate a tangible object which continues to influence the world even after Incandenza Sr.'s mind has been destroyed—the cartridge. As for John Wayne, his application for citizenship in *first* world, as it were, might ultimately have been based on the extreme antipathy he felt for his fellow peers and Americans in general. Perhaps he did not win the WhataBurger because his outburst deprived him of the pent-up anger and intensity which made him an ideal athlete.

Infinite Jest: Triangles, Cycles, Choices & Chases

David Hering

In an interview conducted for KCRW Radio's Bookworm program in 1996 following the publication of *Infinite Jest*, the following exchange took place between David Foster Wallace and host Michael Silverblatt:

> **Silverblatt**: It occurred to me that the way in which the material is presented allows for a subject to be announced in a small form, then there seems to be a fan of subject matter, other subjects, and then it comes back in a second form containing the other subjects in small, and then comes back again as if what were being described were—and I don't know this kind of science, but it just—I said to myself this must be fractals.

> **Wallace**: It's—I've heard you were an acute reader. That's one of the things, structurally, that's going on. It's actually structured like something called a Sierpinski Gasket (…) it went through some I think "mercy cuts," so it's probably kind of a lopsided Sierpinski Gasket now. But it's interesting, that's one of the structural ways that it's supposed to kind of come together (...) it looks basically like a pyramid on acid. (Interview, Bookworm 1996)

A Sierpinski gasket is a fractal and an example of a "self-similar set" (see Fig. 1). The process of constructing a Sierpinski gasket can potentially go on indefinitely (or perhaps more appropriately, infinitely). I argue that Wallace's schema occurs within *Infinite Jest* not only at the level of narrative construction but also, with recourse to several thematic examples and latterly an extended analysis of a specific sequence from the novel, as a series of implicit and explicit geographical shape templates employed to illustrate and dramatize the themes of choice, absence and addiction.

Fig. 1

Greg Carlisle's discussion of the novel's division into 28 distinct chapters is an appropriate starting point for my analysis. *Infinite Jest* follows broadly a pattern of 28 chapters, containing subchapters, which gradually grow in size, and are chronologically non-linear. The novel begins with 15 chapters in 179 pages and climaxes with just 1 chapter in 173 pages (*Elegant Complexity* 17). This begins to illustrate the triangular "fractal" form discussed above.[1] The reader gradually becomes aware of an increase in the size and focus of the chapters as they read, and the initial smaller chapters—relatable to the smaller triangles of the gasket shape— are later retrospectively understood to form part of the overarching structure so we are ultimately aware of the gargantuan system of relationships that operates across the entire novel. The final, enormous chapters, which length-wise could constitute entire novels in themselves, bring much of the novel's thematic content together and also hint at the solution of several overarching mysteries, while not persuasively solving any of them. These chapters relate to the overarching larger triangles of the gasket, that is, understanding of these final chapters necessitates a previous understanding of the component parts of the gasket—the previous, shorter chapters.

However, Wallace's deliberate obfuscation of straight answers to the principle enigmas of the novel reminds the reader that they are regarding a schema characterized as much by absence as by presence, and if we look again at the Sierpinski gasket, we may note that each configuration of three triangles is also accompanied by the apparent visible absence of another triangle. A number of extremely important events within the novel are entirely absent from the text. An appropriate example: a series of linked incidents involving the death of James Incandenza are absented and referred to so elliptically (and often in contradictory accounts) that it is basically impossible to form a definitive picture. The first is James' suicide, which apparently involved him putting his head inside a microwave oven, the aftermath of which was discovered by his young son Hal. An evasive conversation about

---

1 (Wallace has also spoken of how he regards the processes of discovery in mathematics and the hard sciences as being "pyramidical. They're like building a cathedral'"[Interview, McCaffery 133]).

the discovery between Hal and his brother Orin suggests initially that Jim's head might have exploded, but this runs contrary to another reference by Hal to a mysterious incident entirely absent from the main narrative where he is digging up James' interred head with Don Gately. Gately is the novel's second principle protagonist, and a man who has basically no knowledge of or contact with Hal within the main narrative. Additionally, the suggestions that Jim may have had the master copy of "Infinite Jest" buried inside his head, and also that his head contains a mysterious gyroscopic device, create a plethora of confusing absences for the reader in relation to these incidents. *[margin note: Maintain orientation]*

Additional narrative absences appear on a micro scale. An item of clothing may be used to identify a character rather than a name (Poor Tony Krause's wig and coat, for example), and on occasion a character will be introduced in part (a first-person voice, without any physical attributes identified) before their later appearance in body or name. The reader's inference, rather than a direct authorial command or identification, will then serve to identify them. This can therefore be characterized as a narrative strategy of absence (of details deliberately withheld) and inference (of enough suggestion to allow the reader to conjecture, if not definitively). If we look again at Greg Carlisle's discussion of how the Sierpinski Gasket is constructed—"an iterative process of cutting smaller triangle-sized holes out of larger triangles" (*Elegant Complexity* 20) we can begin to understand the process by which Wallace's narrative schema operates, as an initially complete structure within which details are then methodically absented to prompt the reader into a process of inference. To quote Wallace, "this process is a relationship between the writer's consciousness and her own, and that in order for it to be anything like a full human relationship, she's going to have to put in her share of the linguistic work" (Interview, McCaffery 138).

Wallace's employment of the triangular structure does not limit itself to an implicit narrative strategy. Specifically delineated triangular shapes, both present and absent, make appearances at important junctures throughout *Infinite Jest*, with the reinforcing effect of making events within the narrative itself physically resemble the geometric schema for the overall narrative. As well as the appearance of several specific visual triangular shapes within the novel—for example the concentric triangular pattern of the CITGO sign (which is significantly described as "a triangular star to steer by" [*Jest* 476]) and the young James Incandenza's body forming one side of the outline of a "right dihedral triangle" (495) as he helps his father to examine a faulty mattress—there are also implicit triangular shapes in *Infinite Jest* which recall the absent triangles essential to construction of the Sierpinski Gasket. Two examples of this: Mario Incandenza's stance when braced against his cantilevered police lock creates an implied triangular shape formed by the front of his body, the ground and the lock (the apex of the triangle is marked by Mario's heart), and the punishing Star Drills practiced by the ETA students (456) trace triangular shapes across the tennis courts.

Wallace also employs the image of a "massive pseudocartographic right triangle" (571) to illustrate the process of annular fusion, the enormous self-contained waste-based energy system

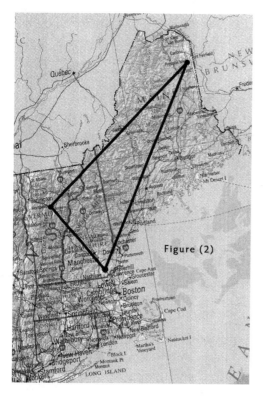

Figure (2)

employed by O.N.A.N. The triangulated process is also a cycle, a "type of fusion that can produce waste that's fuel for a process whose waste is fuel for the fusion" (572). The locations of the waste plants form a triangular shape across what was New England (see Fig. 2) and would initially appear to present a self-sufficient system that generates no excess waste. However, it is discovered that the process is so efficient that it removes all inhibitors to plant and animal growth in the area, necessitating the further dumping of toxins to control the lush flora and fauna that spring up at a moment's notice. What has initially appeared to be a system that operates efficiently as a self-contained, insular cycle has actually spiraled dangerously out of control, with terrible incremental entropic repercussions for all around it. The image of the triangular cycle of annular fusion here is significant thematically, as it conflates a delineated outline of a triangle with the image of a cycle, a process that is more commonly geometrically associated with a circle. [2]

The young James Incandenza's description of a simplified image of the process of annular fusion as "someone (trying) to turn somersaults with one hand nailed to the floor"(503) initializes the idea of the annular process in the reader's mind as both a cyclical process and a pattern of behavior in which the individual is physically restrained, their movement dictated by a personal obstacle which refuses to release them from a specific path. The shape described by James Incandenza here is circular, and the cyclical process of annular fusion is later described as both circular and triangular in nature. This is an essential further conflation of geometry with theme, because within Infinite Jest Wallace also employs the triangle, the circle and the cycle to describe processes of recollection, narrative construction, addiction and personal choice.

The "absences" in the Sierpinski gasket, in addition to representing the absence of key episodes within the narratives of the protagonists, also relate to the depictions of psychological oblivion, either willed or unwilled, that pervade the novel. Many of the novel's principal characters are addicts, both lapsed and recovering, mediating between awareness and denial that they are trapped within a cycle of addictive behavior, and in some instances the addicts have been through the cycle of addiction and recovery many times before. Consider the triangular and cyclical process of annular fusion described above in relation to the destructive cyclical behavior of an addict, whereby an ostensibly self-contained and directed process

2 This image also highlights the plethora of references within the novel to the delineation of maps and geographical inclinations: the map/territory arguments in the Eschaton game (333) and indeed the game itself, the conflation of maps and either heads or bodies (see the oft-quoted expression to eliminate one's map) and the numerous and highly detailed references to areas of Boston, to which I will return later in this analysis.

eventually causes traumatic repercussions outside of the originally delineated area. The image of a continuously determined circular path can also represent an imprisoning structure which prohibits free movement outside of a cycle of behavior, exemplary of the type of process that N. Katherine Hayles refers to in her analysis of *Infinite Jest* as "recursive feedback loops" (684). Such a path is determined by both chemical and psychological addiction—the addict can be aware of their imprisonment while unable to free themselves under their own power, going continuously around and around the cycle of addictive and self-destructive behavior. A graphic illustration of this occurs when Don Gately tells Joelle Van Dyne about an occasion on which he walked a critically injured man around in circles to try and keep him conscious, only for the man to eventually die (*Jest* 532).

The oppositions inherent within a character trapped inside such a state are as follows: the urge to leave the destructive path of the cycle against an apparent choice to remain constricted by the familiarity of the cycle's self-centered or solipsistic processes. However, in *Infinite Jest* a circular or cyclical motion can also anticipate unification rather than disorientation. Wallace presents the work of the Alcoholics and Narcotics Anonymous groups in *Infinite Jest* as an attempt to reclaim the image of the circle, making the choice to employ circular motifs in a manner that acts against solipsism rather than perpetuating it. Perhaps the best example of this is the "traditional huge circle" (503) employed by the NA group attended by Ken Erdedy and Kate Gompert. By employing the image of the circle as a process of unification and identification with others, the "vicious" circle or cycle of addiction and solipsism is recontextualized and disarmed, and we have a circular image defined by a connecting of individuals that opposes that of the solo imprisoned somersaulter nailed to the floor. Much of the recovery process also depends upon the addict's knowledge of the danger of any personalized cycles of behavior. Joelle notes that there can even be a part of the recovery process where "the cycle becomes annular and insidious"(535) if the addict gives themselves away to feelings of insecurity. Essentially, it is the addict's awareness of the possibility of another kind of circle, one outside of his or her own personalized "route," that leads to their escape from the determined path of addiction.

94

ie one labyrinth to another,
h/w

David Hering

These dimensions of spatiality and physicality in *Infinite Jest* are also explicitly connected to the concept of personal freedoms. The eponymous film cartridge reduces those who watch it to a state of permanent infantilization. Anti-O.N.A.N terrorists wish to use the cartridge in a terror campaign against the citizens of O.N.A.N., but during an extensive conversation between the Canadian terrorist Remy Marathe and federal agent Hugh Steeply the necessity of terror tactics to inflict *Infinite Jest* on the general populace is questioned. Marathe suggests that rather than violent imposition of the cartridge, the A.F.R. need only make the cartridge available to people. "There will be then some choosing, to partake or choose not to," says Marathe. Subsequently describing O.N.A.N. as a "confusion of permissions," Marathe lectures Steeply on how "someone let your peoples forget it was the only thing of importance, choosing." Marathe suggests that the concept of personal freedom that is perceived as essential to the American character is in fact corrupted and has become solipsistic, "a freedom-from: no-one tells your precious individual U.S.A. selves what they must do....what of freedom-to?" (319-320).

Marathe's dissection of the differences inherent in national definitions of freedom presents on a macro scale the individual problems of the aforementioned addicts. Marathe posits that "How to choose any but a child's greedy choices if there is no loving-filled father to guide, inform, teach the person how to choose?" (320). The idea of "freedom-from" appeals to the addict, trapped in a cycle of behavior. "Freedom-from" suggests both an apparently unlimited physical space and also potential psychological entrapment in the definition of the self against the other, that is, the illusion of a chosen path. In fact, without "freedom-to," such a path becomes the aforementioned solipsistic cycle with only the illusion of choice, a trap within which one becomes locked into pathological, infantile behavior.

I believe that a graphically concise dramatization of the critical points that I have just argued—that is, the reflection of the novel's triangular and circular schemas in the behavior of its characters, the importance of absence and reader inference in the narrative to depict and comment upon cycles of behavior and solipsism, the making of choices, the geographical notion of choice and the chooser's subjection to overarching structures—appears around two-thirds of the way

95

through the novel. An episode occurs depicting a frenzied series of simultaneous events involving several characters in the area between Central Square and Inman Square in Cambridge, MA, an area in which Wallace lived during his brief research tenure at Harvard in the late 1980s. To communicate the analysis of this sequence as clearly as possible, it is necessary to provide a brief summation of the situation and characters:

- Poor Tony Krause has discharged himself from Cambridge Hospital following a detox seizure and is heading to a shop owned by the Antitoi brothers, located—following Wallace's descriptions—somewhere in the area between Prospect Street and Broadway (*Jest* 689).
- Ruth Van Cleve and Kate Gompert are walking along Prospect Street, their bags being eyed by Poor Tony Krause (698).
- Randy Lenz is following two Chinese women, looking at their bags, the other way along Prospect Street (716).
- Matty Pemulis is in a Portuguese restaurant right next to Inman Square, and sees the beginning of the action from the window (682).

Both Krause and Lenz snatch the bags of their prospective victims and run away, Poor Tony pursued by Ruth Van Cleve. The

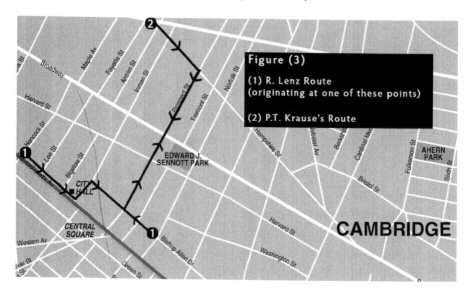

Figure (3)

(1) R. Lenz Route
(originating at one of these points)

(2) P.T. Krause's Route

actions of both Krause and Lenz broadly mirror each other in relation to the location of Prospect Street (see Fig. 3), though this mirroring appears to descend into chaos when both men disappear into a hellish system of labyrinthine alleyways off the main thoroughfares, and Wallace's fairly lucid geographical descriptions disappear. The climax of both men's journeys are, again, absent from the narrative, though much later (845) we discover that their journeys (and lives) both ended in the electronics shop run by the Canadian Antitoi brothers, where they have both been subjected by A.F.R. terrorists to the lethally entertaining film cartridge.

The behavior of the characters in this sequence is subject to the geography of the streets that surround them, though Wallace also embeds within that city geography a suggestion of physical restraint placed upon the individual by a state of addiction and pathological behavior. Both Krause and Lenz instigate separate chaotic chases, and move from clearly delineated spaces to more confusing geographical areas (and eventually to death—a permanent state of absence), through an apparent moment of personal choice—their separate decisions to commit theft. Physical subjugation—both that imposed by the physical environment and also through personal choice—is represented in this sequence through an overt and covert employment of shape diagrams, principally circular and triangular in nature.

Wallace has already established the circular motif as representative of personal restraint and pathological behavior and the sequence contains several circular allusions or movements. Lenz sees a man firing a suction arrow at the wall of a building, then "drawing a miniature chalk circle on the brick around the arrow, and then another circle around that circle, and etc., as in a what's the word" (718). The narrative voice, which incorporates Lenz's prejudices, and which has been foregrounded as ignorant already through a series of racist observations about the Chinese women, remembers the word later in the narrative ("Bull's-eye"[719]) The distance between the observation and the definition, and the fact that the circular image is only eventually perceived by the narrator as having a centripetal function, suggests a focus directed only upon the immediate center and a lack of awareness of the other potential association, that of the concentric circles. In a narrative that has already suggested a circular motion as analogous to an imprisoning cycle of pathological behavior, concentric circles suggest something even more impenetrably inescapable. The significance of the concentric circle image at this point in the narrative suggests that the addict Lenz's notion of choice (to steal the bag or not) is in fact only a delusion of choice, trapped within several unrecognized concentric circles of addictive or pathological behavior.

Consider the order of the narrative during the street sequence. Matty Pemulis notices Krause briefly on the street around Inman Square (683). Subsequently Poor Tony is depicted in a later chapter in more detail walking alone from Cambridge Hospital to the junction of Inman Square (690) where Matty Pemulis sees him before heading down Prospect Street. Poor Tony subsequently sees Kate Gompert and Ruth Van Cleve walking. In subsequent chapters the reader receives details of the two women and the reason for their walk (692). Shortly after this, the reader is presented with Randy Lenz at the other end of Prospect Street (716), widening the scope of the geography of the sequence, before the two subsequent bag-snatch chases finally converge the narrative threads, as Lenz hears Krause's rolling of the barrel at Van Cleve (728). The reader is presented with small details of a sequence involving multiple personae which steadily increases in scope before converging to reveal its "shape," an example of the fractal narrative outlined above in the Sierpinski gasket structure.

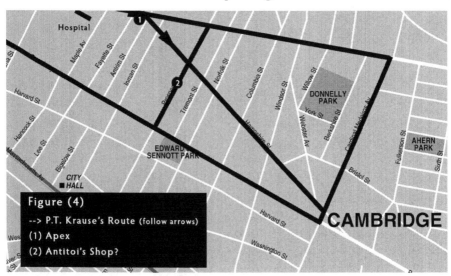

Figure (4)

--> P.T. Krause's Route (follow arrows)

(1) Apex

(2) Antitoi's Shop?

If we now look closely at the map of Cambridge (see Fig. 4) and trace Krause's route from the hospital to Inman Square, it can be observed that Krause's entry in Inman Square is also his entry into the apex of a north-west pointing triangular shape made by Beacon Street/Hampshire Street, Cambridge Street and Prospect Street. That triangle in turn exists as a component of an even larger north-west pointing triangular shape made by Beacon/Hampshire Street, Cambridge Street and Cardinal Medeiros Avenue. Inman Square is also at the apex of an even larger north-east pointing triangular shape made by Beacon Street/Hampshire Street, Cambridge Street and Broadway. Finally, all of these triangular shapes are subsumed within a gigantic north-west pointing triangular shape comprised of Cambridge Street, Cardinal Medeiros Avenue and Broadway. Although Lenz approaches initially from outside, the principal significant action, and the Antitoi's shop, are located within the large triangle. By apparently choosing to enter the initial small triangular area, Poor Tony finds himself subjected to events beyond his control occurring within the overarching larger triangles, drawing an analogy between this sequence and the annular triangular cycle addressed earlier, where a structure created initially through choice runs entropically and destructively out of control and into unexpected chaos. Poor Tony enters into the apex of the initial small triangle and is swept into a series of events that steadily increase in size and complexity to incorporate the largest triangular shape. His movements have existed in this sequence between two fixed points of oblivion (the seizure at the beginning, the paralysis and death induced by the cartridge at the end) which encourages the argument for this sequence as a kind of miniaturization of the whole novel's fractal schema. Several events within the triangle—notably the bag snatch and the two characters deaths—are absences, which must be inferred by the reader and comprise part of the larger structure, a construction created "as much out of what's missing as what's there"(681).

A final, admittedly more speculative detail, but an interesting conjecture nonetheless. If angle bisectors are drawn through each

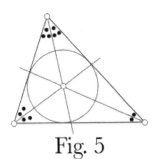

Fig. 5

David Hering

vertex of a triangle, we discover that the three bisectors converge in a single point, which is known as the triangle's incenter (see Fig. 5). The incenter is the center of the triangle's incircle, which touches all three sides of the triangle. We can therefore speculate that the incenter of the Cambridge triangle appears to be located (see Fig. 6) in the area of Prospect Street where the Antitoi's shop is suggested to be (the

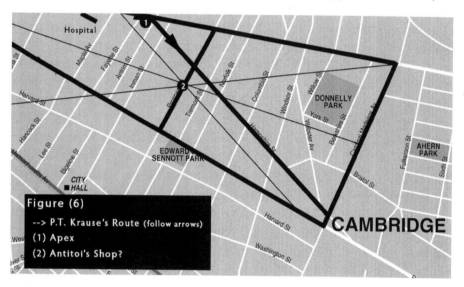

Figure (6)

--> P.T. Krause's Route (follow arrows)

(1) Apex

(2) Antitoi's Shop?

sequence in the Antitoi's shop also occurring at the exact midpoint of the novel, centering the Antitois in the overall narrative schema). The shop forms the center of a circle or cycle of entrapment operating within an overarching triangular schema of action and also containing within itself references to other concentric circles, thus relating a physical and geographical example of a triangular and circular mapping schema for *Infinite Jest*.

· Further: if Antitoi's shop is the center, it is also the de-/anti-center. For the shop contains a funhouse of mirrors that entangle all the connecting characters/ situations in a labyrinth of reflexivity/refraction/ reflection, infinitely duplicated and ultimately entrapping

100

"Yet Another Example of the Porousness of Certain Borders": Chaos and Realism in *Infinite Jest*

Kiki Benzon

"All writers," states Alain Robbe-Grillet in *For a New Novel*, "believe they're realists. None ever calls himself abstract, illusionistic, chimerical, fantastic, falsitical . . . . [I]t is the real world which interests them; each one attempts as best as he can to create 'the real'" (176). In the recent literary avant-garde, this realist drive has gained considerable momentum: the conventions of "high" postmodernism (self-reflexivity, irony, parody, pastiche) are being replaced by tropes and modes that confront and express—rather than evade or satirize—sites of sociopolitical contestation and stagnation. David Foster Wallace's *Infinite Jest* reflects this transition from a conspicuously metafictional, irony-driven sensibility to a deliberate attempt to, in his words, "do something real American, about what it's like to live in America around the millennium" (Interview, McCaffery 138). While what Wallace calls "big-R Realism," born in a nineteenth century Darwinian context, emphasizes linear causality and psychological coherence, Wallace's own aesthetic strategy foregrounds indeterminacy, recursion and flux. As chaos theorists have established in physical, biological and social studies, "complex and fluctuating phenomena [are] the rule rather than the exception" (Favre 147). Thus the unwieldy and quasi-cyclical structures in *Infinite Jest*, rather than signifying distortions of cultural realities, in fact express the "real" and "porous" contours of the late-capitalist environment. Wallace's "chaotic fiction" is thus a kind of literary realism, apposite for rendering experience in what Joseph Conte calls the "postmodern milieu of dispersion" (12). In looking at various forms and themes in *Infinite Jest*—particularly, the reiterative and indeterminate operations (and attendant rituals and wastes) at Ennet House and Enfield Academy—I will argue that Wallace's literary chaotics, far from being a product of Pynchon-clone "crank-turning" (Interview, McCaffery

135), produces a mimetic—if multitudinous and turbulent—depiction of contemporary life in America.

Emerging from a postmodernity that values heterogeneity and simultaneity above historical, ideological and psychoanalytic "master narratives," much millennial fiction resists coherent characterization and narrative continuity in favor of more malleable or fractured representations. Novels like Don DeLillo's *Underworld* (1997) and Mark Z. Danielewski's *House of Leaves* (2000) subvert linear and progressive notions of causality and history, representing individual and collective experience through anachronistic, often polyphonic narrative networks. But *Infinite Jest* is unique within the late-postmodern canon because, while the novel's many plots and subjects spiral out from an undetectable point of narrative origin and systems of addiction, inheritance and political-ideological conflict behave alternately deterministically and stochastically, the novel exudes a thick and gritty humanism that overrides its status as merely a technical performance. Rather than portraying characters as systems—through hyperbolic historiography, parody or allegory—Wallace positions characters *within* systems, evincing at once the rigidity of established patterns and codes, as well as points of potential rupture within these established codes.

In *Infinite Jest*, we are given a set of "character clusters" whose behaviors reflect the greater recursive cultural and philosophical systems depicted in the novel at large. The focal cluster is the Incandenza clan, a luminous, hyper-real example of The American Family, comprised of eccentric and variously capable prodigies. The patriarch, James Incandenza—or, as his sons call him with appropriate closed-circuitry, "Himself"—runs the professional gamut of avant-garde film director, nuclear researcher, and tennis school headmaster, generating the same destruction with each successive incarnation until he does Himself in by way of a microwave suicide. James and his fabulously competent wife, Avril—a.k.a. "the Moms"—run the Enfield Tennis Academy, "the product of negotiated compromises between Avril's academic hard-assery and James's . . . keen sense of athletic pragmatics" (188). Their extreme personalities are reproduced in three sons: Mario, the "hideously deformed" cameraman-child; Hal, the tennis champ-*cum*-lexical genius; and Orin, the disillusioned romantic, tennis-then-football star. But although each son, fractal-like, presents

102

another iteration of his parents' solipsism and obsessiveness, the system has its pores; dynamics within the Incandenza family and the Enfield Tennis Academy emerge across town at Ennet House, a drug and alcohol recovery facility that is presided over by the gigantic former addict Don Gately. The institutional resonance is pointed because, as Wallace said in an interview with *Salon*, "sport and the idea of dedication to a pursuit [are] kind of like an addiction" (5). Inhabitants of both camps are enmeshed in a drug/sport-mediated curriculum toward quelling a kind of existential woe that is variously characterized in the novel as anhedonia, unipolar dysphoria, and "clinical, involutional, or psychotic depression" (*Jest* 675). Addiction becomes symptomatic of and an antidote to woe, so that behaviors in both academic and recovery settings arise always in relation to drugs—as agitated abstention at Ennet House, or covert self-medication at Enfield. The inter-institutional connection is deepened still by romantic and professional associations, the scope of which is often invisible to those involved in them: Joelle van Dyne, for example, is an Ennet House inmate and member of U.H.I.D (Union of the Hideously and Improbably Deformed) but was once Madame Psychosis, the enigmatic radio hostess who provided late-night fantasy fodder for the two younger Incandenza boys and the namesake for Michael Pemulis's acquired street-drug, DMZ. Dyne was also girlfriend to the eldest Incandenza son, Orin (who allegedly dodged flying acid so that it splashed onto and hideously deformed Joelle's face instead) and was an actor in several of Himself's films, including the lethal and looping "Infinite Jest." Through such narrative seepages, single identities become multiple, their behavioral and psychological systems resonating in numerous contexts despite the time and space that separate them.

Infinite Jest testifies to the permeability—the "porousness"—of seemingly rigid boundaries both geographical and social. As Michel Serres contends in "Dream," "What fluctuates is order and disorder. What fluctuates is their vicinity and common border, their relationship and mutual penetration" (233). In *Infinite Jest*, tennis becomes a crucial metaphor for what Serres calls the "interpenetration" of order and disorder. Supplying a conspicuous dialectic between the rigidity of baselines and boundaries and the infinitely variable trajectory, speed and rotation of the ball, tennis enacts a chaotic aesthetics:

Were he now still among the living, Dr. Incandenza would now describe tennis in the paradoxical terms of what's now called Extra-Linear Dynamics. And Schtitt, whose formal knowledge of math is probably equivalent to that of a Taiwanese kindergartner nevertheless seemed to know . . . that locating beauty and art and magic and improvement and keys to excellence and victory in the prolix flux of play is not a fractal matter of reducing chaos to pattern. Seemed to intuitively sense that it was not a matter of reduction at all, but—perversely—of expansion, the aleatory flutter of uncontrolled, metastatic growth (82)

Tennis, as E.T.A. coach Schtitt contends, is about "*not*-order, *limit*, the places where things [break] down, fragmented into beauty" (82). Like the incalculable trajectories of the narrative and its many occupants, tennis is "no more reducible to delimited factors or probability curves than chess or boxing"; it is at once "mathematically uncontrolled but humanly *contained*" (82, italics original). Confronting the infinite variability of his medium, a player works to effect an artistic "containment," which paradoxically enlarges both the aesthetic potential of the game and his own creative agency. The competitor works alone, mimicking the directions and gestures of an adversary, effectively doing battle with something that is almost his reflection. Thus the dichotomous rigidity and fluidity of tennis exist not only on the tangible "canvas" of the court but also within the psychological operations of its players, heightening Hal's "[e]xistential individuality, frequently referred to in the West. Solipsism" (113). Hal's disposition—simultaneously contemplative and escapist, assiduous and flippant—fuses the game's dialectic of order and flux. The psychological implications of tennis and its tropes are dramatized in Hal's recurrent dream, in which he is "standing at the baseline of a gargantuan tennis court":

The lines that bound and define play are on this court as complex and convoluted as a sculpture of string. There are lines going every which way, and they run oblique or meet and form relationships and boxes and rivers and tributaries and systems inside systems: lines, corners, alleys, and angles deliquesce into a blur at the horizon of the distant net. (67)

In Hal's dream, the lines that ought to "bind and define" play assume the "metastatic" convolution that would normally be characteristic of the movements of ball and players. What should be fixed in Hal's unconscious is distorted and conditioned by traits of the game's flexible elements, demonstrating the psychic "expansion" occasioned by the sport. Further, the adversarial aspect of tennis is changed from one involving two opposing players (Hal muses, 'Even the "we" is theory: I never get quite to see the distant opponent, for all the apparatus of the game') to one of parental scrutiny, as Hal sees "[i]n the stands stage-left the white sun-umbrella of the Moms; her height raises the white umbrella above her neighbors" (68). Like the court lines, which should delineate the limits of play but whose "mess" renders it impossible to know "where to direct service," the Moms's presence is highlighted by a bright white umbrella but she herself is rendered obscure under its "circle of shadow" (68).

The pattern of expulsion and resurgence that is dramatized in tennis play emerges in various contexts throughout the novel. As Hayles states, *Infinite Jest* records the "underground seepages and labyrinthine pathways through which the abject always returns in recursive cycles of interconnection that inexorably tie together the sanctified with the polluted" ("Illusion of Autonomy" 687). A central metaphor for this recursive destruction and generation is annulation, a process of nuclear fusion which works by "bombarding highly toxic radioactive particles with massive amounts of stuff even more toxic than the radioactive particles." Essentially, it is "a fusion that feeds on poisons" (*Jest* 572). In the recursive process of annulation, toxicity and waste become synonymous with fertility and replenishment. When deployed in the Great Concavity, annulation "turns out so greedily efficient that is sucks every last toxin and poison out of the surrounding ecosystem, all inhibitors to organic growth for hundreds of radial clicks in every direction" (573). Waste land is transformed, through the fact of its own toxicity, into supremely fertile and luscious terrain. Wallace's dump testifies to the pesky resilience of that which we wish to discard. As Marathe pointedly says, "What goes around, it comes back around . . . [that's] the nature of filth" (233). So the feral infants of the Concavity/Convexity, as described in James A.L. Struck Jr.'s term paper for his History of Canadian Unpleasantness class, "feed on the abundance of annularly available edibles the overgrowth periods in the region represent, do deposit titanically outsized scat, and presumably do crawl thunderously about, occasionally sallying south of murated retention lines and into the populated areas of New New England;" though the report later qualifies the point, stating that the massive infants, "formed by toxicity and sustained by annulation" are essentially "passive icons of the Experialist gestalt." (1056). The infants represent the greater processes that produced them, the group responsible for the Great Concavity/Convexity waste "disposal" system itself, O.N.A.N., ironically evoking onanism—the futile ejaculation of one's seed onto the ground. The organization's name, with its dichotomous implications, indicates that catapulting noxious material away is, simultaneously and insidiously, a pollution of one's own soil.

The film cartridge, "Infinite Jest," is the thread linking the inmates of E.T.A and Ennet House; it both epitomizes and embodies the recursion that characterizes the psychological and physical processes in the two institutions. The film opens with two figures going about a revolving door, unable to make contact with one another, but perpetually pushing forward in a vain attempt. This cyclical idea is then echoed by a figure, Death, who explains that the woman who kills you re-emerges as your mother in the next life. The film then depicts a disconsolate "mother" figure leaning over her infant child, repeatedly pleading "I'm sorry" in various ways; shot from the blurry perspective of the crib-bound child, this segment plays upon deep psychic operations concerning the (im)possibility of deviation from Oedipal structures and produces in the viewer an irresistible "pleasure"/ addiction which makes it impossible to turn away from the screen. Ensnared in an identification with the physical and psychological recursion of "Infinite Jest," the viewer, utterly consumed by what he or she sees, loses all compulsion to do anything but watch the film and consequently dies in his or her own excrement. The absorption of subjects into the film's narrative loops threatens to affect more than the handful of viewers we see expire in their living rooms: Quebecois militants plan to release the cartridge upon Americans to avenge the Great Concavity/Convexity dumpsite on Canadian soil into which the U.S. deposits its waste via giant catapult. The lethal loops of "Infinite

Jest" correspond to cycles of effluence and its reprisals that operate on individual (biological and psychic) and social (waste and international relations) levels. Its properties are at once generative and "natural," insofar as recursion is "necessary" in nature, but they are also a potent means of destruction.

Wallace's work mines the "porousness of certain borders"—to borrow from the short story title in his collection Brief Interviews With Hideous Men—by focusing on the anomalous elements of apparently continuous and coherent systems and amplifying these anomalies to the point where idiosyncrasy becomes the rule rather than the exception. Infinite Jest conveys the porousness of myriad borders—from physical borders like the "spangled mess" of tennis court lines in Hal's dream to national borders such as those that delimit the Great Concavity/Convexity. While these distortions may superficially appear to be sites of psychological and political disaster, their chaotic properties in fact generate orders which are more stable or complex than preceding ones. The novel is riddled with cyclical operations of this kind, where instability and destruction is balanced against an emergent productivity and order: annular fusion, for example, is an exercise in rampant toxicity, but it "can produce waste that's fuel for a process whose waste is fuel for the fusion" (572); ONAN doctors "[treat] cancer by giving cancer cells themselves cancer" (572); Marathe, the terrorist, is "a kind of triple agent or duplicitous double agent" who is "pretending to pretend to betray" (995). These self-referential systems generate energy and new information, illustrating that while systems might be odious in themselves, their "pores" may be sites of creativity.

Wallace applies this thesis in the structural composition of Infinite Jest by punctuating his narrative with extensive endnotes, introducing ruptures that are at once confounding and enlightening. The notes—variously offering elaboration, clarification, crucial information, redundant digressions and, sometimes, entire scenes several pages long—produce yet another dimension of circuitry and narrative turbulence in the novel. In an interview with Charlie Rose, Wallace explained the endnotes' purpose, saying, "it seems to me that reality's fractured right now, at least the reality that I live in. And the difficulty about writing . . . about reality is that text is very linear and it's very unified. . . . I, anyway, am constantly on the look out for ways to fracture the text that aren't totally disoriented" (Interview, Charlie Rose 1997). Critics have interpreted Wallace's "fracturing" paratext in various ways: Frank Cioffi claims that the "constant flipping between text and notes . . . [is a] near aerobic activity" and as such forces the reader into a "performance of disturbance" (169); Timothy Jacobs conceives the endnotes as a way of making the reader "engaged with his work—as opposed to the 'passive spectation' that television prescribes," generating a "participatory aesthetic" where "readers adopt the narrative and physically reconstitute it as their own" ("American Touchstone" 225-6); and in "The Panic of Influence," A.O. Scott calls the endnotes an expression of "quasi-Oedipal hostility" which attests to the author's in anxiety over "the obstacles of writing" (39). In any case, *Infinite Jest* requires more from readers than simple movement of the eye; as Espen Aarseth says of ergodic literature, "nontrivial effort is required to allow the reader to traverse the text" (1). But as much as it may have philosophical (or psychological, obsessive, fetishistic) implications, an endnote per se is fundamentally a technical device, a means of supplying related or explicatory material to the text proper without having to interrupt a flow in the prose—though a note may actually give rise to a rather cavernous fissure. In the tradition of OuLiPo, Wallace uses a quasi-mathematical strategy to expand the written work, both actually (in terms of the novel's word count) and potentially (via the further confusion or clarity the notes provide). Unlike the footnote which can be perceived in a simple vertical glance, the endnote requires a physical negotiation with a text and the temporary abandonment of place in the narrative proper, such that the reader becomes embroiled a recursive performance—what Douglas Hofstadter calls a Strange Loop, where "by moving upwards (or downwards) through the levels of some hierarchical system, we unexpectedly find ourselves back where we started" (10). Often, a reader's digression to the note necessitates further digression, as some notes spawn their own attendant notes and many notes contain medical, mathematical and linguistic jargon or archaic diction that only a consultation of the OED will make lucid. The reader is thus forced into a position of repeated "intermediariness," herself confirming through action the porous borders of the text she is experiencing.

Chaotic indeterminacy and "orderly-disorder" thus inform the narrative structure of *Infinite Jest* and the cyclical and irresolvable social formulations it contains: characters, items, thoughts and symbols circulate perpetually throughout the narrative domain at large, their patterns and behaviors not leading toward any ultimate, quantifiable result or objective "solution" but, rather, conveying meaning in their very unwieldy reverberations. Wallace builds a kind of "chronoschism," Ursula Heise's term for stories which are perpetually "dividing, bifurcating and branching off continuously into multiple possibilities and alternatives" (55). These "methods produce . . . a prodigious density," LeClair explains, "because parts do not disappear into conventional and easily processed wholes" and "disrupt the tranquilizing flow of conventional fiction" ("Prodigious Fiction" 35). This formulation—a "disruption of tranquility" achieved through a process of reiterative folding—counteracts the "anesthesia of form" (Interview, McCaffery 138) that Wallace associates with traditional, "big-R" realist fiction and its valuation of linear causality, stable subjectivity and, indeed, stable ontology, particular with respect to authorship.

The theoretical tension at the center of Wallace's work seems to concern a dual inclination toward "realism" and self-conscious, ironic, or performative writing, which can be loosely termed metafiction. Indeed, Wallace simultaneously employs and derides both literary approaches. In his discussion with McCaffery, Wallace criticizes "big-R Realism" because, he says, it "is soothing, familiar and anaesthetic [and] . . . drops us right into spectation" (138). What Wallace sees as the anaesthetic effect of "big-R Realism" results from its implicit thesis that "real" phenomena and processes are inherently coherent and thus can be delineated by analogously coherent language systems; structure in realist texts, according to LeClair, "stays close to the subject-verb-object syntax of the kernel English sentence and to the causality of linear processes" (The Art of Excess 21). Like television, whose channels offer an illusory freedom of choice but only one "real" option—spectation—classical realism is, according to Wallace, "engaging without being demanding" (Interview, McCaffery

44). Realist texts might imply social and psychological imperatives through the representation of "real" conditions and may be imbued with potential to "enlighten" and/or instruct, but whatever is imparted inevitably stems from an epistemological hierarchy in the author's mind; "reality" in such works is prescribed and determined, encoded by the specific ideology of the writer who conveys qua constructs it. The straight, often temporally linear depictions of characters who appear to independently determine their destinies is, then, an aesthetic trick—a trick to which contemporary readers, dwelling in a atmosphere of irony and interconnectivity, have decidedly caught on: as Lyotard contends, "so-called realist representations can no longer evoke reality except as nostalgia or mockery" (74); the supposition that there is a single and definitive reality to evoke is merely another master narrative, a cultural fiction useful in limiting diversity and facilitating social control.

"The literature of referent, of 'psychological glow,'" according to Wallace, then, "has finally come under constructive attack . . . and exploded into defraction" (Interview, McCaffery 150). But utter "defraction," Wallace is quick to point out, can be as unsatisfying a narrative mode as "big-R realism." The complete shattering or the laying bare of literary conventions is, at base, akin to the depictions of the realist author: a hegemonic and restrictive means of representation in its own right. Further on in his interview with McCaffery, Wallace explains:

We've seen that you can break any or all of the rules . . . but we've also seen the toxicity that anarchy for its own sake can yield. It's often useful to dispense with standard formulas, of course, but it's just as brave to see what can be done within a set of rules. . . . There's something about free play within an ordered and disciplined systems that resonates for readers. And there's something about complete caprice and flux that's deadening. (149-50)

The dispensation of literary "rules" may, Wallace suggests, be "useful" as one stage in the productive reworking of aesthetic practice but, as an end in itself, simple defraction is as hollow a ruse as big-R. Timothy Jacobs proposes that "effective (and affective) art must render things as they are, not in the Realist school of literary representation, but in the real experiences of daily human existence" ("American Touchstone" 225). Wallace concurs in his interview with Laura Miller:

I've always thought of myself as a realist. . . . The world I live in consists of 250 advertisements a day and any number of unbelievably entertaining options, most of which are subsidized by corporations that want to sell me things. The whole way that the world acts on my nerve endings is bound up with stuff that the guys with leather patches on their elbows would consider pop or trivial or ephemeral. I use a fair amount of pop stuff in my fiction, but what I mean by it is nothing different than what other people mean in writing about trees and parks and having to walk to the river to get water a hundred years ago. It's just the texture of the world I live in. (Interview, Salon.com)

According to this self-analysis, it is merely the millennium-specific content, the "pop stuff" in Wallace's fiction that distinguishes it from other versions of realism. It may be that televisual frenzies and toxic waste dumps are simply updated versions of Zola's charcuteries and Tolstoy's battlefields. But Wallace's realism extends beyond simple reflection and rendition of the visible phenomena of contemporary life, incorporating the visceral responses to the ways in which these phenomena act on one's "nerve endings." The real, then, is known not only by its observable artifacts and structures but also through its effects upon perceiving subjects.

Wallace's chaotic fiction, then, is neither a contemporary stab at traditional realism nor a gamey metafictional exercise, but it is a mobilization of the two modes toward an expression of actual, "lived" experience. The synthesis of realist sensibilities and chaotic structures may be conceived of as a kind of "radical realism," a genre propounded by the "tall, lexically gifted and etymologically conscious wraith" in *Infinite Jest* whom LeClair takes to be a surrogate of Wallace himself ("Prodigious Fiction" 2). The wraith calls for the portrayal of "real life's real egalitarian babble of figurant crowds, of the animate world's real agora, the babble of crowds every member of which [is] the central and articulate protagonist of his own entertainment" (Jest 835-836). Realism becomes "radical" when, instead of erecting an orderly interpretation of "real agora," the incoherent and disorderly "egalitarian babble" is embraced and enacted through carefully chosen narrative strategies. Accordingly, Wallace's fiction offers an anti-confluential, turbulent, multitudinous representation of systems and experiences which, in turn, disrupt the passivity of a "spectator" qua reader by problematizing the real. Its mimeticism exists not on the level of representational "mirroring"—though detailed depictions of the material world are a constitutive element—but rather via the manner in which the texture, structure and tone of the narrative assumes the chaotic properties which pervade physical and cultural spheres. Brian McHale evinces a similar intuition in Postmodernist Fiction when he states that postmodern writing "turns out to be mimetic after all, but this imitation of reality is accomplished not so much at the level of its content, which is often manifestly un- or anti-realistic, as at the level of form" (38). Through its chaotic constitution—manifest on the levels of both form and content—*Infinite Jest* affirms that the perpetual, fundamental tension between order and disorder is precisely where "the real" resides.

"Impervious to U.S. Parsing": Encyclopedism, Autism and *Infinite Jest*

Matt Tresco

Why does Hal Incandenza, the protagonist of David Foster Wallace's novel *Infinite Jest*, have the ability to "summon a kind of mental Xerox of anything he'd ever read and basically read it all over again" (797)? How does he "consume libraries" (12) and recite the definition of any word from the OED, such as "implore" or "conversationalist" when asked? (28) Such abilities would appear to make Hal the ideal reader of *Infinite Jest*'s fragmentary and a-chronological structure, a structure which is rich in detail and suspicious of neat, comforting resolutions. The challenging nature of *Infinite Jest* has generated guides such as Greg Carlisle's *Elegant Complexity* and Stephen Burn's *Infinite Jest: A Reader's Guide*, which aim to clarify the "central" action, as well as explain some of the allusive referencing in the novel. The reader seems to be condemned to re-read the novel "over and over," as Hal's brother, Orin, is said to watch clips that were filmed by his girlfriend, Joelle: "He saw something different each time he rewound, something more" (298).

The most remarkable quality of *Infinite Jest* is its structure. Stephen Burn describes the novel as belonging to a tradition of difficult novels, such as those written by Pynchon, Gaddis and Joyce, particularly through its interest in epistemology and conceptions of the social whole. Burn speaks of *Infinite Jest*'s "vast size, encyclopedic knowledge, and elusive plot" (18). Discussions of an encyclopedic genre, or an "encyclopedic mode" (40) relate back to the work of Edward Mendelson and Franco Moretti: the former redefined the national epic as "encyclopedic narrative" for the information age, introducing criteria which described in somewhat limiting terms what constituted such a work; Moretti, on the other hand, acknowledged that the terms "modern epic" (his term) and encyclopedic narrative were virtual synonyms describing the same phenomenon (Moretti 4n). Both agree that the specificity of "epic," relating to ancient and mythical roots, describes inadequately large, allusive modern novels, but whereas Mendelson expected the arrival of a postnational "epic" (arguably a contradiction in terms, but something he believed was suggested by Gravity's Rainbow), Moretti, following Georg Lukács, sees any genuine "modern" epic as thwarted by the rise of the heterogeneous nation-state which turned writing the epic into an exercise in irony. It is through this latter sense I wish to explore *Infinite Jest*'s sense of encyclopedism, but within the changing ideas of the encyclopedic in the last twenty years, particularly how it has been imagined in the figure of the autist.

For Stephen Burn, as Moretti, the encyclopedic project is an impossible, elusive quest. As the encyclopedia strives to totalize, Burn sees the encyclopedic novel as being preoccupied with an arboreal cataloguing project ("a positive project" [20], but it is also a positivist project), whose structure would appear to be deficient—another "modern epic" that overreaches its possible achievements. Ostensibly, *Infinite Jest* confirms the reservations on the possibility of totalization in the postmodern era outlined by Jameson and Lyotard: Burn speaks of its fragmentary, "elusive plot" (18) (think of the conversation between two relatively minor characters, Marathe and Steeply, which is split into twelve segments between pages 87-648) and "the mystery of Hal's condition [that] eludes classification" (40). Yet eluding classification may itself be a positive project insofar as it enables connections and new ways of seeing between differentiated objects—something suggested by one aspect of Hal's "condition" (one aspect, that is, out of a range of different competing mindsets he experiences) and the structure of the novel itself. Hal tells us in "The Year of the Depend Adult Undergarment," in which most of the novel's action occurs, that his current mode of perception has acquired a flowing, filmic quality, in contrast to the static, ordered memories of his childhood, in which "memories of Weston seemed like tableaux. They seemed more like snapshots than films" (950).

Considering autism as a narrative form comes with certain risks which include distinguishing it from clinical autism and, where it is identified as typifying the mode of the thought processes in an individual, distancing it from describing a psychological type.1 Thus, parallels can be drawn with Deleuze and Guattari's schizoanalysis which asserts the dominance of parts—impersonal, fragmented "schizzes"—above a coherent psyche (Deleuze and Guattari 42-43). These create open, proliferating connections and experiences that are not to be "decoded" in psychoanalysis as a description of the mind. Deleuze and Guattari defined schizophrenia against autism, which at the time they were writing retained much of its clinical specificity, with the latter being an artificial type or "artificial person" (26) constructed through the clinic and also through someone identifying him- or herself as a discrete person. But it is not necessarily the case that that the defining trait of the autist is an overly-centered ego, or that they experience desire as a "lack," or that they succumb to fixed images of the self. Hans Asperger notes that the first clinical use of the term was by the Swiss psychiatrist, Eugen Bleuler, in the early twentieth century. Here, in 1944, Asperger quotes Bleuler, noting that autism (or "schizophrenic autism") is a subtle variation on schizophrenia, or dereism:[2]

> The schizophrenic patient loses contact with reality to varying degrees. He ceases to care about the real world. He shows a lack of initiative, aimlessness, neglect of reality, distractedness, but also impulsive and bizarre behaviour ... One finds "whimsical obstinacy", that is, the patient wants something and at the same time the opposite. One finds obsessional acts, automatic acts, automatic commands etc. Schizophrenic patients often live in an

---

1 For a useful account on the historical construction of autistic spectrum disorders, see Majia Holmer Nadesan"s *Constructing Autism*. London: Routledge, 2005. For an example using autism as a trope to discuss modernist texts, see Lance Olsen, "Diagnosing Fantastic Autism: Kafka, Borges, Robbe-Grillet," in *Modern Language Studies*, Vol. 16, No. 3, Summer, 1986, 35-43.

2 The extent to which Asperger was eager to pathologize all non-scientific thought is seen in his perceiving of dereistic thought "in everyday life, for example, in superstition or pseudo-science". Frith remarks that Bleuler went further, using autism "to describe "not only ... schizophrenic patients but ... normal people. "Autistic thinking turns the boy playing soldiers into a general, the girl playing with her doll into a happy mother ... it enables the dreamer to express his wishes and fears." (38 n.4)

[handwritten margin note: "Is 'giving yourself up to yourself'"]

Matt Tresco

imaginary world of wish fulfillment and ideas of persecution.
(38)

Bleuler also notes that the autist is "insufficiently externally motivated," although this appears to refer to an inability or unwillingness to communicate out of the self, not necessarily over-interest in the self or self-absorption. Also, wishing for opposite things simultaneously suggests that the autist perhaps hasn't chosen to make him- or herself a person, as Deleuze asserts. Furthermore, the kind selfhood in discussion here is not one revolving around sociability. In Deleuze and Guattari's example of Büchner's Lenz, Lenz is not particularly "sociable" with people; rather, it is into natural objects that his consciousness slips and his ego disperses. Reading *Infinite Jest* as an "autistic" text may involve identifying the problems of its (un-)readability, its emphasis on the specialization of knowledge, and consequently its incommensurability with other knowledge systems—a form of loneliness or isolation—which does not make the novel "reducible" into a single, neat "total" system in the same way as the former "paranoid" tropes of American fiction were used to explain Pynchon, William Burroughs, and Philip K. Dick.

A comparable situation may be found in the opening pages of *Infinite Jest*. The most famous remark in the opening moments of the novel is the paragraph (a single sentence), "I am in here,"[3] uttered by Hal prior to his admissions interview at The University of Arizona. The sentence prefaces an attack or seizure, but it is an odd thought. Is Hal thinking that he is in himself (where "here" equals his own body), or that he is located in the room itself ("wood-walled, Remington-hung, double-windowed against the November heat")? Either way, if his ego is so stable, why say it? Yet as the interview progresses, Hal's attack is marked by taciturnity. He discerns a "panic at feeling misperceived," but the form this assumes in Hal's head is a kind of encyclopedic eloquence:

> "I could, if you'd let me, talk and talk … I believe the influence
> of Kierkegaard on Camus is underestimated. I believe Dennis
> Gabor may very well have been the Antichrist. I believe Hobbes

---

[3] See also the near-repetition of this remark on page 13.

is just Rousseau in a dark mirror. I believe, with Hegel, that transcendence is absorption. I could interface you guys right under the table", I say. (12)

Yet this reaches the ears of those present as "Subanimalistic noises and sounds." It is assumed that autists have a stable ego (where "autos" equals "self"), but this "autistic" experience of Hal's, which maps onto the descriptions of Asperger and Bleuler, suggests that this may be because taciturnity leads to a perceived self-sufficiency. Instead, "autism" here becomes a model for communicative difficulty: "I'd tell you all you want and more, if the sounds I made could be what you hear" (9).

One way in which communicative difficulty is manifested in the structure of *Infinite Jest*, I wish to argue, is through its unusual use of endnotes. In particular, one does not find a clear distinction between body text and endnote, with important information allocated to the former and the "waste products" relegated to the latter. Rather, the arrangement of material lacks an obvious organizing principle, with suggestive information, such as that the rebranded "Year of Glad" is "the very last year of O.N.A.N.ite Subsidized Time" hidden in a single note (1022 n.114). Similarly, a number of endnotes are "chapter length," some of which, it has been argued, contain "narrative that is more important to the ongoing novel than the passage to which the note is attached" (Boswell, *Understanding* 120). Thus, the narrative expresses the same confusion and anxiety about what is "in here" as Hal in his interview. To take an example, I will examine footnote 110, the largest footnote in the novel, standing at eighteen pages, and see how this apparently operates as subsidiary material to the main text beginning on page 310.

Hal Incandenza is studying in the classes at E.T.A. which are run especially for tennis students. Between the intrusive "WETA" intercom student radio and some background information on the groups of the anti-O.N.A.N. insurgency provided by the narrator, Hal muses that "the only really challenging prorected class for [him] is turning out to be Mlle. Thierry Poutrincourt's "Separatism and Return: Québecois History from Frontenac Through the Age of Interdependence":

Poutrincourt's lecture-voice has gotten quieter and quieter as history's approached its contemporary limit; and Hal, finding the stuff rather more high-concept and less dull than he'd expected—seeing himself as at his innermost core apolitical—nevertheless found the Québecois-Separatism mentality almost impossibly convolved and confused and impervious to U.S. parsing, [endnote 110] plus was both com- and repelled by ... a queasy feeling ... as if someone had been reading mail of Hal's that he thought he'd thrown away. (310-11)

One may conjecture that Hal's "queasy feeling" is due to another blurring between the public and private, perhaps that his mother, Avril, has Québécois ties through the E.T.A. with insurgent groups in ways too tangled for him to imagine at present. We are then led to endnote 110, which promises further information on this, although it is arguably a chapter in its own right, written not as scholarly explanation, as endnotes often are, but in a narrative prose style, beginning "Q.v. here later in the same day ..." Here we are presented with a portrait of the evening in the tennis club. The tennis matches are finishing; Mario, Hal's other brother, is preparing a film to be shown the following day (Interdependence Day, 11/8), and Hal notices a message on his phone left by Orin stating that he would ring back, and noting, incidentally, that "every single one of Ms. Dickinson's canonical poems could be sung without loss or syllabic distortion to the tune of "The Yellow Rose (of Texas)." Thus, the focus oscillates, shifting continuously as between the Intercom and Poutrincourt in the main text:

The odd enclosed echo of locker rooms everywhere, junior or pro. "On my volcano grows the Grass A meditative spot," and so on. The fleshy pop of a professionally snapped towel on adult skin. A black man's falsetto laughter. Orin's recorded voice said he'd just grabbed an odd free second to inquire what Hal's machine might make of this fact. (1005 n.110)

Here, reproduced on a micro level, are the disjointed switches that the reader experiences between paragraphs and chapters (notably the broken narrative of Marathe and Steeply). At the end of the next paragraph of the same endnote, Hal's phone "twitters again," promising either the detail on Hal's connections with Québec, or, at least, Orin's voice, but we do not hear Orin. Instead, on page 1006, there is a new subchapter heading, announced in block capitals, characteristically too long to quote in full, containing a letter from Avril to Orin—a letter which requires its own set of endnotes. Orin's reply to this letter follows (a letter purporting to have been written by Orin's management company), and finally the telephone conversation gets underway. Any consideration of Québécois separatism, however, is postponed for another two-and-a-half pages, until Orin mentions the "Samizdat" in connection with their father (the Samizdat is defined as "any sort of politically underground or beyond the pale press or the stuff published thereby"(1011 n.110), although Hal suggests that it may be connected to his father's "anti-Reconfiguration" films, made as an amateur filmmaker—which one learns about in a different set of endnotes—rather than the potentially lethal film that shares its name with the novel's title. The conversation continues for another eleven pages, amid further E.T.A. interruptions (notably by fellow tennis player Michael Pemulis), describing Orin's conversation with Helen Steeply for Moment Magazine, and considering why she, Helen, might be interested in linking anti-O.N.A.N. groups and their father's work with the term Samizdat. Yet just as it is implied that Hal is about to realize the potential for his father's films in large scale terrorist activity ("anti-U.S. insurgency so far's been too hapless and small-potato," he says), Pemulis disconnects the conversation and the chapter ends in mid-word. (1021 n.110)

Why include these small details at all, even in an endnote? The first time reader would do well to spot the relevance of the topics discussed and identify how they are arguably integral to the novel. The reader may not link Orin's conversation with Steeply to Steeply's work for the U.S. Government; or recognize the nature of the relationship between the U.S. Government and the A.F.R.; or know that the A.F.R. are pursuing the Samizdat; or recognize that the terms "Samizdat," "the Entertainment," and "Infinite Jest" are largely interchangeable; or be aware that for certain groups "Infinite Jest" has particular relevance to terrorist operations. Indeed, the web is so complicated that the narrative tries to communicate these associations at once, but in doing so, it sounds like Hal babbling on the admissions interview floor. It is here that the phrase "impervious to U.S. parsing" is instructive. Besides the aforementioned communicative problems I described in relation to autism (parsing as interpretation, the general sense of the term parsing), the absence of parsing suggests the absence of an ordering or categorizing principle. Parsing in its stricter sense refers to dividing the parts of speech into formal components, the tree model, which Hal recognizes is insufficient for understanding the logic of the wrangling of Québec, Canada and the U.S. Indeed, much of the U.S. itself, post-"Re-Configuration," is impervious to parsing, its borders now a huge rubbish dump, surrendered willingly to neighboring territories, the abandoned land apparently populated by giant feral infants and stampeding hamsters. The details presented in this particular endnote appear to lack a higher ordering principle—a loop, a cycle, a mythical method, etc.—and Wallace appears to be undiscerning, in one sense, about what is inserted in the endnotes. The reader can turn to endnote 143, for example, which reads simply, "Sic.", and feel aggrieved that this ought to have appeared in the main text. Similarly, a number of the endnotes, such as endnote 1, refer to medical/drug knowledge, although similar, more detailed explanations on similar topics often appear in the main text (compare with the final few pages of the novel, in Gately's dream). The medical history of characters is also split (Hal in endnote 76; Mario on pages 312-7). These and other examples throughout the novel suggest there is no obvious "hierarchy" of information, no map allowing the connection of threads. Similar, recent examples include Wallace's essay "Host"—an investigation into radio "shock-jocks"—in which footnotes are represented in the body text through a series of arrows and information flows (appropriately for a piece against tendentiousness, the small details are unavoidable; one cannot skip the notes as though they were buried at the foot of the page), and Jenny Boully's novella *The Body*, which consists entirely of footnotes, the main portion of each page being left blank.

A precedent for this form of cognition—the bending of inside and outside, of body and peritext—is suggested by Borges" short story, "Funes, the Memorious." The story describes the "infallible" memory of the teenage Funes after a horse riding accident leaves him with an eidetic memory. Borges reports that it was "difficult for [Funes] to understand that the generic term "dog" embraced so many unlike specimens of differing sizes and forms" (104). The dog, seen in profile one minute, is perceived as different, seen from the front, the next, leaving him in a world of "almost contiguous details." Like Funes' memory, the endnotes in *Infinite Jest* approach the state of contiguous details. If the flow of detail makes generic terms incomprehensible then the former arboreal "encyclopedia" can no longer be said to stand. Similarly, Funes' inability to abstract mirrors the reader's experience of reading *Infinite Jest* only to miss what is important and recurrent in the novel's minor details. Instead of pursuing a general knowledge, knowledge becomes specialized by necessity, like Funes' highly esoteric systems of enumeration. Yet there is never a totally de-hierarchized structure in this world; objects are never perceived as so singular that they cannot be thought of meaningfully in relation to other objects. Rather, it allows for questioning the stability of genera, of definite types. Recent rises in the diagnoses of autism and other conditions concerning information processing, such as ADHD, may indicate a reaction against esoteric specialization that has strayed too far from the center of a culture. Autistic spectrum disorders, with their emphasis on different, "outsider" status, complement a form of corrupt, readymade postmodern theory which explains the perceived disparateness of social interaction. Accounts of "autism" that have entered the popular consciousness, especially Barry Levinson's Rain Man (1988) show a savant brilliant in certain fields but inept in routine financial matters. Autistic skills are invariably portrayed as being narrow in focus yet closely aligned to the encyclopedia: it is when the protagonist (such as Raymond Babbitt) experiences situations not described in reference books that he or she encounters difficulties.

Consequently, I want to suggest that modern conception of the encyclopedia, particularly Wikipedia, challenges earlier arboreal models.[4] It is possible for the encyclopedia to no longer imply totalization and containment, but release and an enlargement of possibilities. Structurally, both Wikipedia and *Infinite Jest* are always threatening to overspill, to negate the purpose of their organizing principles, if indeed they ever really had any. At any moment, the encyclopedia may become the anti-encyclopedia, an infinite

---

[4] For a treatment of various images and models of the encyclopedia, see Eco (*Semiotics* 68-86).

procession, similar, I would argue, to the "infinite"-ness of *Infinite Jest*. As always when one reaches the end of a novel of such magnitude, one asks, "Why did it stop exactly where it did?" and "Could it have continued for another thousand pages?"

Infinite Jests: David Foster Wallace & Laurence Sterne

Christopher Thomas

> "I'm talking particularly about the art of the Sixties, which abandoned a lot of conventional techniques in favor of black humor and a new emphasis on irony, You hadn't seen irony like that, really, since the pre-Romantics."—David Foster Wallace, Interview, *Whiskey Island*

Timothy Jacobs's 2007 essay on the connections between David Foster Wallace's *Infinite Jest* and Dostoevsky's *The Brothers Karamazov* makes a strong case for the stylistic and thematic influence of an author whom we know Wallace studied widely. Jacobs argues that, while the allusions to Dostoevsky are less overt and frequent than those to Hamlet, they are no less significant and layered. This essay will seek to make further historical connections with Wallace, focusing on formal and stylistic similarities between *Infinite Jest* and Laurence Sterne's *Tristram Shandy*. It will also provide a backdrop for new questions about thematic concerns of both works and how these two authors engaged with their respective contemporary cultures. Wallace's literary ancestry is often-documented as stretching back one generation to Pynchon, Gaddis, Nabokov, and Barthelme, et al. Some critics go back yet further to Joyce, and most cite DeLillo and Barth as his most immediate predecessors. Informative and helpful as this is, it seems worthwhile to push further into history for a broader view.

My interest in connections with Sterne was borne out of what seemed like obvious cosmetic and tonal similarities, but the true depth of the connection was not apparent until further study of the cultural contexts within which each work was produced. One might frame post-war US as a sort of Enlightenment era—belief in the potency of rationality and knowledge; and a focus on containing, categorizing, and appropriating information; reverence for technology. One might imagine Sterne's contemporary, Samuel Johnson, feeling right at home in the information age (where he might find employment with the Google book project). What truly links Sterne and Wallace is their mutual tendency to expose (often hilariously) the fatuity of contemporary beliefs and the limitations of current approaches to philosophical problems.

In his essay, Jacobs set out to prove that "Wallace has patterned *Infinite Jest* so meticulously after Dostoevsky's *The Brothers Karamazov* that in many significant ways, *Infinite Jest* is a rewriting or figurative translation of *The Brothers Karamazov* into the contemporary American idiom and context" ("Brothers Incandenza" 265). In contrast to his discussions of Dostoevsky, Wallace never wrote about Sterne. Additionally, from the limited cache of interviews, reviews and readings we have on record, Wallace did not mention Sterne. So there is, to my knowledge, no published acknowledgment of interest or influence. That said, close textual examination reveals a tendency in Wallace to employ stylistic flourishes that are distinctly Sternian.

The most obvious similarities between *Infinite Jest* and *Tristram Shandy* center around the connections both texts have to Hamlet, specifically the character of Yorick, "a Fellow of infinite Jest" (Hamlet 287). The parson Yorick has a large role in *Tristram Shandy*, and arguably represents the voice of Sterne himself, but the significance of his presence in both texts goes beyond simple historical reference. It highlights both authors' concerns with issues of patrimony and heredity and patricide, both as narrative themes and as part of a larger cultural dialectic (that is, how writers engage with their artistic forefathers and contemporaries). As Hamlet holds the skull of his boyhood companion, he contemplates questions of familial vs. non-familial influence, human nature, and the genealogy of character (i.e. "how did I become the man I am?"), all of which are central themes for Sterne and Wallace.

Textual comparisons between these two works provide speculative evidence that Sterne was an influence on Wallace, especially stylistically and formally. Clear as this case may be, it is still basically conjecture. However, a passage in the waning pages of *Infinite Jest* provides a qualitatively different sort of evidence for this influence.

Just as Sterne made a habit of making direct and indirect textual references to influential writers and thinkers (most frequently,

Locke, Swift, Cervantes, Montaigne, Rabelais), Wallace also makes such references, at times overtly (as with William James), but often quite obliquely. The short appearance of ETA custodians Kenkle and Brandt late in *Infinite Jest* displays a more direct reference to Sterne, which comes in the form of a stylistic mimic, as well as a direct topical nod from the narrator. In his qualification of the relationship between James Incandenza and the custodial duo, Wallace describes their initial meeting late one night on Boston's train system (the "T") where Incandenza was so drunk Brandt had to carry him home. Wallace's parenthetical aside contains the initial reference: "(Kenkle recalls that night's discussion being about the human nose as an erectile organ, but the only really sure bet is that it was one-sided)" (874). Readers of *Tristram Shandy* will recall the prominence of the human nose as both a topic for lengthy prognostication by Walter Shandy, but also as the subject of one of the book's longest digressions, Walter's translation of the fictional pedant, Slawkenbergius, whom he lionized because he "could perceive that the point of long noses had been too loosely handled by all who had gone before" (Sterne 189). The human nose and the significance of its length is one of Walter's most passionate and all-consuming hobby-horses.

Indeed, the human nose is arguably the most prominent thematic symbol in all of *Tristram Shandy*. It is the site of much of Sterne's parody of the prolix pedantry of his contemporaries, and, with the persistent focus on the importance of length, provides a sexual undertone and bawdiness that lurks throughout. This is evident in the quotation immediately above. The nose is a thinly veiled phallic symbol and is "too loosely handled" by all but Slawkenbergius, whose "grip" on the subject insinuates the masturbatory quality of his writings (a critical discourse Wallace was all too familiar with himself).

If Wallace wanted to give a direct nod to Tristram, the human nose is the perfect reference—speaking of it as an "erectile organ" carries strongly Sternean overtones. Also significant in this passage is the description of the discussion as "one-sided." Tristram Shandy and *Infinite Jest* are both replete with one-sided conversations--diatribes or monologues housed within a dialogue, where the non-participatory character functions as humble, subservient audience, and whose thoughts and opinions are ignored and deemed inconsequential by the sermonizer. These comical passages contain many of the thematic elements that connect the two works (the Hobby Horse, solipsism, etc.), but they are also strong indicators of the stylistic influence Sterne had on Wallace.

Kenkle's first lines land with distinct Sternean wit. We catch him in the middle of a diatribe about US holidays that we know has been going on for some time, since on the previous page, Hal narrates, "Even in the stairwell I could hear Kenkle discoursing on their Thanksgiving plans" (873). Brandt, though continually addressed, never has a chance (or cause) to respond, a fact which seems to suit both: "His major attraction for Kenkle seemed to consist in the fact that he neither walked away nor interrupted when Kenkle was speaking" (873). By the time Hal reaches them, Kenkle is discussing Christmas:

> And then the Yuletide season, Brandt my friend Brandt -- Christmas -- Christmas morning -- What is the essence of Christmas morning but the childish co-eval of venereal interface, for a child? -- A present, Brandt -- Something you have not earned and which formerly was out of your po-ssession is now in your po-ssession -- Can you sit there and try to say there is no symbolic rela-tion between unwrapping a Christmas present and undressing a young lady? (874)

Several stylistic elements stand out. First, the frequent use of the em-dash, most distinctly after a terminal punctuation mark (as with "for a child? -- A present ..."). Sterne frequently employed this technique, and it is part of what makes reading him difficult for modern readers. One might wonder, if this is quoting spoken language, what we are supposed to make of a dash after a question mark. What does that sound like? How is that enunciated, and by what grammatical system does the writer--the documenter--choose to represent this spoken language in this way? Questions such as these abound for modern readers of Sterne. They are part of how the reader engages with Sterne's text, and they represent another distinct similarity in approach between Wallace and Sterne. Wallace also takes this technique of "unpronounced" or "unpronounceable" textual markings in a new direction with the use of quoted ellipses in dialogue. Characters in *Infinite Jest* are frequently attributed with simply "..." in response to a comment or question. The technique is pushed further at times when the ellipses come back-to-back in dialogue, as with Hal and Mario:

> "That's a good one!"
> "Shush."
> ". . ."
> ". . ."
> "Hey Hal? What's an insomniac?"
> "Somebody who rooms with you, kid, that's for sure."
> "Hey Hal?"
> ". . ." (41)

These markings insinuate a conversational pause with a specific cadence that is familiar in spoken language but that is difficult to represent textually. As with Sterne, Wallace is testing the limits of language. (Wallace extends this investigation with his use of "Q" in *Brief Interviews With Hideous Men*.)

Kenkle's discussion of Christmas is followed up by a contextual narration from Hal, who describes the night James met Kenkle and Brandt on the T, and how James later used the duo in one of his experimental films. After this short description from Hal, Kenkle resumes his diatribe:

> For I am a missionary man, Brandt, is what I am -- Brandt -- as in give me the straight-forward venereal in-terface of missionary congress or give me nihil and zilch -- You know what I am saying? -- Give me your best thoughts on the alter-native positions, Brandt --Brandt -- For me, for my part at least, I say nix and nihil on the rear-entry or you might hear it termed Dog- or Canine-Style interface so favored in huts, blue car-tridges, Tan-tric etchings -- Brandt, it's animal-istic -- Why? -- Why you say? -- Brandt, it is an ess-entially *hunched* way to have interface -- She hunches, you hunch over her -- Inor*dinately* too much hunching, to my own way of -- (874—875, italics original)

Thematically speaking, Wallace is referencing Sterne quite adeptly here by illustrating the notion of the associative nature of the human mind--a central psychological theme in Tristram Shandy. Kenkle begins speaking about their plans for Thanksgiving, which brings him to thoughts of Christmas, and how Christmas gifts are sexualized symbols, which brings him to prognosticating on the superiority of missionary over "Canine-Style" interface--from Thanksgiving to doggy-style in just four steps.

As it is with Walter Shandy, sexuality seems to be one of Kenkle's hobby-horses, but it would seem like an oversight to attribute Kenkle's character to be a direct mimic of Walter. He certainly exhibits several of Walter's flourishes--his loud, flamboyant speaking voice, his pedantic, authoritative tone, and the tendency of his thoughts to be dominated by his hobby-horse. But it seems that Wallace has created a sort of hybrid character here, one that is part Walter and part Tristram Shandy himself. Most reminiscent of Tristram's voice is Kenkle's repeated address to his interlocutor. For Kenkle, this is Brandt--for Tristram, it is us, the reader. Much has been made of Sterne's varied approach to this. He moves from "good folks" to "Sir" to "Dear reader," "dear sir," "madam," etc., but the constant acknowledgment of and engagement with the reader is a trademark of Tristram Shandy that Wallace is also clearly employing here.

Similar diatribes abound throughout Sterne's text. Several illustrate the directness of Wallace's reference in Kenkle and Brandt:

> In the case of *knots*,----by which, in the first place, I would not be understood to mean slip-knots,----because in the course of my life and opinions,----my opinions of them will come in more properly when I mention the catastrophe of my great uncle Mr. *Hammond Shandy*,----a little man,----but of high fancy: ----he rushed into the duke of *Monmouth's* affair:----nor, secondly, in this place, do I mean that particular species of knots, called bow-knots;----there is so little address, or skill, or patience, required in the unloosing them, that they are below my giving any opinions at all about them.----But by knots I am speaking of, may it please your reverences to believe, that I mean good, honest, devilish tight, hard knots (Sterne 137-8, italics original)

The authority in Kenkle's voice above is also clearly present here where the narrator speaks with absolute certainty and confidence in his mastery of the topic at hand. This, of course, is part of the satire that runs through *Tristram Shandy*--self-proclaimed experts laying out the law on subjects insignificant. Tristram again:

> Button-holes!----there is something lively in the very idea of 'em----and trust me, when I get amongst 'em----You gentry with great beards----look as grave as you will----I'll make merry work with my button-holes----I shall have 'em all to myself----'tis a maiden subject----I shall run foul of no man's wisdom or fine sayings in it. (238)

Again, the bewildering interest in a subject so pedestrian and unremarkable. The following excerpt shows Tristram extolling his father's virtues in his translation of Slawkenbergius, and in his general expertise in anything to do with noses. This passage's similarities with Kenkle's seems to lie more in the stylistic elements--the timbre we imagine in the voice, the meter, and the peculiar emphasis added with italics, capitalization and bold text:

> And to do justice to *Slawkenbergius*, he has entered the list with a stronger lance, and taken a much larger career in it, than any one man who has ever entered it before him,----and indeed, in many respects, deserves to be *en-nich'd* as a prototype for all writers, of voluminous works at least, to model their books by,---- for he has taken in, Sir, the whole subject,----examined every part of it, *dialectically*,----then brought it into full day; dilucidating it will all the light which either the collision of his own natural parts could strike,----or the profoundest knowledge of the sciences had impowered him to cast upon it,----collating, collecting and compiling,----begging, borrowing, and stealing, as he went along, all that had been wrote or wrangled thereupon in the schools and porticos of the learned: so that *Slawkenbergius* his book may be properly considered, not only as a model,----but as a thorough-stitch'd DIGEST and regular institute of *noses*; comprehending in it, all that is, or can be needful to be known about them. (189, italics original)

All of the above passages are from the voice of the narrator, Tristram Shandy. If we think of Kenkle as a mimic of Tristram, then the character of Brandt turns out to be us, the reader--constantly addressed and involved, but never responding within the text. Kenkle and Brandt disappear from the storyline as quickly as they appeared, but their existence, and Kenkle's monologue, represent what seems like a direct reference to Sterne's flamboyant, arrogant yet likeable characters.

David Foster Wallace and the New Sincerity in American Fiction

Adam Kelly

I

My point of departure for this article is the widespread agreement, which has by now become almost a cliché among readers, fans, and critics, that David Foster Wallace affirmed and embodied sincerity as a crucial value in his life and work, perhaps even as that work's defining feature. Whether one is inspired to this thought by Wallace's critique of irony and the call for "single-entendre principles" in "E Unibus Pluram" (Supposedly 81), by the regular thematic treatment of sincerity in *Infinite Jest*, or simply through the feeling one gets from the voice of Wallace's prose in one's own head, the notion of sincerity has from early on marked discussions of his work at all levels of debate. On the back cover of Wallace's first collection *Girl With Curious Hair*, for example, Madison Smartt Bell describes the stories therein as "serious and sincere," while in an influential mid-career assessment, A.O. Scott identified "the feedback loop of irony and sincerity which animates so much of Wallace's writing." Since Wallace's early death, this attribution of sincerity has becomes particularly ubiquitous: in a major recent assessment, Jon Baskin remarks that "it would be difficult to imagine a writer more committed and sincere in our time," while in his long biographical essay for the *New Yorker*, D. T. Max refers both to "Wallace's opaque sincerity" and to "the robust sincerity of his writing" (Max). With this broad consensus in mind, I want to ask two critical questions here: firstly, in terms of literary and intellectual history, what does this attribution of sincerity to Wallace mean? And secondly, is there something fundamentally new about Wallace's sincerity, a re-working of the concept as a complex and radical response to contemporary conditions?

In attempting to answer these questions, a good place to start is Lionel Trilling's 1972 study *Sincerity and Authenticity*, in which Trilling offers historical outlines of these two key concepts. He begins by defining sincerity as "a congruence of avowal and actual feeling" (2), and traces its origin to the advent of Renaissance humanism, citing Polonius's famous advice to Laertes in *Hamlet*:

> This above all: to thine own self be true
> And it doth follow, as the night the day
> Thou canst not then be false to any man. (3)

For Trilling, the crucial aspect of Shakespeare's formulation is that truth to the self is conceived of as a means of ensuring truth to the other, and—via readings of Rousseau, Diderot, Hegel and Jane Austen among others—Trilling goes on to suggest that this conception of sincerity would become "a salient, perhaps a definitive, characteristic of Western culture for some four hundred years" (6). But by the twentieth century it had gone into sharp decline, superseded by the ideal of authenticity, which conceives truth to the self as an end and not simply as a means. Whereas sincerity places emphasis on inter-subjective truth and communication with others, and on what Trilling calls the "public end in view" (9), authenticity conceives truth as something inward, personal, and hidden, the goal primarily of self-expression rather than other-directed communication. Thus, the role-playing associated with the theatrical origins of sincerity is repudiated in favor of a plunge into the Conradian heart of darkness; and, indeed, Trilling closely associates the cultural trumping of sincerity by authenticity with the intense but non-confessional exploration of the self characteristic of literary modernism. Connected to this, and equally crucial, is the way the modernist idea of the artist as aloof genius, as persona rather than person, shattered the older, traditional view, perhaps best articulated in Wordsworth's understanding of poets as "men speaking to men." Citing various formulations by Eliot, Joyce and Gide, Trilling suggests that the modernists' aesthetic of impersonality means that "the criterion of sincerity, the calculation of the degree of congruence between feeling and avowal, is not pertinent to the judgement of their work" (7), a position, he argues, that would go on to become enshrined by the New Critical denigration of intention, so central to any conception of sincerity, as a fallacy in the study of literature. And the initial reactions to modernism—the existentialist and absurdist literature of mid-century Europe (which we might note draws its bearings from Heidegger's notion of authenticity as a concern with the "ownmost self" [eigenste Selbst]), as well as American Beat writing and confessional poetry—only added to the privilege afforded to authenticity, in that any demonstrable awareness of a public self, again an important characteristic of sincerity, becomes associated with bad faith or an artificial dishonesty.[1] This state of affairs leads Trilling to write of the "anachronism" now involved in the notion of sincerity, how when we speak the word, "we are likely to do so with either discomfort or irony" (6). Yet what Trilling could not anticipate in 1972 was that irony was in the process of taking over, and with the rise of poststructuralism in the academy, and of postmodernism in the arts, the surface/depth model of the self assumed by both sincerity and authenticity would soon be superseded by the privilege afforded to the inaugurating powers of capital, technology, culture, and especially language.

This is where David Foster Wallace comes in. That Wallace from early on characterized his artistic project as a response to the contemporary prevalence of irony in American literature and culture is well-established, and there is no need to reconstruct the argument of "E Unibus Pluram" here. But what I want to suggest is that Wallace's project ended up even more far-reaching than he claimed it would be in that key early essay, and that from *Infinite Jest* onward it became primarily about returning to literary narrative a concern with sincerity not seen since modernism shifted the ground so fundamentally almost a century before. In his essay comparing Dostoevsky's fiction to "our own lit's thematic poverty," Wallace commented upon this shift: "The good old modernists, among their other accomplishments, elevated aesthetics to the level of ethics—maybe even metaphysics—and Serious Novels after Joyce tend to be valued and studied mainly for

---

[1] It is important to note here Trilling's contention, pace Donald Davie and others, that although the modernist doctrine of the persona was challenged by the English and American poets that followed high modernism, this did not mark a return from authenticity to sincerity, "because it does not involve the reason that Polonius gives for being true to one's own self: that if one is, one cannot then be false to any man" (9).

their formal ingenuity" (*Lobster* 272). According to Wallace, this modernist legacy has formed part of a more general "intellectualization and aestheticizing of principles and values in this country," one of the things, he argued, "that's gutted our generation" (Interview, Salon.com). As a contrast to the modernist concern with authentic forms of representation, Dostoevsky is explicitly presented by Wallace as an ideological writer who possesses the required "degrees of passion, conviction, and engagement with deep moral issues that we—here, today—cannot or do not permit ourselves" (*Lobster* 271). Yet elsewhere Wallace often made it abundantly clear that it could not simply be a question of contemporary literature's returning to the precise kind of sincerity he saw as informing Dostoevsky's fiction. In one of his last interviews, he claimed that while terms like "moral" and "ethical"—concepts that have to do, like sincerity, primarily with not being false to others—might be apt for describing the era of Dostoevsky or the European Romantics, these terms had become thorny and problematic for those born in the age of television (Interview, Bookworm 2006). For Wallace, any return to sincerity must be informed by a study of postmodernist fiction, in order to properly take into account the effects wrought by contemporary media, particularly TV and advertising. He told another interviewer that "the biggest thing [...] that was interesting about postmodernism is that it was the first text that was highly self-conscious, self-conscious of itself as text, self-conscious of the writer as persona, self-conscious about the effects that narrative had on readers, and the fact that readers probably knew that. It was the first generation of writers who'd actually read a lot of criticism, and there was a certain schizophrenia about it" (Interview, Charlie Rose 1997). Coming himself from an American generation that had attended college when critical theory was at its zenith, and with these highly self-conscious writers as his direct precursors, Wallace found that he could not reject their insights for older and more naive forms of communication.[2]

---

[2] Wallace highlighted the importance of critical theory for the writers of his generation in his first published essay, arguing that one of its effects was to show that "the relations between literary artist, literary language, and literary artifact are vastly more complex and powerful than has been realized hitherto" ("Fictional Futures" 14).

Instead, most crucial for the contemporary artist is to recognize "not just what's true for me as a person, but what's gonna sound true—what's going to hit readers or music-listeners [...] as true in 2006, or 2000, or 1995," all while taking into account a cultural context that is "vastly more complicated, difficult, cynical and over-hyped than it used to be" (Interview, Bookworm 2006).

But let us pause for a moment here, because if we wish to discuss Wallace's sincerity, it is clear that we are faced with a complication from the outset. If, according to Wallace, a writer must anticipate how his work will be received by readers in a complex culture, and thus about communicating what sounds true, rather than simply what is true, is he really being fully sincere? Is this "a congruence of avowal and actual feeling," or even an endorsement of "single-entendre principles?" Is there not a schizophrenic and/or manipulative quality at work here that counteracts the good intentions of the artist as communicator of truth? As Trilling recognized, and as Ernst van Alphen and Mieke Bal make clear in their introduction to the recent collection *The Rhetoric of Sincerity*, sincerity as a concept has from the beginning been wracked by this kind of difficulty, has never, in fact, evaded its theatrical connection to a notion of performance. "In a traditional sense," van Alphen and Bal tell us, "sincerity indicates the performance of an inner state on one's outer surface so that others can witness it. But the very distinction between inner self and outer manifestation implies a split that assaults the traditional integration that marks sincerity" (3). Moreover, in the age of theory, this characteristic split between inner self and outer performance is further complicated, and even displaced, by the interrogation and re-evaluation of basic concepts of selfhood, intention, and performativity. With this in mind, it might appear that the notion of sincerity becomes inutile, but such is not the case according to van Alphen and Bal: "Sincerity cannot be dismissed [...] because it is an indispensable affective (hence, social) process between subjects" (5). Rather than dismissal, what is required is "a new theorization of the concept" (17), a rethinking of sincerity's rhetorical basis, with particular regard to be paid to the formidable role of new media.

Both sincerity and authenticity, as Trilling defines them, assume a wholeness to the inner self, a lack of internal division regardless of what shows on the outside. The force of appearance/reality and surface/

depth distinctions is fully at work in both concepts, so that when André Gide famously remarks that "One cannot both be sincere and seem so" (qtd. in Trilling 70), this rejection of outward sincerity still involves a commitment to the wholeness of inner being that remains a characteristic of authenticity. David Foster Wallace's fiction, in contrast, asks what happens when the anticipation of others' reception of one's outward behavior begins to take priority for the acting self, so that inner states lose their originating causal status and instead become effects of that anticipatory logic. Former divisions between self and other morph into conflicts within the self, and a recursive and paranoid cycle of endless anticipation begins, putting in doubt the very referents of terms like "self" and "other," "inner" and "outer." Wallace's artistic method for dealing with this infinite cycle—this mirror or bind or aporia— involves a complex, contemporary logic; it is at this point, therefore, that I want to re-describe that method as the operation and promotion of a "New Sincerity." But before exploring examples from Wallace's fiction, and looking at his influence upon his contemporaries, I will first attempt to outline the principles underlying his New Sincerity with reference to the thought of Jacques Derrida.[3]

II

Although Wallace is usually most closely aligned philosophically with Wittgenstein, what connects him to Derrida is the similar set of historically novel concerns they shared, and their comparably acute responses to the period in which they wrote. Specifically, what most binds the two writers is their common recognition that the twin problems of narcissism and communicative uncertainty had, by the late twentieth century, become endemic in the

---

[3] I should note here that the term "New Sincerity" has been employed before, by Jim Collins in a 1993 article on film theory. However, Collins uses the phrase to characterize early-nineties films, such as *Dances with Wolves* and *Field of Dreams*, which reject a postmodernist awareness of mediation in favor of the direct revision of American myths of origin. In Trilling's terms, this would be better described as a rejection of irony in favor of authenticity rather than sincerity, and indeed there is little to link this genre of film to the kind of new sincerity I identify with the work of Wallace and his contemporaries.

connected spheres of Western culture and Western philosophy. For both writers, in their different ways, these problems had to do with an obsession with univocal meaning, which still framed understanding even in a supposed age of irony. For Derrida, responding to this situation meant taking issue with what he called "the ethico-theoretical decision of metaphysics," a decision at the core of philosophy that "postulates the simple to be before the complex, the pure before the impure, the sincere before the deceitful, and so on" (Hägglund 46). For Wallace, these same hierarchical oppositions had become metaphysically unsustainable for Americans of his generation through that generation's prolonged exposure to advertising, a previously peripheral discourse that had risen to paradigmatic status as the main form of public communication in the West. The most basic feature of advertising is that it addresses the other only as a means of highlighting the charms of the self. It is thus fundamentally narcissistic, and yet cannot easily be dismissed, because it has the effect of revealing the potential narcissism involved in all forms of communication. In the age of advertising, it becomes impossible to separate in an absolute manner those communications genuinely directed toward the benefit of the receiver from those that serve primarily to draw attention to the sender. To attempt such a separation is to desire the recovery of a pure sincerity, understood as the lost wholeness of intention associated with speech and presence. More useful, in Derrida's view, would be to construct a logic that can account for impurity and impossibility, that can respond to what he called "the increasingly powerful historical expansion of a system of general writing, of which the system of speech, consciousness, meaning, presence, truth etc., would be only an effect, and should be analyzed as such" ("Signature" 20). Wallace, who recognized that Derrida had "successfully debunked the idea that speech is language's primary instantiation" (Lobster 84), agreed that the effect advertising had of highlighting the complexity and impurity of all discourse could only be responded to by acknowledging one's own implication within this "system of general writing." One must begin by recognizing the lack of any transcendent, absolute, Archimedean point from which to judge the authentic from the inauthentic, the sincere from the manipulative, truth from ideology, and so on.[4]

  As a discourse that reads itself and tries to anticipate and direct its own reception, advertising is never innocent, and Derrida and Wallace likewise feel compelled to produce texts that display impatience with rhetorical innocence and self-justificatory claims of detachment or transcendence. They both develop a writing that relentlessly interrogates its own commitments, and a logic that reflects back on itself to the greatest degree possible. In doing so they aim to offer a critical alternative to what Paul Ricoeur termed a "hermeneutics of suspicion," the prevailing approach to literature and culture that emphasizes what it sees as the blindnesses caused by ideological investment, historical ignorance, and psychological repression. One problem with this approach is that it fails to recognize that under the sign of advertising, when traditional depth has been displaced by a syntagmatic chain of signifiers, truth should no longer be understood as simply existing beneath the surface, a contingent absence that can be rendered present via the processes of critique. In contrast, truth may be uncannily on the surface, impervious to those processes. In many ways, the America Wallace depicts in his fiction has exactly this character, is already radically over-exposed, with many secrets appearing in open view. In *Infinite Jest*, for instance, the transparently comic machinations of Johnny Gentle's Clean U.S. Party bear remarkable and prescient resemblance to the rather blatant ways in which the real-life Bush administration would carry out torture and invasion without appearing overly concerned to argue that what it was doing was lawful or morally right. Similarly, the open manner in which John Wayne and Avril Incandenza carry out their affair pre-empts Michael Pemulis's attempts at blackmail, which are based on the false presupposition that suspicion produces results.

---

[4] This is why, in "E Unibus Pluram," Wallace regularly reiterates that his argument is not a lament or diatribe against TV and advertising, but rather an attempt to understand their power and suggest a response. Paul Giles calls this Wallace's "movement beyond a straightforwardly oppositional critical perspective" (333), and it is a crucial aspect of Wallace's innovative approach to non-fiction.

Adam Kelly

For both Derrida and Wallace, a second problem with the hermeneutics of suspicion, in its exposure-centered emphasis on authenticity rather than sincerity, is that it falls damagingly short of accounting for the persistence of the truly valuable in human life—traits such as love, trust, faith and responsibility. Yet in order to avoid the hermeneutical pitfalls outlined above, both writers find they can approach these traits only through the frame of paradox. Whence the crucial importance of double binds in the work of both writers. Wallace claimed in interview that "Interesting and true stuff in my life seems to involve double-binds, where there is a decision between two alternatives, but neither is acceptable" (Interview, Bookworm 1996), and the logic of the double bind is evidently a basic structure in his work, particularly in *Infinite Jest* (where one character even sets an exam in double binds [307-8]) and in *Brief Interviews with Hideous Men*, where the majority of stories constitute riffs on basic double-bind scenarios. Meanwhile, in late texts such as *Given Time, The Gift of Death and On Cosmopolitanism* and *Forgiveness*, Derrida developed a logic that highlights and addresses the double bind at the heart of concepts such as the gift, the secret, hospitality and forgiveness. A gift, for example, is structured by a paradoxical relation between, on the one hand, calculation, conditionality, and a self-conscious awareness of impurity—the gift as exchange, as a means of getting something in return, even if what one gets is only a moment of self-approval—and, on the other hand, the incalculable, the unconditional, a relation to the other that goes beyond all forms of cognition, manipulation, narcissism and self-promotion. Without this unconditionality, this openness to a horizon beyond anticipation, there can be no such thing as a true gift, and yet such unconditionality proves impossible to separate fully from conditionality, from the self-conscious anticipation of how the other will understand the gift, and how one understands it oneself. The two poles thus become interminably entangled in any action, and we can never know for certain, according to Derrida, if any single event of giving or receiving is the genuine article or not. And this impossibility of knowledge is not contingent, but fundamentally structural to the idea of a gift, something Wallace demonstrates with comic brio in the short stories in *Brief Interviews* that focus on the spiralling paradoxes involved in gift-giving ("The Devil is a Busy Man" and "Suicide as a Sort of Present" are two

139

examples). Like Derrida, Wallace places gift and economy in conceptual opposition: in interview, he contrasted "an artistic transaction, which I think involves a gift" with "an economic transaction, which I regard as cold" (Interview, Bookworm 2000). Yet Wallace also admits that no artistic gift can exist without economy, and has phrased this in terms of the writer's sincerity: "There is, in writing, a certain blend of sincerity and manipulation, of trying always to gauge what the particular effect of something is gonna be" (qtd. in Lipsky).[5] This suggests that sincerity has the same structure as the gift: it can always be taken for manipulation, and this risk is fundamental—it cannot be reduced by appeal to intention, or morality, or context—because true sincerity, if there is ever such a thing, must take place in the aporia between the conditional and the unconditional. Or in Wallace's terms, sincerity must involve "intent" but cannot involve "motive." This is a fraught distinction, and even the writer him- or herself will never know whether they have attained true sincerity, and the reader will never know either. And yet true sincerity happens, is in fact made possible by the impossibility of its certain identification.[6] As Derrida makes clear on many occasions, what is at stake here is not primarily a question of knowledge, because knowledge can always be challenged by the claim to a deeper level of reading and exposure, in a chain of spiralling and ironic infinity. For Wallace, consciousness is precisely this kind of "infinite jest," making absolute cognitive certainty concerning the difference between intent and motive impossible to finally ascertain.

---

[5] It is worth noting that Wallace, along with contemporaries such as Jonathan Franzen and Jonathan Lethem, have expressed their admiration for Lewis Hyde's *The Gift* as a model for contemporary artistic practice. Yet, as Derrida implies in *Given Time*, Hyde's conception of the gift is less radical than these writers' own exploitation of the gift-structure in their work: "As for the unconditionality evoked by Lewis Hyde in *The Gift* […], it is explicitly limited to gifts among close friends, relatives, and most often close relatives. Which is to say that it is not what it is or claims to be: unconditional" (17-18n8). For more on the crucial role of gifts in Wallace's work, see Zadie Smith's essay in her collection *Changing My Mind* (257-300).

[6] Thus Jane Taylor rightly observes of sincerity that "its affects and its effects must remain beyond calculation, must exceed rational description and instrumental reason. Sincerity cannot be deployed. Whenever 'sincerity' names itself, its ceases to exist" (19).

III

This distinction between intent and motive is drawn from *Infinite Jest*. On the one hand, Wallace suggests that intent is a basic human feature when we are told that the eyes of those who witness the film *Infinite Jest* become "Empty of intent" (508).[7] On the other hand, Orin's seduction of his "Subjects" is described as *"sincerity with a motive"* (1048, italics original), and elsewhere, concerning the AA Crocodiles, we are told that "Sincerity with an ulterior motive is something these tough ravaged people know and fear" (369). This latter quotation suggests that the distinction between intent and motive, and any possible affirmation of sincerity, can only be made by a particular kind of listener. More generally, it suggests that the possibility of sincerity depends upon its becoming dialogic in character, always requiring a response from the other to bring it into play. One mark this leaves on Wallace's fiction is in his treatment of voice. Voices within Wallace's work that are understood in terms of their potential sincerity—such as those of Madame Psychosis in *Infinite Jest* and of the Granola Cruncher in the final "Brief Interview"—tend to resist positive description: "not bored or laconic or ironic or tongue-in-cheek. It's reflective but not judgmental, somehow" we are told of the transmitted voice of Madame Psychosis (189). Because all telling can be understood as a pose, there is no way to present sincerity positively in cognitive terms.[8] Moreover, the technical elements of Madame Psychosis's presentation—her demand for five minutes of dead air before and after her show, along with her ritualized and portentous opening—seem calculated to control the impact of her self-

---

[7] This emphasis on the human importance of intent also returns us, of course, to Wallace's quarrel with the modernist/New Critical rejection of "intention" as a factor in the judgment of literary art.

[8] This is why sincerity can only be evoked through attestation, rather than direct description. Thus the hideous man in the final brief interview insists on the power of the Granola Cruncher's delivery of her story while only being able to describe that delivery negatively: "She was not melodramatic about it, the anecdote [...] nor affecting an unnatural calm. [...] She seemed truly poseless in relating it, open to attention but not solicitous—nor contemptuous of the attention, or affecting a disdain or contempt" (*Brief Interviews* 253).

presentation on air, putting in doubt her sincerity. Yet this technicity functions (paradoxically) in the service of a vital "unknowing" quality that it takes Mario Incandenza, "the least cynical person in the history of Enfield MA" (184), to detect. "One of the reasons," the narrator tells us, "Mario's obsessed with her show is that he's somehow sure Madame Psychosis cannot herself sense the compelling beauty and light she projects over the air, somehow" (190). Through Mario's response, we glimpse the possibility of a more affirmative understanding of Madame Psychosis's voice. For him, the voice has "the low-depth familiar[ity] [of] certain childhood smells" (189), and the word it brings to his mind is "haunting" (191). In *Spectres of Marx*, Derrida suggests that an alternative to the metaphysics of presence is to think concepts through a "hauntology," and Psychosis's lack of bodily presence, her invisibility even to the student who produces her radio show, suggest the disembodied haunting, the spectral uncertainty, that marks her particular brand of intent without motive, of sincerity. But that sincerity can only be attested to, not proven, always requiring the listener's own response to the haunting call of the other.[9]

Of course, approaching sincerity in Wallace's fiction means taking account not only of his treatment of character's voices, but also of the term's relevance as a description of his own narrative persona. As early as *Girl With Curious Hair* this had become a key issue for Wallace. Lines that occur in the final paragraph of "Westward the Course of Empire Takes Its Way"—"See this thing. See inside what spins without purchase. Close your eye. Absolutely no salesman will call. Relax. Lie back. I want nothing from you" (*Girl* 373)—with their creepy tone of sales-speak, yet the resonance of genuine communicative truth-telling they hold within the story's context, already demonstrate Wallace's acute awareness of the co-implication of sincerity and spin. But the clearest working out of this bind in Wallace's fiction is "Octet" from *Brief Interviews With Hideous Men*. The

---

[9] The attestation of sincerity need not be provoked purely by the affective quality of the voice, as it is for Mario. It can also involve a conscious decision, as it does for Madame Psychosis herself in a later passage at an AA meeting: "He's got your autodidactic orator's way with emotional dramatic pauses that don't seem affected. Joelle makes another line down the Styrofoam coffee cup with her fingernail and chooses consciously to believe it isn't affected, the story's emotive drama" (710).

key section, "Pop Quiz 9," begins "You are, unfortunately, a fiction writer" (123), and is addressed to the self, reading at times like an anguished diary entry. In it, a writer is concerned about the successful communication of a "weird univocal urgency" (126) he feels in the conception of "a cycle of very short belletristic pieces [that are] supposed to compose a certain sort of 'interrogation' of the person reading them, somehow" (123). But because this interrogation requires the writer to "break the textual fourth wall and kind of address [...] the reader directly," it inevitably ends up resembling the fourth-wall-puncturing that takes place in postmodernist metafiction, in which the writer congratulates himself for not manipulating his audience, but by doing so achieves precisely the opposite, "viz. not interrogating you or have any sort of interchange or even really talking to you but rather just performing in some highly self-conscious and manipulative way." Anxious that he cannot seem to put himself in the place of a reader who is completely other to him, Wallace's narrator ties himself up in knots about these issues, soon concluding that "none of this real-narrative-honesty-v.-sham-narrative-honesty stuff can even be talked about up front" (125n2).

What this suggests, in effect, is that in Wallace's fiction the guarantee of the writer's sincere intentions cannot finally lie in representation—sincerity is rather the kind of secret that must always break with representation. In this, we can see the surface and depth model conventionally assumed to characterize secrecy displaced by structures of difference and deferral. For Derrida, the conditional secret, describable in terms of unveiling, within the logic of surface and depth, is about power—power lies in knowledge of the secret and the ability to uncover the truth it hides (*Gift of Death* 63-64). Most narrative, just like most political discourse, is structured by this kind of conditional secrecy. In contrast, the unconditional secret beyond representation would resist power and knowledge, instead inducing weakness and epistemological humility, the kind of weakness and humility that Wallace's alcoholics must accept if they are to find a way out of their cage. "Nobody's been able to figure AA out," *Infinite Jest*'s narrator tells us (349), and it is this kind of secrecy, a secrecy hiding no knowledge that can be exposed, which allows AA the chance to succeed, but which also accounts for its structural similarity to Fascism.

Both ideologies require a surrendering of the will, "an almost classic sort of Blind Faith in the older guys" (351), a faith in the sincerity of their withholding of the secret. Indeed, the real secret here lies in never knowing whether the secret involved is conditional or unconditional, whether the sincerity of the "older guys" involves motive or intent. This constitutive openness to the possibility of what Derrida terms "the best and the worst" means that the secret beyond representation requires a blind response from the other to legitimate it; in "Octet," this other is the actual reader of the text. Far from the drive to "mastery" that Tom LeClair has argued marks the greatest American postmodernist fiction, Wallace's double bind in "Octet" allows only a "completely naked helpless pathetic sincerity" (131), a weak appeal to the reader to look beyond the text's self-conscious pre-empting of its own reception.[10] It is only this reader (rather than the writer Wallace addresses as "you") who will "be able to tell [what] you're doing; even if she can't articulate it she'll know if you're just trying to save your own belletristic ass by manipulating her—trust me on this" (132n9). The last four words of this phrase are vital, because they repeat the maneuver of reinscribing trust in the very place where knowledge is claimed. This is why "Octet" must end with the demand, or appeal,

---

[10] LeClair claims that the "massive novels" of the postmodernist generation "master the time, the methods of fiction, and the reader" (*The Art Of Excess* 1). Their role is to "judge us, our minds and memories and membership of American life" (2). The fiction of the New Sincerity promotes an entirely different model of writer-reader relations. In Wallace's terms, this difference is perhaps best understood through the distinction he makes in "Authority and American Usage" between the Logical Appeal and the Ethical Appeal. The latter, which accounts for the "genius" of Bryan A. Garner's *Dictionary of Modern American Usage*, and also characterizes Wallace's own genius, is explained thus: "What the Ethical Appeal amounts to is a complex and sophisticated 'Trust me.' It's the boldest, most ambitious, and also most democratic of rhetorical Appeals because it requires the rhetor to convince us not just of his intellectual acuity or technical competence but of his basic decency and fairness and sensitivity to the audience's own hopes and fears" (*Lobster* 77). This unremitting consideration of the reader's position accounts for Wallace's lack of complacency, his recognition that the gift of trust is always open to abuse, and his conscious fear that humility can shade into self-regard at any moment (or even that humility might already be a form of self-regard, as when Geoffrey Day tells Don Gately of his abhorrence of "this AA tactic of masking condescension behind humility" [*Jest* 1001]).

"So decide" (136). Even though this phrase is directed, diary-like, at the writer's self, it can only be answered by the reader, the text's true other. In the spiraling search for the truth of intentions, in an era when advertising, self-promotion and irony are endemic, the endpoint to the infinite jest of consciousness can only be the reader's choice whether or not to place trust and Blind Faith. In Wallace's terms, the greatest terror, but also the only true relief, is the passive decision to relinquish the self to the judgment of the other, and the fiction of the New Sincerity is thus structured and informed by this dialogic appeal to the reader's attestation and judgment.

In a pithy formulation, Steven Connor has quipped that "[b]eing modernist always meant not quite realizing that you were so," whereas "[b]eing postmodernist always involved the awareness that you were so" (10). Within these terms, I would suggest, being a "post-postmodernist" of Wallace's generation means never quite being sure whether you are one, whether you have really managed to escape narcissism, solipsism, irony and insincerity. Again, this uncertainty is structural, allowing as it does for a genuine futurity that only the reader can provide. Hence Zadie Smith, in her introduction to a recent collection of stories by Wallace and his contemporaries, is right when she claims that their texts are primarily "attempting to make something happen off the page, outside words, a curious thing for a piece of writing to want to do" (Introduction xx). It is only by invoking this future off the page that dialogue can be engaged, and that both reader and writer can be challenged by the dialogic dimension of the reading experience. This call for a two-way conversation characterizes not only Wallace's work, but all the fiction of the New Sincerity. For example, Richard Powers, perhaps the most scientifically-focused of major post-boomer writers, has nonetheless described reading as "a kind of secular prayer, a conversation you hold with someone whose world is not yours" (Interview, Bookworm). Similarly, Michael Chabon has argued for the reclamation of the term "entertainment" from its "narrow, debased" connotation of passivity, to serve instead as "a two-way exchange of attention, experience, and the universal hunger for connection" (14, 17). In the work of younger writers whom Wallace has influenced, these dialogic concerns abound. For instance, Joshua Ferris's novel *Then We Came to the End* only breaks with its first-person plural narrative "we" in its revelatory final two lines—"We were the only two left. Just the two of us, you and me" (385)—while in Benjamin Kunkel's debut *Indecision*, a coming-of-age novel that can be read as tracing his generation's turn from authenticity to sincerity, Eden is described at the end of the novel as a place where there is no third person, where there is "Only you and I, I and you" (203). This direct acknowledgement of reader by writer, and vice versa, is captured by the final line of Dave Eggers's *What is the What*: "All the while I will know that you are there. How can I pretend that you do not exist? It would be almost as impossible as you pretending that I do not exist" (535). Or as Wallace himself once put it: "Some [contemporary writers] are involved in transactions requiring genius, but it seems to me to be sort of required on both sides" (Interview, Bookworm 2000). Note the language here: reading is a transaction, an economy like any other in which goods are sold and received, but at the same time an element of genius allows the transaction to go beyond the economic, into the realm of the gift of sincerity. Like sincerity, this genius must remain a secret beyond representation, beyond theoretical definition, tied as it is to the very excess of writing itself. As Derrida remarked, in a line that could have been written for Wallace: "Sometimes theoretical arguments as such, even if they are in the form of critique, are less 'destabilizing,' or let's just say alarming, for 'metaphysical assumptions' than one or other 'way of writing'" ("Strange Institution" 50). Wallace's "way of writing," and his reconfiguration of the writer-reader relationship, displaces metaphysics while retaining a love of truth, a truth now associated with the possibility of a reconceived, and renewed, sincerity.

"Quote unquote love... a type of scotopia": David Foster Wallace's *Brief Interviews with Hideous Men*

Christoforos Diakoulakis

In this paper I would like to attempt a brief reading of David Foster Wallace's "Brief Interviews with Hideous Men #20," the fourth and last homonymous short story from his homonymous collection of short stories. A love story —a story about a love story, to be more precise; the narrative of a love narrative/the narrative that is love, quote unquote; and as such, I would like to argue, an exemplary (if there is one), a proper "love story."

For "love" is surely not a proper name; it is just a banal, corny testimony to an irreducible, ungraspable experience. Of course, there is no such thing as "real" love; surely, every "I love you" is essentially pornographic. "The most worn down of stereotypes... [E]very other night, on TV, someone says: *I love you*," as Roland Barthes notes with exasperation (*A Lover's Discourse* 151). "Love" is nothing but a fabrication, a figure, an invention if you will; *it is* a story —untruth.

David Foster Wallace, however, will not make do with a postmodern cynicism that self-righteously proclaims the end of propriety, purity, intentionality, meaning, truth and so forth. In fact, as we shall see, his whole work is constituted out of just this resistance: to irony, to debasement, to a nauseous, abysmal self-reflection, to the veneration of the hollowness of language —in short, to the mandates of his intellectual inheritance. Wallace will rather speak of "love," of "what it really feels like," because he knows it is only that, the recital of love, a story, a declaration of love, here and now, which preserves its possibility. Too intelligent and too sincere to claim he can somehow hold on to or salvage love's authenticity, its "genuine" signified, Wallace will nevertheless choose to yield to this dreadful void, to immerse himself in the impossible. He knows that a face-off with the dreadful, unconditional assumption of one's fundamental loneliness and incommunicability is all the hope there is: stories are all we have to connect with each other. For Wallace, the surrender to love's "inauthenticity," to its fictitiousness, to its vulgarity, to its terrifying meaninglessness, is alone what safeguards the truthfulness of its experience. What would love be, after all, if one could arrest love, understand love, learn love as such, repeat love in itself, say "I love you" and really mean it, just distinguish "real" love and leave it at that? And inversely, what would love be if one denied love and never said "I love you?" It is precisely this testament to love's inexistence and un-graspability, the sacrifice of love through language, through a trite little narrative which *always* inevitably fails to do justice to the singularity of one's "true" feeling, which corrupts love indeed –Wallace knows it is nothing but the submission to the story of love/the story that is love, nothing but "love" that makes love as such possible. Simply put, one *must* reduce love to "love" and so betray love, in order to make love possible. One *must* tell a "love story" in order to love. "Love" is the necessary presupposition of love. This is the hypothesis of "Brief Interviews with Hideous Men #20."

In his early essay "E Unibus Pluram: Television and U.S. Fiction" (1990), Wallace argues that postmodern fiction has exhausted its potential to have an impact on contemporary, televisual culture. He concludes:

> The next real literary "rebels"… might well emerge as some weird bunch of *anti*-rebels,… who dare somehow to back away from ironic watching,… [w]ho treat of plain old untrendy human troubles and emotions… with reverence and conviction. Who eschew self-consciousness… These anti-rebels would be outdated, of course, before they even started… Maybe that'll be the point… Real rebels… risk disapproval. The old postmodern insurgents risked the gasp and squeal: shock, disgust, outrage, censorship, accusations of socialism, anarchism, nihilism. Today's risks are different. The new rebels might be artists willing to risk the yawn, the rolled eyes, the cool smile… the parody of gifted ironists, the "Oh how *banal*." To risk accusations of sentimentality, melodrama. Of overcredulity. Of softness… Who knows. (*Supposedly* 81-82)

The rather schematic confrontation which Wallace forecasts in those few sentences becomes precisely the conflict that runs through the narrative of "Brief Interviews with Hideous Men #20." The narrator, on the one hand, embodies what Wallace understands to be the postmodern mentality: a very intelligent, well-educated man, who treats with grim sarcasm and relentless irony any assertions that refer to a "pure meaning" or point affirmatively at some "true feeling." On the other hand, the woman he eventually falls in love with represents the realist, "anti-rebel" mentality; she is the one that has a truly banal, sentimental, melodramatic story to tell. Expectedly, the narrator places her instantly in a certain calculable type of women, predicts and parodies all her views and scorns her apparent naivety. Worst of all, he points out, the woman used

> ...well, the quote L-word itself several times without irony or even any evident awareness that the word has through tactical overdeployment become trite and requires invisible quotes around it now at the very least. (250)

The narrator hastily assumes that the woman is referring to some kind of identifiable content that the word "love" supposedly encompasses. Yet, he will soon find out that she is rather testifying to an irreducible event, to an experience, a story she is now about to recount.

While hitchhiking, the woman is picked up by a psychotic man, who soon exits into a secluded area and confesses to her that he intends to "brutally rape, torture and kill her" (251). The woman

> determines that her only chance of surviving this encounter is to establish a quote connection with the quote soul of the sexual psychopath... [S]he believes that sufficient love and focus can penetrate even psychosis and evil and establish a quote soul-connection, unquote, and that if the mulatto can be brought to feel even a minim of this alleged soul-connection there is some chance that he'll be unable to follow through with actually killing her (256)

"Oh, how banal!" responds the reader, along with the cynical narrator. And yet: staring all the time "directly into the sexual psychopath's right eye-the eye that is accessible to her in his aquiline

149

profile" (257), attempting to "empathize with the sex offender's psychosis and rage and terror and psychic torment," focusing "very intently" on him and telling him "what she saw in his soul" (258), "not resisting, not even considering resisting, using all her energy and focus to sustain the feeling of connection with his conflicted despair" (263) and finally "aided by spiritual resources far greater than her own" (262), the woman does manage to prevent the man from murdering her. In fact, the man vomits once he steps out of the car and starts "crying and chewing his lower lip like a frightened child, making small lost noises" (264). While he is raping her, the woman is "stroking the back of his head and whispering small little consolatory syllables in a soothing maternal singsong" (264), and the man weeps in her arms and attempts "to stroke her head in return" (268). Once the rape is finally over, the man stabs "the ground dozens of times with desperate savagery" (270), drops his knife, gets back into his car and drives away.

Now, what did really happen? Of course, it would be silly to assume that the woman actually achieved to connect with the soul of her rapist. But, still, what did really happen? Isn't the event that took place necessarily irreducible to any description? The narrator maintains that "[i]f I had asked a you-type question such as did she really *feel* loving as the mulatto was raping her or was she merely *conducting herself in a loving manner* she would have gazed blankly at me and had no idea what I was talking about" (266, original emphasis). What happened is neither identifiable with an intention nor ascribable to a meaning nor reducible to an explanation; as the narrator now puts it, the woman and her rapist "were connected by something far deeper and more elemental than what we limitedly call quote unquote love, what from her perspective she calls connection" (263). Isn't it then irrelevant how one describes, names or explains it? And yet, is it not necessary to describe, to name and to explain? Isn't it this that saved the woman's life? Is it not necessary to be naïve enough to fail, to surrender to the other, in order to make the other and oneself possible, in order to make love possible?

In an astonishing passage in "Sauf le Nom," Jacques Derrida defines love, as if in passing:

[H]ere love is probably only a particular figure for all that this letting can affect (without, however, affecting it). But why not recognize there love itself, that is, this infinite renunciation which somehow surrenders to the impossible [*se rend à l'impossible*]? To surrender to the other, and this is the impossible, would amount to giving oneself over in going toward the other, to coming toward the other, to coming toward the other but without crossing the threshold, and to respecting, to loving even the invisibility that keeps the other inaccessible. (*On The Name* 74)

This seems to be precisely what the narrator ultimately realizes in the story's finale:

I did not care whether it was quote true. It would depend what you mean by true... it seemed true even if it wasn't. That even if the whole focused-soul-connection theology, that even if it was just catachrestic New-Age goo, her belief in it had saved her life, so whether or not it's goo becomes irrelevant, no? ...I kept saying her name and she would ask What? And I'd say her name again... can you see why there's no way I could let her just go away after this? ...Why it didn't matter if she was fluffy or not terribly bright? Nothing else mattered. She had all my attention. I'd fallen in love with her. I believed she could save me... I knew she could. I knew I loved. End of story'. (270-71)

Redeemed from the harrowing awareness of his necessary imprisonment in language, from the infinite suspicion of every name, the narrator now realizes that precisely because every name is improper, precisely because "every other is every bit other," as Derrida's famous dictum states, the sacrificial testimony of the other is simultaneously the necessary presupposition of its possibility. The narrator is saved when he realizes that love is possible, that every other is possible, *on condition* that one acknowledges that the other is inaccessible and unattainable, *on condition* that one assumes the responsibility to sacrifice the other's singularity and say the other's name, again and again.

Throughout the story, the narrator increasingly identifies with the psychotic man's emotional turmoil. For the latter, the rape is "is his twisted way of having a, quote, relationship... [A] soul-exposing connection with another human being terrifies him that *he* will become the victim" (259, emphasis original); now the narrator admits that this is not

> all that substantively different from a man sizing up an attractive girl... and artfully deploying just the right rhetoric... until she's... totally under his emotional control... when what he really wants is to be in some absolutely antipodal spot from wherever she is from now on... [A]n all too obvious part of the reason for his... maybe somewhat victimizing behavior is that the potential profundity of the very connection he has worked so hard to make her feel terrifies him (259)

In consequence, the woman's silly, little narrative of "love" and "soul-connection" affects the narrator in exactly the same way it affected the psychotic man; by the end of it he is as much transformed. "The story's emotional impact . . . was . . . profound and unprecedented" (269), he asserts. "I was moved, changed" (270), "I realized I had never loved anyone."(267) "Well I don't mind telling you I'd begun to cry, at the anecdote's climax. Not loudly but I did (...) I was weeping for myself" (269). "Believe that I felt the mulatto's fathomless sadness, then." (268) "And all this was going on simultaneously." (266) That which connected the woman with the sex offender, "something far deeper and more elemental than what we limitedly call quote unquote love, what from her perspective she calls connection" (263), now connects the woman with the narrator: a "love" story. It is the same "love story" in fact, which in yet another repetition connects thereon the narrator with his apparently cynical addressee, as it also connects Wallace with his reader and me with you. "It feels as if she's back there by the road. A type of scotopia.' (263)

Which brings us back to the beginning:

> And yet I did not fall in love with her until she had related the story of the unbelievably horrifying incident in which she was brutally accosted and held captive and very nearly killed."

Q.

> "Let me explain. I'm aware of how it might sound, believe me. I can explain. In bed together, in response to some sort of prompt or association, she related an anecdote about hitchhiking and once being picked up by what turned out to be a psychotic serial

sex offender who then drove her to a secluded area and raped her and would almost surely have murdered her had she not been able to think effectively on her feet under enormous fear and stress. Irregardless of whatever I might have thought of the quality and substance of the thinking that enabled her to induce him to let her live. (245)

These are the story's opening lines, and they call for our most concentrated attention as everything seems to be played out here. "And yet I did not fall in love with her until she had related the story of...": already, in the very first sentence, a declaration of love and its justification: a story is why, asserts the narrator; the story that a woman related to him is why he fell in love with her; a narrative is –in place of– the reason of love. "Let me explain. I'm aware of how it might sound, believe me. I can explain," he adds immediately. Yet his second remark turns out to be nothing but a repetition of the first: the declaration of love, this time latent in the ellipsis of the final sentence ("Irregardless of whatever...to let her live"), and its justification, in the form of a second succinct mention of the woman's story. In place of the promised explanation to his covert interlocutor (Q) the narrator cannot but tell her (in the course of the story it becomes evident that the interlocutor is female) the story that this woman told him, since the reason he fell in love with her is *nothing but* that story. A narrative will have made love possible in the first place.

Having now gone through the rest of Wallace's story, one realizes that these first few lines constitute in fact its sound summary. What succeeds those two remarks, which repeat each other and the story of another, is yet another repetition of what has already been recounted in them. In his attempt to explain why he fell in love with that woman, the narrator only repeats her narrative once more; no other explanation, only the narration of a narrative in place of love's justification. As soon as it starts, then, "Brief Interviews with Hideous Men #20" has concluded: from the outset, everything is decided. Wallace's story induces the reader therefore to turn her attention from the "what" to the "how," that is, from *the event recited* to the *event of the recitation* itself. In 'How to Avoid Speaking: Denials' Derrida notes "[t]he 'how' always conceals a 'why'" (*Languages* 15); and indeed, Wallace's story unfolds on account of an essential aporia –like all literature: why recite the story again? Why recite the story in the first place? "And yet I did not fall in love with her until she had related the story of..." Why love? The response to this question constitutes the narrative of "Brief Interviews with Hideous Men #20"; love, quote unquote, will have made narrative possible in the first place.

"I know how this sounds, trust me... I know what you're bound to ask. Ask it now... I don't care... I knew I loved. End of story.'" (271) These are the narrator's final words, repeating the story's takeoff and bringing us back to the start of an interminable recitation of the origin of love; interminable because of never having begun without ending with the same movement, always already repeating itself. The story is over and the narrator's interlocutor has not understood —"I don't care... I knew I loved": after all, she could have never understood. The narrator admits his failure and acknowledges now that the failure was in truth prescribed, that his endeavor to justify love has always been impossible: "love" is unidentifiable, other than itself; it has always been just a story.

A declaration of love, the narrative that is "love," sets the story in motion; it makes the story possible. And yet, by the same token, that declaration of love also causes the story to eventually fail, to miss itself. As soon as the narrator names "love," he finds himself confronted with the question of love's "content" —its referent, meaning, identity, source —paradoxically obliged to respond *inadequately*, to fail and betray love, in order to justify that which must be unconditional and indeed unnameable in order to be what it is. "Love" will have always inevitably carried with it the parasitic question "why love?" —here embodied by the covert interlocutor— as the mark of the unbridgeable gap separating "love" from love. But it remains—this dreadful parasite will have simultaneously been love's chance: one's impossible attempt to get rid of it, as horrifying as it might be, the vain attempt to describe love without explaining *it*, to verify love without proving *it*, to name love without naming it —*this*, a narrative, will have *eventually* allowed one to connect with the other. The inevitable betrayal of love, its violent vulgarization, a love narrative/the narrative that is love, will have made the experience of love itself possible.

In place of a proper conclusion, allow me to cite a short excerpt from Jacques Derrida's unpublished seminar on "je t'aime":

"Je t'aime" is not a description; it is the production of an event by means of which, claiming not to lie, claiming to speak the truth…, I tend to affect the other, to touch the other, literally or not, to give the other or to promise the other the love that I speak to him or her… This performative declaration creates an event in manifesting, in attesting to that which it speaks, in bearing witness to it; and that to which it testifies is not elsewhere, but here and now, nearly merging with the act that consists in saying it. (qtd. in Miller 137-38)

Love is neither identifiable with the word that "bears witness to it" nor reducible (just "nearly") to "the act that consists in saying it." Love is the imaginative experience that this act and this word, a declaration of love, like the ruins of something irrevocable, just might give rise to, unquote.

"That Is Not Wholly True"
Notes on Annotation in
David Foster Wallace's Shorter Fiction
(and Non-Fiction)[1]

Iannis Goerlandt

> He loves nothing better than a vertiginous plunge to the foot of
> the page. He is the self-appointed president-for-life of the
> American Subscript Society. To Wallace, a footnote is the
> equivalent of the concert pianist's cadenza, the moment he can
> depart from the score and dazzle us with his virtuoso gifts.
> (McCrum)

One of the formal idiosyncrasies of David Foster Wallace's
prose is its extensive use of footnotes. It is not only his fiction that has
triggered fervid reactions: the sheer mass and intricate structure of the
annotation systems in his non-fiction, both his essay collections and
Everything & More, have given rise to animosity as well.[2] What these
sweeping observations obscure, however, is the understanding that
although similar to a certain extent, in their different textual settings
the various annotation systems serve different ends, especially on the
level of textual performance. Starting from a brief discussion of the
notes in Wallace's non-fiction, this paper will focus on the role of the
footnotes in five short stories from the collections *Brief Interviews with
Hideous Men* and *Oblivion*.

Before going into these texts in more detail, it is relevant to
briefly sketch the research context. Apart from the widely received
findings of Marshall Boswell and Greg Carlisle, I can refer to a recent

---

[1] The following is in part a revised summary of my paper "Fußnoten und
Performativität bei David Foster Wallace: Fallstudien."(in Metz and Zubarik
387-408).

[2] Not to mention playful parody (Campbell) and tributary/commemorative imitation
(consider Blumenbach; Goerlandt/Rovers; Martone).

paper presented by the Swiss scholar Magnus Wieland in 2008 during the second conference on annotation in literary texts hosted by the University of Erfurt. One of Wieland's topics was the annotation system in "A Supposedly Fun Thing I'll Never Do Again," which mirrors the essay's interest in cleanliness and waste management: the notes are employed to keep the "main" text "clean" of excess information—they are banned to the foot of the text and as such are equivalent to the frantic efforts to keep the m.v. *Zenith* agleam, while underneath the sewage system builds up its fearsome force. However, many of these notes themselves are presented parenthetically, which marks them as belonging "potentially to the main text." At the same time, many passages in the main text come in parentheses and can therefore be deemed "potential footnotes." On a performative level, Wieland argues, Wallace's essay is a re-enactment of the cruise experience for its readers: "either a text simply accepts the fact that it is immanently and inherently 'impure', or it 'ejects' these impurities, but by doing so renders them visible—which is the principal insight about the whole cruise business as well" (12; translation mine).

Waste Management and Rhetorical Distance

Wieland is right to regard "A Supposedly Fun Thing" as the culmination point of Wallace's early series of footnoted essays. Relating his cruise experience, Wallace self-consciously employs the full range of how textual suspense and humor can be achieved through annotation. This becomes clear when comparing the annotation systems in the other pieces from his first essay collection: in "E Unibus Pluram," the notes were still mere academic references, and while in the essays on David Lynch and Michael Joyce the notes are a joyous mix of source references and explanatory asides, only in some respects they can be considered facetious mirror images of the main texts' argumentative structures.

In "David Lynch Keeps His Head," Wallace uses *trivia tidbits* both in the footnotes and the main text (most commonly at the end of each chapter), a narrative device he will later also employ in *Everything & More*, in the guise of the "If You're Interested" parts. At certain points, however, extra information is added as a sub-chapter (for example chapter 9a [*Supposedly* 166]), as a new chapter that actually extends a preceding chapter (chapters 11 and 14 [169;189]), or as a sub-chapter to such an extension (chapter 11a [191]), quite markedly even at a wrong place in the chapter sequence, which in turn gives rise to questions of referentiality. The footnotes mirror these techniques by ejecting additional information from the "main body" of the note, not by meta-footnotes, but by adding a new parenthetical level. The most interesting of the numerous instances is note 25 (180), because it additionally marks the meta-parenthetical sub-comment with a paragraph switch.

"A Supposedly Fun Thing," however, takes annotation to a whole new level, not only by the sheer number of notes, which causes the essay's narrative structure to turn into a capricious hierarchical jungle, but also by numerous rhetorical tricks. For a text so explicitly concerned with the performative appeal and ethics of essay-writing, some examples of these rhetorical devices are worth mentioning.

The memorable introduction of Wallace's tablemates at Table 64 in a note (280 n32) features a humorous discrepancy between its length of almost three pages and its introduction as a "a fast footnote" (281 n32). This note is a key example of "textual waste" being stacked up so high that it spills over and pushes aside the "main" text—it visualizes the fact that the annotations are indispensable for understanding the narrative as a whole in that they claim the main text's principal typographical locus, the "main" page.

This type of spillover is equally manifest in the essay "Authority and American Usage" (as well as in *Everything & More*), which has sections marked as "INTERPOLATIONS." Some of these are presented as part of the main text but are simultaneously asterisked, sometimes even daggered, and set in a smaller type (*Lobster* 113-6). These "INTERPOLATIONS," presented as excess material midway between the "main" argument and the more "aside"-like annotations, stand as examples of a rigorously employed mechanized hierarchical annotation system that ultimately *obscures* textual organization.

In "Host," with its reintroduction of the marginal gloss, Wallace shows how proliferating clarifying contextual information eventually undercuts hierarchical patterning.[3] In a comment on her design for *Consider the Lobster*, typographer Marie Mundaca remarks that Wallace "wanted to stress the immediacy of communication and the speed of thought that occurred in the studio" ("The Influence of Anxiety"). Structurally, the lay-out functions as the equivalent of the problems related to "determining which sources to pay attention to and how exactly to distinguish real information from spin" (*Lobster* 285). Mundaca adds that she and Wallace initially "had some very intense discussions regarding the semiotics of the leaders (the lines going from the text to the boxes) and the tics and the line width of the boxes." The main problem here is that of "anchoring" (Bunia, qtd. in Metz and Zubarik 16), namely the semiotic value of the locus of referentiality, or, more concretely, in the differences between the anchor (the footnote mark), the anchoring point (the place in the main text where the anchor is set) and the anchor's context (the actual content that the gloss refers to). These differences are especially clear when comparing the *Atlantic Monthly* version and the book version. Whereas the former employs color highlighting of (part of) the anchor's context to establish the reference and then simply lines up the highlighted boxes in the margin, the latter shifts focus to the relative semantic weight of the notes by placing them in-line, sometimes again pushing

---

[3] Naturally, Wallace is not the first to use excessive, multi-layered annotation (see the bibliography in Metz/Zubarik and on http://www.amrandebemerkt.de/bibliographie.htm), but whereas the footnotes and glosses in e.g. Pierre Bayle's *Dictionnaire historique et critique* (1697) serve distinctly different ends (both annotation and a critique of secondary sources; see Grafton 189-211), and whereas the annotation in e.g. Mark Z. Danielewski's *House of Leaves* (2000) has (even typographically) discernable narrators, Wallace's texts referred to in this paper (most often) have only one narrator. As a result, excessive annotation in Wallace's works is especially hard to follow, since the multiple layers, though on the narrative plain hierarchically distinct, carry an equal weight. Wallace was well aware of this effect, as shows in the 1997 Bookworm interview with Michael Silverblatt: "[...] Michael Pietsch [...] pointed out to me that it seems about a third of the footnotes—particularly in the Lynch thing, and the cruise thing—were cut out—because he can nail when I have forgotten that the footnotes *have to be read exactly the same way the text does*. To me they become sort of corollaries or afterthoughts, but for the reader actually they're even more demanding because reader has to stop, hold his or her place in the text, go down, you know, read the interpolation and then return to the text." (italics mine)

away the "main text," playing with the rhythm of reader focus and the indistinctness of the reference points.

Wallace is a master at balancing where to place notes, always minding the prosody of his prose. Let us consider the first notes and asides in "A Supposedly Fun Thing," namely the comments on [1] the "very bright blue" vs. there being a blue "beyond *very, very bright blue*" (256/7), [2] the little glowing fish that like to swim between the ship's hull and the pier (257), [3] the notable difference between "shooting skeet" vs. shooting "*at* skeet" (257-8), [4] the ship's maximum cruising speed in knots vs. not knowing what a knot is (258), [5] Mr. Dermatis henceforth being referred to as "Mr. Dermatitis" (258-9), [6] the grudge against Mr. Dermatis (258 n1), and finally [7] the note on no wag being able to resist mentally rechristening the ship as the m.v. *Nadir* (259 n3). The keywords here are distance, refocusing and timing for unexpectedness and maximum effect. A comparison of this passage with the one in *Harper's* reveals that Wallace decided to employ rhetorical distance by alternating between distance in the main text [1-3] and by using notes [4-6-7]. The most important instances are the skeet shooting and the knots (in the latter alternation, Wallace even copies the typography by introducing the parentheses in the note[4]), and the double rechristening, the first of which is presented in an immediate apposition, the second in a direct note. The technique of distancing, which is part of the essay's overall structure, as themes are introduced to be picked up again in the course of the narrative (not unlike a series of parentheses being opened and gradually closed), can be seen to be already governing the rhetorical distribution of content in the opening scene and the first notes.

Two additional examples can clarify how the principle of distancing is at the root of the essay. The first example is sub-footnote 72a (306-7), in which Wallace describes how he, ignorant of the recent scandals with waste disposal, ends up asking Mr. Dermatis more information on the *Zenith*'s Vacuum Sewage System, how his

---

[4] In *Harper's* the remark is simply tacked into the main text: there, the skeet shooting scene does not precede it, so there is no need for an additional typographical annotation layer.

tablemates "scream with mirth at [his] clay-footed naïveté" (305 n72; with the sub-footnote anchored after the word "scream") and how he starts to fear that the Greek staff will somehow use the toilet to assassinate him. There is no intrinsic need to repeat the comment about the scream's nature, as this was part of the discussion of his tablemates in the aforementioned "fast footnote" (281 n32), and no discernable reason why this very brief addition should be ejected from the main text. Therefore, it seems to be *the whole textual span* between the anchor and the actual sub-footnote 72a that is somehow labelled "(literally)." It is the semiotic and referential blurredness of footnote referencing which strengthens the humorous effect: the addition evokes Wallace's VSS paranoia by making it more "real," so to speak by planting a "literal" image in the readers' minds that will be become ultra-vivid in all respects, not unlike Conroy's "vast lapis lazuli dome of the sky" (287 n36).[5]

The second example is footnote 119, a brief comment on the clause "guys in the Guy division have to slide out on a plastic telephone pole slathered with Vaseline" (336-7). The footnote inserts a laconic "(the pole)," which combines rhetorical distance with a boundless "drive for disambiguation" to maximize a humorous effect: it is the note itself that sparks the question who or what was slathered with Vaseline.

Reader-Annoyance in *Brief Interviews with Hideous Men*

This "drive for clarification" is the governing principle in many of Wallace's early footnoted fiction. However, in his short stories, this drive is put to work on a wholly different level.

In "The Depressed Person," Wallace unveils the protagonist's "obsessive self-absorption" and "voracious narcissism," whence she is "particularly unlikable" (Boswell, *Understanding* 204-5). Many readers of the original publication in *Harper's* objected to Wallace's depiction of

---

[5]A similar effect is achieved in footnote 125, in which Wallace brackets off his appreciation of Cruise Director Scott Peterson as a "dweeb" (341) by means of a parenthesis sketching how Wallace anxiously hopes for marital retaliation by Mrs. S.P.

depression, but they failed to see, as Boswell indicates, that the woman "more than anything else" is a victim "of her own reliance on quick fixes for narcissism, which she has mistakenly, and self-aggrandizingly, diagnosed as depression" (206).

However, the real "problem" of the text is the way in which the narrator adopts and/or simulates the protagonist's subjective stance and idiolect. One means by which this is achieved is the obstinate repetition of the phrase "the depressed person" (179 times in the main text, 99 times in the footnotes), a phrase which is only rarely questioned, and only rhetorically, for instance in the following passage:

> She was asking sincerely, the depressed person said, honestly, desperately: what kind of person could seem to feel nothing —"*nothing*," she emphasized—for anyone but herself? Maybe not *ever*? The depressed person wept into the headset telephone [...] (57)

The embedment of the question "what kind of person" between the verbally similar epithets casts doubt on the self-assessment of "depression" and on the reliability of the story's adoption of this phrase, even in the story's title: readers are invited to re-evaluate the nomenclature's validity.[6] The most important means, however, is the adoption of the protagonist's obsessive speech and thought processes manifest in the insistence on clarifying sequences,[7] even when the anaphoric or cataphoric elements explained are at most semi-ambivalent:

> The depressed person also shared with long-distance friends [...] the painful realization that she had never once actually come right out and asked the therapist what she (i.e., the therapist) was thinking or feeling at any given moment during their time together, nor had asked, even once, what she (i.e., the therapist) actually thought of her (i.e., of the depressed person) as a human being, i.e. whether the therapist personally liked her,

---

[6] See Sánchez 246 for general comments on the "canonizing function" of titles.

[7] Similar clarification sequences (both as parentheses and as subordinate clauses) can be found throughout the text, albeit not always as concentrated as in this passage. In total, there are 86 such instances, 39 of which concern "the depressed person," 11 "the therapist," and 7 "the friend".

didn't like her, thought she was a basically decent v. repellent person, etc. (52 n6)

A good illustration of the fact that this indeed is a narrative adoption of the protagonist's voice is the following passage, in which the deictic element "here" assumes a double meaning and points both to the referred scene and the insertion's locutionary act itself:

> [...] an abuse clearly connected—*here* the depressed person nearly always *inserted* that her therapist concurred with this assessment—to the bottomless, chronic adult despair she suffered every day [...] (32, emphasis mine)

Another form of annotation acting as clarifying sequences are the footnotes, which dramatize "the layered nature of the woman's obsessive self-absorption, in which thoughts have tangents that themselves become winding thought helixes running parallel to the first-order line of self-consciousness" (Boswell, *Understanding* 204-5). Some of these hyper-reflexive "narrative tangents" (Carlisle, "Wallace's Infinite Fiction" 32) are concocted very intricately. Consider e.g. the therapist's "tic of placing the tips of all her fingers together in her lap," which thus form "various enclosing shapes"—the DP dislikes this habit "chiefly because it drew her attention to the therapist's fingers and fingernails and caused her to compare them with her own" (36). This observation is picked up on the next page: analogously to the therapist, who doesn't seem to pay attention to what the DP is saying, the story's first footnote draws the attention away from the therapist's response:

> The therapist[1] was diligent [...] in supporting the depressed person in exploring how these beliefs about how she "seemed" or "came off" to others made her feel.
>
> [1] The multiform shapes the therapist's mated fingers assumed nearly always resembled, *for the depressed person,* various forms of geometrically diverse cages [...]. The therapist's fingernails were long and shapely and well maintained, whereas the depressed person's fingernails were compulsively bitten so short and ragged that the quick sometimes protruded and began spontaneously to bleed. (37, emphasis mine)

This note confirms that the DP is "chiefly" concerned with the nails, a comparison which is self-agonizing but of course also very narcissistic. Moreover, the footnote interrupts the course of the narrative exactly when the therapist wants to react to a very complex avowal: the annotation system thus simulates the self-absorption at the heart of the DP's reactions. In what follows, the "hand-in-lap"-problem is played out in ever more paranoid configurations (41, 44 n4, 45 n4, 46 n4, 52 n6(A)).

Another interesting case is footnote 6(A), which is introduced as part of a double anchor:

> [...] the therapist had challenged the depressed person to identify whether the overheard slur had made her (i.e., the depressed person) feel primarily more angry, lonely, frightened, or sad.[6,6(A)] (51)

Because the anchor is structured paratactically, 6(A) cannot be called a pure sub-footnote. Again, this is a narrative simulation of a peculiarity of the protagonist's "wild consciousness" as indicated in the note's first sentence:

> As a natural part of the grieving process, sensuous details and emotional memories flooded the depressed person's agonized psyche at random moments and in ways impossible to predict, pressing in on her and clamoring for expression and processing. (52 n6(A))

Unexpectedness also is a key feature of the referentiality of this particular footnote. Despite the fact that there is no sub-footnote anchor in footnote 6, note 6(A) can be considered to be also referring to the preceding note 6 (which deals with the neurotic urge to offer "honest" and long-winded clarifications) on the basis of the numbering scheme. The narrative thus subtly and ambivalently simulates self-reflexivity as second-order narration.

Other telling examples are footnotes 2 and 8: both are parenthetical appositions that one normally would have expected in the main text, but that are here put at the foot of the page. Noticeably, these clarification sequences still are presented parenthetically, e.g. the very brief note 2, which refers to a sentence of almost 350 words:

> [...] the depressed person [...] had reexperienced long-pent-up and festering emotional wounds, one of which[2] being a deep vestigial rage [...]
>
> [2] (i.e., one of which purulent wounds) (39)

It would have been possible to integrate the parenthesis into the main text without a significant change in complexity, especially in view of the fact that the sentence has two more *id est* sequences. Adopting the parentheses in the note hence is another example of hyper-reflexivity doubled on a narrative level.

This "technique of dramatizing the self-reflexive nightmare of hyper-self-consciousness" (Boswell, *Understanding* 204) is equally present in "Death Is Not the End," a story sharing with "The Depressed Person" the theme of narcissism. In "Death Is Not the End," the writer protagonist's self-applauding is expanded and simulated in three footnotes. The protagonist, who shares many traits with the radically self-absorbed "Great Male Narcissists" Wallace would later discuss in his essay "Certainly the End of Something or Other, One Would Sort of Have to Think," is implicitly criticized through the painfully detailed stasis of the narcissistic gaze that loses itself in endless repetitions. One of the points the story makes is that the end lies in this stasis, not in death itself. However, doesn't the "neutral," "non-evaluative" narrative stance cause the story itself to degenerate into "uncritical celebration of this self-absorption both in [it]sel[f] and in [its] characters" (*Lobster* 53), rendering it as little attractive as the gaze is simulates? The final footnote marks this stasis by refuting the alleged incomparability of "the whole enclosed tableau of pool and deck and poet and chair and table and trees and shrubbery" (*Brief Interviews* 3) and comparing it to the story itself, which is equally motionless and inescapable:

> [...] the silent living enclosing flora's motionless green vivid and inescapable and not like anything else in the world in either appearance or suggestion.[3]

[3] That is not wholly true. (3)

Both the repetitious addiction to details in "Death Is Not The End" and the hyper-reflexive narration in "The Depressed Person" do not ironize the speech of their protagonists, rather, they present it unflatteringly, adopt it and expand it. Because of that, their respective narrative techniques *reproduce* their protagonists' irritating idiosyncrasies. If we want to read these stories as a critique of certain forms of thought and speech, these texts can only succeed if we as readers disapprove of them and reject them *as texts*. My thesis[8] is that these two stories exploit the annoyance many readers feel when having to deal with excessive annotation: with an hardly bearable and at times nauseating simulation, these texts are designed to induce a knee-jerk reaction in their readers, namely an intense rejection of this "the gaping trap of logolatry" (Goerlandt/Herman 11).

Wallace's preoccupation with this problem is highly visible in "Octet," *Brief Interviews'* most saliently footnoted text. The structure of this story, a series of shorter "Pop Quizzes" aiming for a certain reader response, is an exploration of the narrative and ethical possibilities offered in "Problems," the title story of John Updike's 1979 collection (see Boswell, *Understanding* 185). Whereas Updike's collection consists of a series of interconnected, sequentially numbered "problems," "Octet" offers but two "successful" quizzes (4 and 7), complemented by the failed PQ6, which has only remained part of the cycle because the succeeding PQ6(A) "depends so heavily on 6's first version" (*Brief Interviews* 124), and the highly self-reflexive PQ9. As Adam Kelly has pointed out (see his paper in this volume), this last Pop Quiz provides the cycle's key question: does hyper-self-consciousness concord with sincerity, and if so, what are the consequences, both the way fiction is written and for the ethics of the relationship between author and readers?

Before going into these questions, it is necessary to investigate to which extent the story's "fancy footwork" (Goerlandt/Herman 11) supports or thwarts the cycle's program. In "Octet," the difference between parenthetical and non-parenthetical footnotes is less pronounced, apart from the fact the parenthetical notes contain less important clarifications that one could have deduced from the text proper. The cycle's footnotes are not numbered sequentially: each new Pop Quiz has its own set of notes, which suggests that the pieces are relatively independent. Also remarkable is the fact that the number of notes in the different pieces is proportional to the level of self-consciousness they exhibit (see Table).

---

[8] (and keeping in mind the question with which Wallace characterizes his sister Amy Wallace Havens in the acknowledgments in *A Supposedly Fun Thing I'll Never Do Again*: "Just How Much Reader-Annoyance Are You Shooting For Here Exactly?" [355])

Pop Quiz	4	6	7	6(A)	9
footnotes / total	0	0	1	4	21
plain	0	0	1	1	6
parenthetical	0	0	0	3	12

Probably the most important of the 21 footnotes in PQ9 (a conspicuous sequence number in an *octet* if ever there was one) is note 2, which deals with the "now-tired S.O.P. 'meta'-stuff" and sketches the literary devices of "classic postmodern rhetorician[s]," viz. "belletrist[s] whose intermural honesty is both formally unimpeachable and wholly self-serving" (125 n2*). "[F]ound buried in a footnote," this passage "nevertheless provides the key to the entire book":

> meta-strategies of any sort are decadent when they are mere "performance" and self-consciously manipulative. The task is here to disclose the self-consciousness as manipulative and thereby enact an actual, two-way "interrogation" with the reader. (Boswell, *Understanding* 187)

"Octet" shows the almost inherent possibility to talk openly about the "how real-honesty-v.-sham-honesty stuff" (125 n2) without becoming manipulative. Because this statement is made in *a sub-footnote to a footnote*, meaning a formal setting suggesting self-consciousness and hyper-reflexivity, the question arises whether this note itself is straightforward and sincere, even (and especially) when the narrator tells the readers (who have to picture themselves in his position as author) that the note in fact perhaps had better been left out altogether ("None of that was very clearly put and might well ought to get cut" [125 n2])— which of course *itself* would have been a manipulative act.

Luckily, there are some ways out of the hyper-reflexive jungle, but unfortunately, they again depend on the reader's willingness to show or refuse sympathy and/or empathy. One (positive) option is to accept the text's long-winded direction of the narrator-narratee relation as being "sincere," as truly direct communication between author and reader (see Goerlandt, "This Is The Sort...," 553-4). In doing so, one wouldn't simply be displaying sympathy for Wallace's difficult position as an author of a "failed" cycle: by switching roles, there would also be *empathy*, even in the face of the story's (explicit) manipulative aspects. The other possibility is to dismiss the cycle as "failed" and avoid being taken in by the narrator. However, the story, coordinated "from back at some gleaming abstract Olympian HQ" (*Brief Interviews* 136), paradoxically *succeeds* in both ways, because either a *hideous man's* scheming is tumbled to, or the story becomes the locus of genuine empathy.

Irrespective of how one interprets this HQ, it is the ethical effects of the "failed" or "successful" Pop Quizzes that are crucial for an understanding of the cycle. Because the Quizzes should facilitate ethical responses, the question is what e.g. PQ4, with its notable absence of all forms of obtruding annotation, communicates. In this quiz, which deals with two drug addicts leaning against a wall of the "Commonwealth Aluminum Can Redemption Center" (an ominous name) on a cold January night, the reader is asked "which one lived" (111). The piece's setting prompts for a decision rather than an answer (hence the "so decide" [136] in PQ9). On a first level, the decision is one for a preference towards a particular narrative scheme and its implications[9] (if the sick addict dies, the piece could indicate that all pity and offered relief ultimately will prove to be futile—if the Samaritan dies, the scene could for instance be used to hail or ridicule the heroism or the stupidity of selfless compassion). The catch, however, is on a second level: the real "interrogation" of the reader this piece does entail the hyper-reflexivity originating in the subsequent notes and permeating the whole cycle. Namely, when the last quiz asks us readers to imagine themselves in the position of an author of a cycle, we should realize that the consequence of adopting this position is that we readers/authors should decide whether we want prompt our readers for what ultimately is a death sentence—regardless of the underlying moral: how ethical is it to force this decision upon the readers and turning them into perpetrators or accomplices?[10] As Wallace stated in the McCaffery interview: "the stuff's a permanent migraine." (142)

---

[9] Incidentally, the same holds true for the first of Updike's "Problems".

[10] This double bind is rendered explicitly in the discussion of James Incandenza's *Accomplice!* in *Infinite Jest* (see Goerlandt and Herman 316 and Carlisle, *Elegant Complexity* 453-5).

Some Footnotes and an Endnote in *Oblivion*

After *Brief Interviews*, Wallace gradually started to consider the footnotes as an annoying gimmick, a burdensome "crutch" (Sheenan 20) he wanted to proceed without. In a 1997 interview, Wallace discussed the "weird kind addictive quality" of footnotes and the fact that he would go "cold turkey from footnotes" (Interview, *Bookworm* 1997), and in 2003, he foretold the decline of the footnote in his upcoming collection *Oblivion*:

> I don't think any of the stories have footnotes, which I'm rather proud of. Got that monkey off my back. I think one story maybe has a couple of asterisk footnotes. You know, there are so few of them that you can use asterisks. (Crain)

Wallace does not employ the references to addiction coincidentally here: in *Infinite Jest*, it was "marijuana thinking" that was the equivalent to hyper-reflexivity (Goerlandt/Herman 9-10). In his last story collection, Wallace will explore new territory, and the few footnotes left will serve other purposes.

In "Mr. Squishy"'s highly complex system of observers, it is ultimately impossible to decide who is manipulating whom. Understanding the narrative is also aggravated by the abundant use of acronyms, typical corporate jargon and the deliberate confusion as to who the narrator of the story is. In the beginning of the story, it still seems like there is more or less a single, reliable narrator, and the footnotes seem to function as helpful explanatory glosses: eight of the thirteen notes simply explain an acronym. The fourth note, however, is slightly different, while it implicitly harks back to the preceding note. Whereas the third note explained the acronym "MAM" as "Manual Adjusting Mechanism" (16*), the fourth note, 16 pages further on in the narrative, comments on the expression "Market Appeal Matrix" in the main text, in that its acronym is "also, somewhat confusingly, = MAM" (31*). Though of course in practice at Team Δy problematical, on a *textual* level, the ambiguity of the double-coded acronym really is *introduced* by this footnote.[11]

Also, the confusion about who is narrating the story becomes very problematic with the sudden appearance of a mysterious "I"-narrator in the middle of a paragraph (14), who thereupon disappears for 42 pages. Then, a footnote picks up this perspective (57†), shattering the illusion of clarification the notes had perhaps conveyed until then. Although another footnote with a narrative position that is hard to ascertain (66*) will ensue, note 57† is crucial because it contains an unexplained acronym, "C.P.D.," the determination of the signified of which could put the story's plot in a new perspective. It could of course mean "Chicago Police Department,"[12] but the text does not fix the meaning.

I believe that in this story the notes indicate and strengthen the intransparency of the narrative position in "Mr. Squishy." Wallace is able to break away from the stifling problem of self-referential speech as we encountered in *Brief Interviews* in order to exploit this intransparency as a non-dramatized device to induce utter uncertainty in his readers, which confirms the story's oppressive atmosphere on all textual levels.

Finally, there is the single footnote in "Good Old Neon" (apart from the commemorative and epitaph-like addition "[→ NMN. 80.418]" [181]). Today, this daring note is almost unbearable to read:

> * One clue that there's something not quite real about sequential time the way you experience it is the various paradoxes of time supposedly passing and of a so-called 'present' that's always unrolling into the future and creating more and more past behind it. [...] What if there's really no movement at all? [...] Meaning that what if in fact this *now* is infinite and never really passes in the way your mind is supposedly wired to understand *pass*, so that not only your whole life but every single humanly

---

[11] Later still, the acronym "MAM" is used twice without additional explication (46), but the context unambiguously reveals that MAM here means "Manual Adjusting Mechanism".

[12] There is also an intratextual possibility, "Creative Packaging Director" (50), but the context of the footnote rules out this option.

conceivable way to describe and account for that life has time to flash like neon shaped into those connected cursive letters that businesses' signs and windows love so much to use through your mind all at once in the literally immeasurable instant between impact and death, just as you start forward to meet the wheel at a rate no belt ever made could restrain—THE END. (179)

Here, the twisted narrative setting of a "David" imagining a "Neal" talking to him about the reasons for his suicide is adopted and extended, namely in its ghastly use of the second person address, which also implicates the reader. The ending of this note does not quite reach the climax,[13] but is hinted at by the explicit *narrative* closure —this really is "THE END."

In the main text, the final paragraph on "David Wallace" deals with self-consciousness in great detail and structurally runs parallel with the aforementioned footnote:

> David Wallace also fully aware that the cliché that you can't ever truly know what's going on inside somebody else is hoary and insipid and yet at the same time trying very consciously to prohibit that awareness from mocking the attempt or sending the whole line of thought into the sort of inbent spiral that keeps you from ever getting anywhere [...], the realer, more enduring and sentimental part of him commanding that other part to be silent as if looking it levelly in the eye and saying, almost aloud, 'Not another word.' (181)

"Good Old Neon" is so remarkable and gripping as a multi-level dramatization of the effects of hyper-self-consciousness, including the level of narrative organization (namely in the sole "end"-note), while the story, in contrast to *Brief Interviews with Hideous Men*, does not lose itself in this hyper-consciousness, and also tries to offer closure, a way out of the nightmare—in expressly and tragically dramatizing "THE END" of hyper-conscious thought.

---

[13] See Carlisle, "Wallace's Infinite Fiction".

Representations of Trauma in David Foster Wallace's *Oblivion*

Thomas Tracey

This essay will focus on representations of trauma in David Foster Wallace's third and last story collection, *Oblivion*; short fiction being a mode in which Wallace excelled and innovated throughout his career. Essentially it will highlight some of the principal narrative techniques that Wallace uses there to explore the nature of human trauma.

Before commencing, it is instructive to call to mind some contextually important points: foremost, that one of Wallace's aims, in the search for a direction beyond postmodernism, was to eschew irony as an end in itself and to initiate an affective reengagement with what he called "the plain old untrendy human troubles and emotions of U.S. life," themes deserving "reverence and conviction." This of course issues from his 1990 manifesto-like essay, "E Unibus Pluram: Television and U.S. Fiction." There, he anticipates an upcoming generation's defiantly *anti*-rebellious endorsement and instantiation of "single-entendre principles" (*Supposedly* 81). Put briefly, Wallace realized that the problematic involutions that came from self-reflexive habits of postmodern thought were very much akin to the way an addict thinks about his substance, and strikingly similar to the encaged way an addict becomes addicted to *thinking* about his substance and his relation to it. *Infinite Jest* treats this theme almost exhaustively; and it is there that Wallace offers up the communal model of Alcoholics Anonymous as an "irony-free" antidote to the mordant rut of the postmodern condition. Confronting the dire and lonely straits of addiction and its attendant ills (whether financial hardship, violence, crime, self-harm, psychological fallout, spiritual despair, familial abandonment, or whatever) is far too mortally serious to ironize with a clear conscience. *Infinite Jest* therefore stands as a precursor to the detailed exploration of psychological trauma we later encounter in *Oblivion*.

Now Wallace's aesthetic has from the outset located art's gestation in our acquaintance with painful experience, his conviction being that art's *purpose* is closely tied to its alleviation. The later Wittgenstein's conception of philosophy as a *therapeutic* form of investigation into life's intrinsic confusions played a vital role in influencing the young Wallace's vision of art's cultural function. As Wallace explained to Larry McCaffrey in a seminal interview for the *Review of Contemporary Fiction*:

> Since an ineluctable part of being human is suffering, part of what we come to art for is an experience of suffering, necessarily a vicarious experience, more like a *generalization* of suffering. (Interview, McCaffery 127, emphasis original)

For Wallace, then, art's *raison d'être* is intimately bound up with what we might generally term traumatic experience. Stemming from this, his oeuvre seeks to explore whether or how a person can establish any kind of moral ground or ethical philosophy in order to approach the leading of a humane, responsible, and civil life in the context of our relativistic age; that is, how one can be fully, humanly alive despite these uncertain, often dark times.

Oblivion is Wallace's first piece of fiction published after 9/11, and across its complex narratives trauma is firmly embedded in the socio-cultural milieu of contemporary U.S. life. Yet it would be rash to explain *Oblivion*'s preoccupations solely in terms of the public trauma of 9/11. As previously indicated, Wallace's artistic project is engaged in a more general meditation upon the nature and dynamics of traumatic experience per se, often explored from a private perspective. In *Oblivion* this is explicitly the case where the experience of trauma touches especially on human memory, dream, and fantasy. Initially it might seem strange that Wallace align trauma with dream or fantasy, until we consider a helpful etymological kinship: trauma is related to *traum*, the German for "dream," and of course Freudian psychoanalysis could make for a familiar touchstone here.

While I'm not primarily concerned with performing a Freudian reading of Wallace, the author's evident conversance with (and occasional strategic deployment of) the psychoanalytic idiom ought not to go unacknowledged. At least two of the eight stories in *Oblivion* involve characters who have undergone analysis or therapy of one form or another. And yet, though his fiction is entirely au fait with the hermeneutics of psychoanalytic theory, it is also patently wary of them. The basis for skepticism is that Wallace considered the Freudian tenet that "etiology and diagnosis pointed toward cure, that a revelation of imprisonment led to freedom" (*Supposedly* 67) authorized the same kind of self-conscious involutions that postmodern irony shared with poststructuralist thought. In other words, the unbounded structure of the so-called "talking cure" could all too easily accommodate a brand of self-indulgent circumlocution and compensatory irony symptomatic of the chronically self-absorbed (one thinks of *Portnoy's Complaint* here). And in Wallace's view, endless postmodern irony was in many respects the imprisoning cage itself. Thus the problem remains unresolved in cases where the "pathology" to be "cured" happens to *be* self-consciousness. The story of "The Depressed Person" in *Brief Interviews with Hideous Men* features as both a classic instance and scathing critique of this predicament. Accordingly, while admitting the sizeable cultural influence of psychoanalysis on the culture in general, for good or ill, we should only conditionally credit its exploitation by Wallace as a serviceable argot.

In *Unclaimed Experience*, Cathy Caruth reminds us that the word *trauma* is of Greek origin, meaning "wound," later coming to connote a wound upon the mind (3). The German *traum* is of course a close cousin of the Greek; and this etymological kinship flags up a significant point of convergence between psychoanalysis and the field of trauma theory. One essential characteristic of trauma that Caruth outlines is the "inherent *latency*" (17) of its experience. Furthermore, the history of a trauma necessarily involves an *indirectness* in its telling (27). Part of this typical indirectness is doubtless bound up with an enigma at the heart of traumatic experience: that is, with the fact that "trauma is not simply an effect of destruction but also, fundamentally, an enigma of survival" (58). Indeed, Caruth reads Freud's formulation of trauma as "a theory of the peculiar incomprehensibility of human survival" (58). She asks what it means for consciousness to survive (and I would suggest that this is closely bound up to Wallace's thematic investment in questions of human consciousness).

Caruth likens a traumatized consciousness to a body in shock, whereby there is a significant "break in the mind's experience of time" (61). With reference to this formulation, it is fascinating to consider the post-mortem narration of "Good Old Neon" as allegorically representing an extra-temporal human subject's post-traumatic attempt indirectly to narrate such an experience. As Caruth further notes, "the trauma of the nightmare does not simply consist in the experience *within* the dream, but in *the experience of waking from it*. It is the experience of *waking into consciousness* that, peculiarly, is identified with the reliving of the trauma" (64). Taking Freud's well-known example of the dream of the burning child (one we should not overlook in light of Wallace's "Incarnations of Burned Children"), Caruth argues for the advantage of a Lacanian reading, as follows:

> If Freud asks, *What does it mean to sleep?* Lacan discovers at the heart of this question another one, perhaps even more urgent: *What does it mean to awaken?* [...] Lacan seems to suggest a paradoxical attempt *to respond, in awakening, to a call that can only be heard within sleep.* (99)

From this perspective, Lacan interprets the dream as "the story of an urgent responsibility, [...] an ethical relation to the real" (Caruth, *Unclaimed* 92). What is significant about Lacan's turn is that it challenges the conventional demarcation of Post-Traumatic Stress Disorder as "a response to an event "outside the range of usual human experience." (130) "Trauma," then, is no longer something beyond the common ken, but an integral component of our lived historical reality, both individual and collective.

In *Testimony*, Shoshana Felman registers "how art inscribes (artistically bears witness to) *what we do not yet know of our lived historical relation to events of our times*" (xx). Reading history as always the history of a trauma, Felman's study serves to re-emphasize the aforementioned *latency* inherent in any historical situation, even during—indeed, *especially* during—its narration in the aftermath.[1] Moreover, history's narrative of belated witnessing frequently occurs as literary testimony, whose specific task Felman understands as being

---

[1] Cf. Caruth: "The historical power of [...] trauma is not just that the experience is repeated after its forgetting, but that it is only in and through its inherent forgetting that it is first experienced at all." (*Trauma* 8).

to open up in that belated witness, which the reader now historically becomes, the imaginative capability of perceiving history—what is happening to others—in *one's own body*, with the power of sight (of insight) usually afforded only by one's own immediate physical involvement. (108)

We can readily compare Felman's perspective on testimonial histories to Wallace's conception of art as a medium for the vicarious experience of human suffering, with literary art being a particularly apt avenue for opening up one's consciousness to that of the other, as outlined in the McCaffrey interview. Wallace's express desire to render the familiar strange again is closely bound up with this recognition of radical alterity inherent in the quotidian.

A good example of this kind of quotidian acquaintance with trauma is the dream of "the face in the floor" in *Infinite Jest* (61-3). A first person narrator experiences "the sudden intra-dream realization that the nightmare's very essence and center has been with you all along, even awake: it's just been….*overlooked*." The narrator senses "the presence of something radically evil," "a distillation of total evil" there in the room.[2] At first it's not clear to the dreamer that the face-in-the-floor is in fact a *dream*; indeed, it is precisely its waking character that is so distressing. A Cartesian dilemma is at work here, a fugal confusion that challenges the certainty of the dreaming subject's sense of self. Furthermore, the floor's face defies conventional linguistic representation: its eyebrows are portrayed in an overstretched manner by the signs "\ /", paradoxically embodying what Caruth has elsewhere identified as "the resistance of language to perceptual analogies" (*Unclaimed* 90) and "the curious resistance of trauma to symbolism" (140). The bewildered reactions of the dreamer upon waking are repeated "just as in the dream." In a discussion of avant-garde film, Caruth has implicitly outlined a status for dreams within trauma theory, one that is equally applicable to this oneiric episode:

the dream here does not so much concern the fact that one might not know *what* one has dreamed as it opens up the possibility that one might not know *that one* is dreaming; that one might see, that is, without knowing it. (*Unclaimed* 36)

---

[2] This anticipates the "demonic face" of Father Karras in "The Soul Is Not a Smithy."

This perspective will gather force when we come to examine Wallace's use of dream in "Oblivion."

It is important to note that *Oblivion*'s persistent exploration of the dynamics of consciousness, chiefly from the aspect of pointedly traumatic psychical experience, is what is perhaps most thematically consistent with Wallace's other work. For our purposes, a reading of two exemplary pieces will help map out the terrain.

I

Many of the principal narrative techniques that recur throughout *Oblivion* are fully operational, and perhaps most explicitly foregrounded, in its second story, "The Soul Is Not a Smithy." Here as elsewhere, Wallace seeks to place the crucial events of each tale *beyond* the frame of the main exposition. This story relates the traumatic events of what ultimately became a hostage situation in which its unnamed narrator was caught up as a schoolboy, when his substitute teacher, a one Mr. Johnson, suffers some kind of nervous breakdown or psychotic episode in the middle of class. As the plot gradually develops, the important actions of the narrative are seen to occur only on the extreme periphery of the narrator's awareness. For while the terrifying events of the schoolroom are unfolding, the narrator has been quite absorbed in his imagining of various narrative tableaux, in layout similar to cartoon strips, in the squares of the classroom's meshed windows.

A call for greater attentiveness to our peripheral surroundings, and a recognition that the most important events of our lives often take place on the margins of our quotidian experience, turns out to be central to Wallace's narrative procedures throughout his oeuvre, but acutely so in *Oblivion*, which invites us to approach its interpretation with this in mind. Wallace's careful cultivation of an understated yet discernible dramatic tension, by means of "nesting" significant informational "stimuli" or "stressors" amidst a plethora of innocuous detail, reveals that the ulterior narratives" "real attention" is always rather "directed peripherally" (*Oblivion* 71). Thus, it is suggested that Wallace's own narrative art behaves in a way similar to the window's tableaux— tableaux whose own traumas obliquely mirror the increasingly distressed ambience of the classroom's hostage situation. One clear typographical complement to this occurs in the sectioning-up of the story into discrete narrative blocks under capitalized rubrics, contributing a spatial dimension to the text, somewhat like a storyboard.

Poignantly, the narrator's apparent obliviousness to the surrounding action may have something to do with his imagination functioning as a form of defense mechanism, psychic armor for coping with the classroom trauma to which he would otherwise be subjected. The obvious entailment is that imagination can provide a psychological outlet, or refuge, from suffering, as the narrator later recognizes:

> Meanwhile, in the inception of the real incident, Mr. Johnson had evidently just written *KILL* on the chalkboard. The most obvious flaw in my memory of the incident as a whole is that much of the trauma's inception unfolded outside my awareness, so intently was I concentrating on the window's mesh squares [...] in retrospect, I believe that the atmosphere of the classroom may have subconsciously influenced the unhappy events of the period's window's mesh's narrative fantasy, which was now more like a nightmare. (84, 92)

In certain respects, the concatenation of apostrophes that structure this final cluster of Anglo-Saxon genitives ("period's window's mesh's") stylistically mirrors the rapid flash-effects of the imagistic narrative tableaux, conceivably in an attempt to emulate the traumatic consciousness at work.

While his classmates are becoming progressively alarmed by the abnormal behavior of their teacher, the narrator, on the other hand, becomes "more and more disturbed by the graphic narrative that was unfolding, square by square, in the window" (88). Here is a notable example: we learn that the nightmarish "claw" that Mr. Johnson forms with his left hand in front of the class (92) is paralleled in one of the window's tableaux. In one panel, we witness the suicidal mother of a local blind girl, Mrs. Marjorie Simmons, whose own hand assumes the shape of a claw just prior to smearing lipstick on her face and asphyxiating on her car's exhaust fumes (93).

It is significant that the narrator emphatically distances his creative imaginings from what is conventionally called "daydreaming," a practice roundly admonished by his teachers. For it is rather suggested that these are actively-constructed storyboards into which intrude involuntary, nightmarish memorial flashbacks that may have their origin in prior trauma. As he explains:

> such single, horrible flashes often appear in bad dreams [...] and often a rapid, peripheral flash of something contextless and awful could be the single worst part of a nightmare, and the part that stayed with you the most vividly and kept popping into your mind's eye at odd moments [...] perhaps because its very instantaneousness in the dream meant that your mind had to keep subconsciously returning to it in order to work it out or incorporate it. As if the fragment were not done with you yet, in much the same way that now, so very much later, the most persistent memories of early childhood consist of these flashes, peripheral tableaux. (94)

Such fragments are as yet "unclaimed" (to adopt Caruth's diction), or not yet "worked through" (to use the psychoanalytic idiom); rather, they are returned to involuntarily and repeatedly. The narrator proceeds to draw a comparative analogy with certain imagistic flashes from the horror film, *The Exorcist*, which he watched many years later with his future wife. In that film, one scene follows the slow, soundless descent of a coin or medal as it falls through a backdrop of black space, suddenly spliced with an instantaneous shot of the protagonist priest Father Karras' ghoulishly distressed visage.

The Exorcist makes for an appositely ironic cultural reference, here, because it humorously invites us to wonder whether the substitute teacher may be in some way demonically possessed—when in fact it is more likely to be a psychotic episode, all the more terrifying because conventionally truer to life.[3] More generally, though, the narrator's celebration of imagination over scholastic drudgery or administrative tedium asks us to consider what it might mean to be ordinarily "possessed" of anything: that is, why one thing rather than another should "possess" our individual attention. It is instructive to note that this question is given some consideration in Wallace's now-famous Kenyon Commencement Speech of 2005 (recently published under the title *This Is Water*). Likewise, in an excerpt from *The Pale King*, titled

---

[3]Although, as Caruth points out: "to be traumatized is precisely to be possessed by an image or event." (*Trauma* 4)

"Wiggle Room," published in *The New Yorker* in March 2009, the question of what to focus one's attention on, or be mindful of, occupies a central role in the narrative. In "Wiggle Room" it is ultimately a matter bound up with the problem of quotidian boredom and how to overcome it (the story takes place in the mundane environs of an IRS Office). Indeed, its thematic preoccupations are echoed by "Smithy," in which the narrator's own father toils under the "deeper, soul-level boredom" of his actuarial job (105). What's so terrifying about the narrator's nightmares of adult life, over and above the supernatural horrors of *The Exorcist*, consists in the grim fact that there can be no maternal reassurance that there exists "nothing like what you just dreamed in the real world" (106).

Oblivion as a state of being is perhaps typically thought of as passive; but the active (if subconscious) censoring of seemingly peripheral though emotionally seminal aspects of their lives comes to haunt most of the principal actors in these stories. Wallace's narratives aver that a self-licensed ignorance of one's situation/condition can all too readily be transformed into a kind of moral oblivion—transfigured like the "demonic [...] face of evil" upon the filially negligent Father Karras—and I would like to suggest that this broader moral impulse has an important bearing on Wallace's literary project as a whole.

The question of possession, then—that is, the possession of a differentiated identity—underlies Wallace's narrative. This comes across most humorously near the tale's end, by way of the narrator's brother's observations as to whom the "*THEM*" of the teacher's lethal imperative may have been referring. The assumption during the media's coverage had been that the "*THEM*" had referred to the captive children as victims of a murderous imperative. However, since serving in what is presumably either the Korean or Vietnam War, the brother points out the possibility that the substitute Mr. Johnson (whose surname corresponds to that of a U.S. President) may have been inciting the class to violence against the threat of some unspecified hostile force. Whether this threat comes from within or beyond the nation's borders is never explicitly stated. Wallace dovetails both possibilities in his repeated use of the defensive term "bulwarks." At one point the narrator evokes the melancholia and primal anxiety underlying suburban domesticity:

at twilight [...] all of the houses became the same color and all of their porch lights came on like bulwarks against something without name. (104)

By contrast, the closing image of the story recounts a "President's Day presentation" (112) in which the schoolchildren re-enact numerous patriotic events from the history of their nation, the last of these involving an unmistakably aggressive image: a bayonet charge "against the papier maché bulwarks of Iwo Jima" (113). At the heart of this Other-directed assault, it is hinted, lies "fear itself, fear itself" (113): a fear that points back the radical otherness of the self; a something without name that lies, in fact, within us.

II

Let us move onto the title story, "Oblivion." Randall, the narrator, recounts the recent connubial tensions which have arisen due to his wife's complaint that he has been snoring so loudly that it keeps her awake. As Randall protests, it is precisely when he knows himself to be awake, and is certain that his wife, Hope, is asleep, that she makes these accusations. Eventually, they decide to visit a Sleep Clinic so as to monitor their behaviors with a view to getting some consensus and closure on the issue. In the meantime, however, Randall is experiencing the inevitable cerebral trauma that attends insomnia and sleep deprivation resultant from the marital saga. One repercussion is that Randall suffers a visual onslaught of deeply discomfiting and "involuntary interior" tableaux (210)—strikingly similar to the rapid filmic flashes to which the narrator of "Smithy" was intermittently subjected—and which serve to layer the traumatic substrata of even the most mundane occurrences of married life.

One example Randall outlines is particularly notable, as its symbolic resonances play a significant part in the ominous atmosphere that surrounds a subsequent story, titled "The Suffering Channel," whose peripheral subject is the terror of 9/11.[4] Let us look at Randall's example, which is worth quoting at length:

---

[4] It should be mentioned, here, that although *Oblivion* is ostensibly a book of separate stories, Wallace deftly weaves a series of motifs across the entire volume, motifs that forebode and echo each other in startling ways, and to great cumulative effect.

Next, in a predictable yet far more disturbing stage of the wave of disorientation, came the appearance of a strange, static, hallucinatory tableau or mental "shot," "scene," *Fata morgana* or "vision" of a public telephone in an airport or commuter rail terminal's linear row or "bank" of public phones, ringing. Travelers are hurrying laterally past the row of phones, some bearing or pulling "carry on" luggage and other personal possessions, walking or hurrying past while the telephone, which remains at the center of the view of the scene or tableau, rings on and on, persistently, but is unanswered, with none of the "bank" of phones" other phones in use and none of the air travelers or commuters acknowledging or even so much as glancing at the ringing phone, about which there is suddenly something terribly "moving" or poignant, forlorn, melancholic or even foreboding, an endlessly ringing and unanswered public phone, all of which appears or seems to occur both endlessly and in, as it were, "no-time," and is accompanied by an incongruous odor of saffron. (194)

The narration's use of conjunctive "or"s has a generally destabilizing effect, as it eschews a categorical description of the situation witnessed; indeed, Randall, despite his best efforts, is at a loss to articulate with the desired precision that which stands before him. Added to this is the rhythmic breathlessness brought about by continual clausal expansion of the sentence, syncopated by commas, inducing a suspenseful tension building to anxiety or panic. These and other similar stylistic features may be seen to recur in *Oblivion*'s prose. Furthermore, the author's locating the action in a quintessentially transient space, in combination with the atemporal aura of this liminal experience, adds an unnerving quality to the atmosphere that is inherently traumatic.

The dream of the ringing phone best encapsulates the imaginary mode and mood of "Oblivion." This quite literal alarm alerts us an atmosphere of subconscious collective crisis, of latent communal trauma; suggesting either something suppressed or something emergent, or indeed something of the two. It is an apposite figure to convey the efforts of latent dream content to make itself manifest. The unwillingness of any one individual to take responsibility, to lift the receiver, evokes the melancholy loneliness that comes of the alienating disunities within a contemporary commuter society.[5] Significantly, Randall directly associates the alarming effect of an unheeded public phone with the private stress he undergoes at his wife's crying out in protestation against his snoring:

> adrenaline coursing through my system (just as when the telephone rings at night, its signal or "ring" *now piercing in a way which daylight never makes it*) (201, emphasis mine)

In a manner similar to his post-9/11 essay, "The View from Mrs. Thompson's," Wallace transposes public trauma into domestic space, dovetailing the collective and communal with a more private, individual anxiety. Later in the story, the Clinic's final test results astonish Randall, since they affirm that he "had, indeed, been, clinically speaking—despite [his] belief or perception of being fully conscious—'technically asleep'" (228). Inscrutably, during the "collective silence" that follows Randall's nonplussed assimilation of this news, the sound of a "ringing telephone somewhere deeper within the administrative offices" (229) of the Clinic, "seemingly unanswered" (230), echoes the anxiety-laden tableau Randall had previously hallucinated. In this respect, Randall's mental activity could be said to imitate the process by which, according to Freud, material from waking life informs the manifest content of dreams.

Throughout *Oblivion* (both story and volume) hidden information and revelatory details gradually yet insistently come to light, emerging from the dark backward and abysm of the human mind. Memory obviously plays a contributory role in the recovery of such apparently forgotten knowledge (its conceptual obverse being a rather Lethean state of oblivion). Insofar as memory takes an active role in the constitution of the self, it also lays a ground for a heuristic ethics based on past experience. This point has particular relevance for Wallace's tale, because the most traumatic elements of the narrative swarm under the surface as suppressed memories of unspeakable acts and fantasies of taboo desire. Evidence for this comes in the form of hysterical accusations of abuse that Hope's stepsister levels at the family patriarch subsequent to a series of recovered memories in

---

[5] On the theme of collective responsibility, cf. "Lyndon" in *Girl with Curious Hair*.

adulthood. In a similar vein, it is revealed that Randall has been harboring incestuous desires for Hope's daughter (and thus his own stepdaughter), the buxomly nubile Audrey (whose favorite bath gel's scent, and whose bustier, it turns out, happen to be saffron!)

Recovered memory and taboo fantasy, then, construct an ambience of traumatizing latencies whose full expression is censored everywhere beyond the licensed theatre of dream (Randall, for example, has a provocative chivalric fantasy of saving the damsel Audrey from the banishment of her Out-of-State College's dormitory—here with a censoriously loaded pun on the architectural term "banishment"). Thus, operating much like artistic sensibility, REM sleep can creatively process certain unutterable desires and traumatic frustrations in ways that its diurnal counterpart, memory, finds irreconcilable.

In correspondence with Don DeLillo, dated "21 March" (2000), Wallace writes:

> Plus also the single best movie I've seen in the last year [is] the Wachowski Bros. "The Matrix" [...], which yes is commercial postmodernism with a capital C, [but] the movie is also an incredible evocation of what's creepy and powerful in Descartes' first two *Meditations on First Philosophy* (no kidding).[6]

Wallace's musings, as ever, blend pop culture with serious philosophy, humorous review with insightful analysis. This passage is instructive not merely for its author's personal opinion on the film in question, but because of his palpable enthusiasm for the contiguous philosophical considerations it provokes. The introduction of the "Cogito" into Descartes' *Meditations* has been equated with the birth of Modern Philosophy in Western culture, and an entire tradition of post-Renaissance thought concerning selfhood has been touched, one way or another, by its influence. The Cogito having such pertinence to questions about the nature of the self, it ties in closely with the theme of selfhood prevalent across Wallace's oeuvre, to which "Oblivion" is no exception. The motivating concept behind Wallace's story essentially resolves into an imaginative response to a crucial dilemma

---

[6] See Works Cited for full reference.

in the Cartesian *Meditations*: how can we be sure that we are awake and not dreaming? Another way of asking this question—or, more precisely, one way of interrogating the real philosophical issue behind this query—presents as: how can one have any certainty (i.e., positive knowledge) about reality (or, the world around one), especially as it pertains to one as an individual, or self?

In certain respects, then, Descartes' meditation can be read as an investigation into solipsism; or rather, a question that interrogates the whole notion of solipsism while at the same time endeavoring to establish incontrovertibly the existence of self. Of course, this relates back to the Cartesian thought experiment that one could imaginably be asleep and yet dream that one is carrying on in a waking state: one extrapolation from this is the notion that people are indeed living in a sort of unconscious oblivion—a mode of unawareness, or coma-like unknowing—from which they must awaken and emerge into a clearer mindfulness about reality.

The question, then, of what is real—put personally, of what we can believe in, believe to be true, with all the complexities involved in what we might mean by "believe"[7]—this question, with firm roots in the Cartesian *Meditations*, is finally unanswered by "Oblivion"; unanswered perhaps because unanswerable. The narrative's finale is not, of course, meant to defend the extreme skepticism that declares that "None of this is real" (237). Rather, the implication (echoed in Wallace's Deciderization essay) is that that which is real, or "true," is that which we choose to value as being so: "truth" is always really "truth-*value*." In this light we may understand Felman's claim that trauma involves a "crisis of truth" (*Unclaimed* 6), coming to appreciate "the complex ways that knowing and not knowing are tangled in the language of trauma" (4).

In conclusion, Wallace's fictions suggest that art allows for the confrontation and communication of feelings otherwise interdicted by ordinary social exchanges. As we have seen with the story "Oblivion," this includes what might be termed "unspeakable" desires and fears. Principal among these are instances of inwardly traumatic experience. It is significant, therefore, that fears are always or shrouded in silence

---

[7] Cf. Wallace's theological inflection on "believe" in his essay on Dostoevsky.

across these narratives: the ghoulish face of Karras that flashes during the falling coin scene in "Smithy" is soundless; as is its narrator's morbid dream of his father's insufferable workplace; likewise, on The Suffering Channel, the cable network venture that gives its name to the closing novella in the collection, "montages of well known photos involving anguish or pain" form a televised loop that emits "no sound" (289). For texts so replete with incessant human speech, such silence makes for striking contrast. Wallace's oeuvre was, from the outset, haunted by the question of the possibility of interpersonal communication. It is thus critical to consider what such silences and other ellipses may signify across these texts.

Indeed, "The Suffering Channel" tempts further exploration of our topic, seeing as its subject involves a very public trauma that has forged itself into the smithies of all our terrorized consciences. Its narrative invokes the latent traumas of our time as much through excision and obliquity as it does through precise prose of considerable descriptive fervor. But alas, it exceeds the scope of this essay. So I leave you with a final thought: one character humorously muses on how a mortified, feigned obliviousness usually attends the intrusion of flatulence into any social gathering—as she opines: "The silence communicates some kind of unease about it" (266). Likewise, in a 9/11 tale which places the immense spectacle of terror beyond its narrative frame, an uneasy silence becomes audible. But I would invite you to discover this for yourselves, perhaps with what has been said here kept somewhere safe in the back of your mind.

Seething Static: Notes on Wallace and Journalism

Christoph Ribbat

On August 14, 1998 Paul Fishbein, President of Adult Video Network Publications, sent a letter to *Premiere* magazine. Fishbein responded to what was going to turn into "Big Red Son," the opening essay of David Foster Wallace's *Consider the Lobster*: a long feature on the *Adult Video News*'s annual awards show, the pornography industry's equivalent of the Academy Awards.[1] In his letter Fishbein first thanks the *Premiere* editors for "devoting approximately 12 pages of your high profile, mainstream magazine to our Adult Video News Awards." He continues in a different tone: "Unfortunately, your funny and beautifully-worded article is also a shoddy piece of journalism, rife with errors and innuendo" (Fishbein).

It is strange that a key spokesman for the adult video industry should find "innuendo" bothersome. And while Fishbein does identify the factual mistakes in Wallace's article, his somewhat scanty catalog may really prove the comparative precision of the writer's reporting.[2] Seen against the plethora of details, facts, names, and scenes listed in Wallace's study of the porn industry's pageant, Fishbein's complaints appear nitpicking at best (and motivated more by the essay's aggressive questioning of pornography's ethics.) Recalling his collaboration with the author on this piece, *Premiere* editor Glen Kenny concedes that Wallace's use of two invented/composite characters (Kenny and porn screenwriter Evan Wright turned into "Dick Filth" and "Harold Hecuba") ran against the magazine's philosophy—he also emphasizes,

---

1 "Big Red Son" was originally published as a feature called "Neither Adult nor Entertainment" in *Premiere* magazine, ostensibly written by the authors "deGroot and Rundlet."

2 Among the ten mistakes Fishbein cites are these: the essay misidentified the "Impressive" booth as the "Xplor booth," the senior editor and vice president of AVN was described as "a co-owner" of AVN, the text confused the winners of the "AVN Breakthrough Award."

however, that *Premiere* magazine's legal department treated the piece like any other journalistic text and thus called for the same standards of painstaking fact-checking. Read in conjunction with Kenny's comment that Wallace's preoccupation in writing nonfiction was "the very simple idea that you should not lie" (Kipp), it is more than probable that his journalistic work adhered to the (albeit flexible) rules of journalism instead of being located in the twilight zone of "truthiness."[3]

We can assume, then, that Wallace's essays aren't "shoddy journalism." Saying more about the intricate questions of research, interviewing, editing, and fact-checking relevant to his magazine work would require in-depth studies both of the author's reporting and of his collaborations with magazine editors. These questions lie beyond the scope of this paper. Nonetheless, it is the purpose of this essay to perhaps stimulate such work and to address a few of the key questions raised by Wallace's journalism. As historians of American writing, literary or journalistic, fictional or nonfictional, how are we going to categorize such pieces as "Getting Away From Being Already Pretty Much Away From It All," "A Supposedly Fun Thing I'll Never Do Again;" the tennis essays, the article on John McCain's 2000 campaign or "Big Red Son?" What are the most meaningful contexts for reading Wallace's nonfiction? How do they reflect previous interactions of journalism and fiction in American letters? In light of the sheer brilliance of his reporting, it is important to connect the field of Wallace studies to ongoing discussions in the scholarship of nonfiction writing. This paper hopes to show that the New Journalism of the 1960s proves helpful here (though not as helpful as some scholars have suggested) and that Robert Boynton's work on the "New New Journalism" of the early 21st century may provide interesting perspectives. Finally, a brief discussion of Wallace's short story "The Suffering Channel" will explore the reflections of journalism in the author's fiction, helping us define an approach to the author's nonfiction.

In the developing field of Wallace studies, not much critical attention has been paid on Wallace and his position in the larger context of late-20th century American journalism. Scholars tend to

---

[3] See Kramer/Call, Zelizer.

follow the author's own statement that the persona he created in his nonfictional work was "a little stupider and schmuckier" than he really was (qtd. in Lipsky). In the aftermath of the writer's death, a number of pieces insisted that his journalism represented "Wallace-light," a more accessible, less tortured version of his prose. An extensive New Yorker feature that appeared a few months after the author's passing quoted from a letter to Don DeLillo in which Wallace states that "the comparative ease and pleasure of writing nonfiction always confirms my intuition that fiction is really What I'm Supposed to Do" (qtd. in Max), alluding to fiction as the more difficult yet ultimately more significant task. David Lipsky's *Rolling Stone* feature on the author states that "the difference between [Wallace's] fiction and [...] nonfiction reads as the difference between Wallace's social self and his private self." The journalism, Lipsky argues, was "endlessly charming, [...] whispering jokes, sweeping you past what was irritating or boring or awful in humane style." In contrast, Lipsky argues, the fiction ranked as "chilly, dark, abstract." He concludes that one "could imagine the author of the fiction sinking into a depression" whereas the "nonfiction writer was an impervious sun" (Lipsky).

This reading obviously privileges the fiction over the nonfiction, treating the journalistic pieces as harmless, perhaps even therapeutic, finger exercises in comparison to Wallace's complex short and long fiction. We will have to ask, of course, whether these interpretations—based on biographical resources, interviews, letters—will ultimately take us to a deeper understanding of the larger ways in which the writer transformed literary journalism. In his published work, David Foster Wallace constructed a much different picture of the relationship between fiction and nonfiction, as seen from the perspective of a (tormented) writer. His introduction to *The Best American Essays 2007*, a volume Wallace edited, meditates on the two genres as follows:

> Writing-wise, fiction is scarier, but nonfiction is harder—because nonfiction's based in reality, and today's felt reality is overwhelmingly, circuit-blowingly huge and complex. Whereas fiction comes out of nothing. Actually, so wait: the truth is that both genres are scary; both feel like they are executed on tightropes, over abysses—it's the abysses that are different. Fiction's abyss is silence, nada. Whereas nonfiction's abyss is

Total Noise, the seething static of every particular thing and experience, and one's total freedom of infinite choice about what to choose to attend to and represent and connect, and how, and why, etc. ("Deciderization" xiv)

Wallace, the private individual, may have had an easier time writing nonfiction than nonfiction. However, Wallace, the published writer, as this passage shows all too clearly, had a keen interest in treating the two genres on the same level. As it is the published writer literary criticism tends to foreground, it is relevant to look at his journalism carefully and to develop contexts in which to discuss his nonfiction.

A larger study of Wallace's position in the field of American literary journalism would have to explore antecedents even in the late 19th century, in the oeuvres of Mark Twain, Henry James, and Stephen Crane, and the ways in which nonfiction and fiction informed each other in these literary projects. As Shelley Fisher Fishkin has pointed out, American writers emphasize experience, looking for ways to describe the world "from scratch" (5), a concept that seems very similar to the naïve persona of Wallace's nonfiction.[4]

Using a narrower focus, the most obvious point of comparison here is the New Journalism of the 1960s and 1970s, largely because Wallace's thematic interests seem so similar to that generation's. Wallace covers the great American election process in "Up, Simba"—Hunter S. Thompson followed the elections in *Fear and Loathing on the Campaign Trail* (so did Joan Didion in *After Henry*). Wallace explores Las Vegas in "Big Red Son"—Tom Wolfe and Hunter S. Thompson also portrayed Southern Nevada. And there are plenty of parallels, of

---

4 In recent years, numerous studies (for a survey see Hartsock) have argued for a more encompassing perspective on literary and journalistic work, a perspective acknowledging the close connection between the fields of fact and fiction and an approach that moves past the privileging of established genres over others. In his history of American literary journalism, John Hartsock has outlined the wide range of texts operating in-between the registers of literature and journalism, an array of subgenres making simple categorizations impossible. As Hartsock puts it, "a critical leap of faith is required when it comes to the nomenclature by which the form will be characterized." (11) His choice is "literary journalism," which seems useful for the purposes of this study.

course, in the way both Wallace and the New Journalists ignored the conventions of journalistic prose, moving away from the routine of the plain, clean, and straightforward as well as the optimistic, the upbeat, and the sentimental toward an experimental, sometimes meandering, often improvised, stream-of-consciousness response to the American scene.

One of the key issues here is subjectivity—not the subjectivity of a common-sense reporter hero, but the shaken, frustrated, disoriented kind. Wallace's journalism needs the alienated Midwesterner Wallace all over his state fair text, needs the clumsy rookie political reporter all over the McCain piece, needs the writer breaking down in tears trying to buy a small plastic American flag on September 12, 2001 at a Kwik-N-EZ-mart in Bloomington, Illinois in "The View from Mrs. Thompson's." This reminds us of the way Michael Herr registered the Vietnam War in Dispatches, the way Joan Didion confronted the American everyday in the White Album. While in terms of style, Didion's terse work does not bear much resemblance to Wallace's essays, her programmatic ideas on writing are reflected by central notions in his nonfiction. "How it felt to me"—this, Joan Didion notes, was the guiding principle of her journalistic work (138). Wallace's take seems remarkably similar.[5]

As John Hellmann has pointed out, the key antagonism between conventional forms of journalism and the New Journalism of the 1960s is "a conflict of a disguised perspective versus an admitted one, and a corporate fiction versus a personal one" (4). While the conventional (pre-New) journalism of the mainstream newspapers "refuses to acknowledge the creative nature of its 'news,'" Hellman writes, the New Journalists "frankly asserted their personal perspectives" (3), often performing a very personal "movement from innocence to experience" (4). In more ways than one, this kind of combination is reflected in what Marshall Boswell has called the "elusive Wallace 'tone,' that paradoxical blending of cynicism and naiveté" (*Understanding* 19). Along similar lines, Phyllis Frus has shown how Joan Didion's political journalism displays the reporter's own

---

[5] "The *Harper's* pieces were me peeling back my skull," Wallace told an interviewer. "[W]elcome to my mind for 20 pages, see through my eyes." (qtd. in Lipsky, n.p.).

political leanings as openly as "the construction of her attitudes," thus allowing for a sort of self-consciousness enabling her to seriously critique the purported neutrality of elite political reporters managing only "modest self-referentiality" (xvi). Frus' reading of Didion's journalism points at some of the most important issues shaping Wallace's reporting on John McCain's primary campaign, a kind of journalism that, like Didion's, uses a "cumulative" strategy (Frus xvi) to move beyond the constructed moments of the campaign circus.

It seems self-evident then to link Wallace's work to the key authors of the New Journalism. In a memorial essay in *Modernism/ Modernity*, Steven Moore proclaims that Wallace "built on the New Journalism of Wolfe and Thompson" (2). Troy Patterson compares Wallace to Norman Mailer, stating that "both produced nonfiction so bold and inventive as to surpass their achievements as novelists" (Patterson). But these comparisons overshoot. There is nothing particularly "bold" about Wallace's nonfiction, at least not the kind of boldness that Tom Wolfe, Hunter S. Thompson, and Mailer developed to establish themselves as maverick heroes in the cultural landscape of the American 1960s. It is not an accident, for instance, that the Hell's Angels were favorite subjects of the New Journalists whereas an Illinois state fair, tennis, and a pleasure cruise rank as the most important subjects of Wallace's reporting. The 1960s and 70s texts often feature a predatory ego out on the prowl, and sometimes, particularly in Tom Wolfe's work, the text's stylistic fireworks serve to emphasize the narrative voice's aggressiveness in a fashion never encountered in Wallace's essays. David Foster Wallace as a journalist was never out to destroy the contemporary novel in the way Tom Wolfe imagined the New Journalism as a dramatic, explosive new art form causing "status panic in the literary community" (15). Even Wallace's foray into pornography takes a much different tone than Wolfe, Mailer or Thompson would have employed to describe their own excursions. His is a voice more baffled than excited, a persona more interested in the moral issues raised by pornography than in the titillating or taboo-breaking features of the event. Nor does Wallace's nonfiction make much use of such New Journalist techniques as complete dialogues, scene-by-scene construction, or varying points of view (see Boynton xvi). His essays foreground paying attention more than reinventing the journalistic wheel.

Obviously, then, Wallace's nonfiction comes out of the New Journalism tradition, but the predecessors we might have to consider here form the quieter faction of that generation: authors like Joan Didion, Michael Herr, perhaps even George Plimpton, all of them much more interested in recording events with a fine, outsider sensibility rather than in the energies emanating from violence and provocative rebelliousness. Most importantly, the solipsism of Thompson's and Wolfe's works seems one-dimensional compared to Wallace's meditations on the self and coming to terms with the "seething static" of the American everyday.

In this respect, Wallace's reportage shares some traits with a new generation of narrative journalists that Robert Boynton, a Professor of Journalism at New York University, categorized as the New New Journalism in 2005. In an influential anthology, Boynton discusses the works of some of the most prominent contemporary writers of nonfiction: writers like Eric Schlosser, Susan Orlean, Ted Conover, Alex Kotlowitz, Adrian Nicole LeBlanc, and Jon Krakauer. Boynton argues that these New New Journalists, often expressing themselves in the long form, the nonfiction book, departed from the aesthetic experiments and the provocative games with the extremes that the New Journalists cherished, moving toward a more patient and a more sensitive approach to what he calls "the bedrock of ordinary experience" (xv). To these writers, he argues, late 19th century journalists like Stephen Crane may be more significant than Tom Wolfe in developing what one of the New New Journalists, Alex Kotlowitz, calls a "journalism of empathy" (Boynton 130). Instead of exploring the colorful and provocative cultural edges of American society, the New New Journalists immerse themselves in everyday experiences and might be sharing this perspective with Wallace, who, as a journalist, also seems extremely interested in the commonplace. As Adrian Nicole LeBlanc points out, the truth is a problematic concept even to these journalists. The strange moniker of this new generation of reporters may not be entirely accidental: Like Wallace, the most innovative New New Journalists carve out a postpostmodern position. The purpose of writing and researching, LeBlanc finds, is that "journalism can lead to a moment of real human connection between the reader and a world that they would not otherwise know" (Boynton 247).

It is difficult, however, to classify Wallace as a chronicler of ordinary Americans. While in the aftermath of the author's suicide, many comments focused on the democratic ethics conveyed by his work, it is important to remember that his early journalism is marked by a distinct kind of disgust with everyday Americans, as displayed, one of several possible examples, in this passage on the "Kmart people" the reporter encounters at the Illinois State Fair:

> Kmart People tend to be overweight, polyestered, grim-faced, toting glazed unhappy children. Toupees are the movingly obvious shiny square-cut kind, and the women's makeup is garish and often asymmetrically applied, giving many of the female faces a kind of demented look. They are sharp-voiced and snap at their families. They're the type you see slapping their kids in supermarket checkouts. [...] I'm sorry, but this is all true. I went to high school with Kmart People. I know them. (*Supposedly* 120-121)

Later in his life, Wallace clearly reshaped this approach to the American scene. His Kenyon College commencement speech prizes attention as a means to shape a compassionate existence (taking a much different view of people encountered in supermarket checkout lines). To a certain extent, his journalism proper also changed from the alienated cursory experience of the everyday to a more attentive and moral perception of American events. Whereas the Illinois State Fair prompts an (albeit self-consciously) cynical reporter to reflect on the supposedly naïve throngs of Midwesterners,[6] "Big Red Son" has an (albeit self-consciously) naïve reporter meditate on political and social issues raised by the porn industry's cynicism. It is a turn toward the "Kmart People," if you will, a turn fully performed in his Kenyon College address, and in many ways a transformation reflecting the larger developments of American literary journalism—from the mercurial subjectivity of the New Journalism to the social conscience of the New New Journalism.

---

[6]As Paul Giles points out, however, the essay also addresses "the cultural hegemony enjoyed by the two coasts" (337).

Boynton, however, observes that "the New New Journalists become part of their [protagonists'] lives," (xiii). And at this point, it is fairly obvious that Wallace does not really belong in this group. Adrian Nicole LeBlanc spent 10 years of her life researching her 500-page nonfiction book *Random Family*, Ted Conover, another immersive journalist, devoted a year of his life to working as a prison guard for his book on a New York State correctional institution. Wallace's journalism, in contrast, is shaped by a quick immersion into and a quick exit from a particular situation—and his pieces usually document the writer's alienation and puzzlement more than his particular expertise and identification with a given context. Also, in stylistic terms, some of the more recent American nonfiction Boynton discusses almost seems like stolid 19th century realism compared to Wallace's pieces.

Perhaps because his connections to the 'isms' of American journalism seem tenuous at best, Wallace's nonfiction may have developed a sort of middle ground between the New Journalism, its aesthetic fireworks and its lack of a social conscience, and the contemporary nonfiction writers and their interest in immersion and lack of interest in overly innovative prose. There is, in Wallace's nonfiction, none of the maneuvering and self-posturing that kept some of the big egos of the new journalism from exploring the social and the everyday instead of just colorful excess. There is, on the other hand, the ability to explore the social and the everyday with an experimental stream-of-consciousness prose that many New New Journalists eschew, perhaps influenced by the mistaken belief that socially aware journalism needs to be written in Dickensian prose. It is entirely possible then, that the impact of Wallace's prose on journalism will be just as lasting as his influence on contemporary American fiction. His journalism, to quote "Big Red Son" entirely out of context, "humbly offer[s] an alternative" (*Lobster* 4).

These brief notes, however, can't do much more than sketch these issues, hoping to prompt more in-depth comparative studies of Wallace's nonfiction pieces and the journalism produced by fellow writers defining their work more clearly as journalism and/or nonfiction. Nonetheless any discussion of the status of journalism in Wallace's work itself would be incomplete it if ignored the way his fiction commented on and imagined the world of journalism that Wallace had experienced ever since working on his Harper's pieces in the mid-1990s. "The Suffering Channel," the novella-length final story in *Oblivion*, ranks as the most important work in this context. And Virgil "Skip" Atwater, its main protagonist, a journeyman reporter for Style magazine, may even be seen as an, albeit cartoonish, stand-in for Wallace, the reporter. He surely shows some distinctive traits: There's the combination of high-cultured sophistication and Midwestern folksiness that is reflected, among other things, in his very name, Virgil "Skip." Like Wallace (though this, again, is an overly biographical reading), Atwater writes "by pouring into his notebooks and word processor an enormous waterfall of prose" (*Oblivion* 250). He "possesses an outstanding verbal memory" (*Oblivion* 271). There is "an artlessness about him [...] and a measure of true empathy" (*Oblivion* 284). Like Wallace, the writer (according to characterizations in journalistic portraits appearing after his death), Atwater is both "old-school" and "low-tech" (*Oblivion* 253). Like Wallace, he is extremely conscientious about writing, revising, rewriting, and he is curious about the everyday nooks and niches of contemporary American culture (if only as "soft news," and always looking for the "UBA," the up-beat angle [*Oblivion* 298-9]).

Reading "The Suffering Channel" from this perspective, informed by the plethora of biographical pieces on Wallace's life and work, it is tempting to think about Atwater as a less troubled writer figure than the one his creator might have been. He is a journalist, not a fiction writer, and this, in some sense, makes him able to focus on his empathy, his craft. He is a failure, to be sure ("his fatal flaw was an ineluctably light, airy prose sensibility" [270]), yet nonetheless far from the troubled self-reflexivity of similar protagonists in *Oblivion*. It is again tempting, then, to follow David Lipsky and think of the fiction writer Wallace as troubled and in pain—and the nonfiction writer as an "impervious sun."

Readers familiar with "The Suffering Channel," however, will know that this sort of analysis is superficial at best. Atwater may seem to embody the attractive, meaningful, pragmatic nature of journalism in a few passages of the story—as a whole, however, "The Suffering Channel" explores journalism's trivial, corrupt, and indeed disgusting aspects. The story unfolds the status games at the editorial offices of *Style* Magazine, locates these offices in the World Trade Center, and sets the narrative in the summer of 2001. All of the protagonists seem doomed. The reader learns of the launching of a new TV station, "The Suffering Channel," a network programming images of pain and suffering and only images of pain and suffering, and thus taking journalism to its cynical extremes. Most importantly, of course, the story unfolds as the journeyman reporter Atwater is trying to pitch a story on a Midwestern Man whose shit looks like sculptures (and whose weird sort of innocence will be exploited by the New York media). The man's wife, "the sexiest morbidly obese woman Atwater had ever seen" (*Oblivion* 250), quasi-rapes Atwater while their car is stopped by an Indiana storm. In arranging this array of dark and grotesque motifs and scenes, the story aims at representing the horror, cynicism, and stupidity attendant to explorations of the banal. It caricatures the human body grotesquely refined by the anorexic aesthetes staffing the elite East Coast magazine and grotesquely vulgar and extremely over-displayed in the Midwest. The final image of the story conjoins these two worlds by showing a Chicago TV studio and a "clear Lucite commode unit atop a ten foot platform of tempered glass beneath which a video crew will record the real time emergence" (*Oblivion* 328).[7]

In his extensive posthumous portrait of Wallace for *The New Yorker*, D.T. Max reads "The Suffering Channel" as the story of "a man for whom great art comes so easily he can defecate it," another example of journalism's alleged simplicity and fiction's complexity. Following Wallace's own take on writing nonfiction as a struggle with reality as "overwhelmingly, circuit-blowingly huge and complex" ("Deciderization" xiv), we may want to change our focus. Clearly, "The Suffering Channel" ranks as Wallace's most significant and ironic statement on the difficult craft of journalism. And just as clearly, this isn't really the story of a man shitting sculptures, but the tale of Virgil "Skip" Atwater, a man who is extremely attentive to detail and whose craft and business, journalism, only perverts this attentiveness. It is the story of a man torn between a fascination for the banal and the fear of being squashed and silenced by it—or, for

---

7 The story ends, however, by alluding to the camera's 'feedback glare [...] a searing and amorphous light" (*Oblivion* 329), thus symbolically announcing (according to Zuzanna Ladyga) the "self-cancellation" in the technological mode.

instance, by the overwhelming, circuit-blowingly huge and complex Midwesterner Amber Moltke, who mistakes the "fluttering motions" of the reporter's hands for "passion" and cushions his body with hers until "anyone trying to look in either side's window would have been unable to see any part of Skip Atwater at all" (288).

Don't Compare, Identify:
David Foster Wallace on John McCain

Paul Jenner

> "No doubt there is a danger of evasion in this spiralling self consciousness..." (Stanley Cavell, *Must We Mean What We Say?*)

> "It's like I can't get enough outside it to call it anything." (*Infinite Jest* 73)

     In a radio interview with Michael Silverblatt, Wallace suggested that, "if there's a thing that a lot of the long pieces in (*Consider the Lobster*) have in common, it's that to a large extent *they are about ideology*." (Interview, Bookworm 2006, emphasis mine). This should remind us that Wallace's signature concern in his essays with how the reader "feels, inside" is meant in part to capture the public and political significance of everyday experience and its affective backdrop. Wallace went on to sketch out the possible "service" that his nonfiction pieces might offer for their readers:

> You don't have time to really sit and noodle—the average person —for long periods of time about what this experience is like, what assumptions you bring to bear on it, what conclusions are to be reached. And for the very few Americans who have a taste for that sort of thing, I think these essays simply provide...here's somebody who really went absolutely to the wall, dropping all the attention filters, trying to pay attention to absolutely everything [...] including his own responses and his own ideological templates and trying his best to figure what the truth is. (Interview, *Bookworm* 2006)

     With relatively few ontological commitments (time, inclination) and in its commitment to the average, this is an attractively minimalist sketch of something resembling critique. It would be premature to object that exposing ideology consists in interrogating rather than dropping our "attention filters," because in fact Wallace's fiction and nonfiction alike perform just such an interrogation. His work is centrally concerned with the question of our attention.

Wallace's assignment to cover John McCain's 2000 presidential campaign for *Rolling Stone* magazine certainly afforded him the opportunity to noodle. Freed from the journalistic constraints of a daily deadline, Wallace had the time (if not the access) to "go to the wall." Hard indeed to imagine more fertile terrain for Wallace to pursue his characteristic concern with unpicking sentiment from the abuses of sentimentality than a Republican primary ("Where do they *get* these giant flags?" [*McCain* 93, emphasis original]). His subsequent report —"the truth as one person saw it"—is less a straightforwardly political piece than a scrupulous meta-political meditation on the possibility of political engagement in a culture of mediation and "absolution via irony" (*Jest* 385). McCain's candidacy offered a lurid limit situation from within which to confront the loosely postmodern assumption that cynicism and naivety are mutually exclusive (*Supposedly* 63).[1]

Wallace's article is at least as much about his *Rolling Stone* audience, the question of their attention and their "willingness to be pleased" as it is about McCain (Cavell, *Pursuits* 231). Writing for *Rolling Stone* was not without its constraints—constraints that tend to structure the form and content of Wallace's analysis. With its "lush photos of puffy-lipped girls with their Diesels half unzipped" (*McCain* 7) any association of *Rolling Stone* with countercultural negation had long since faded. Wallace confesses to borrowing "a friend's battered old black leather jacket" so as to "better project the kind of edgy, vaguely dangerous vibe I imagined an *RS* reporter might give off." But then, as he concedes, "I hadn't read *Rolling Stone* in some time" (*McCain* 8). Space restrictions meant that the eventual article would appear in somewhat truncated form; its inclusion in *Consider the Lobster* gave readers noodle-restored access.

The essay's single-volume republication as *McCain's Promise* allowed readers to compare Wallace's rendering of McCain in 2000 with what they had seen in 2008 when, like one of *Infinite Jest's* characters, McCain bounced "to his version of back" (*Jest* 937). The 2008 race featured McCain's recklessly dramatic, ill-judged decision to

---

1 See also *Infinite Jest* 694.

suspend his campaign—"temporarily setting politics aside" as he put it —and head to Washington to resolve the global financial crisis over the weekend. It would see McCain grab the microphone from a woman who'd exclaimed at one of his signature Town Hall Meetings "I'm scared of Barack Obama…he's an Arab…" to reply "No, no ma'am. He's a decent family man."[2] His campaign, of course, had already linked Obama explicitly to domestic terrorism through his minimal association with former Weatherman Bill Ayers.

It would be nice to regard these examples as speaking of the same finely balanced mix of leadership and salesmanship that so fascinated Wallace in 2000, but it is not at all clear that they do. Even more obviously in 2008 than in 2000, McCain represented—to lift a distinction from Hal's term paper in *Infinite Jest*—a post-modern heroism of "reaction" rather than of "action," a figure even more boxed in by political compromise. As Hal puts it in his term paper, "The jut-jawed hero of action […] becomes the mild-eyed hero of reaction" (*Jest* 142). Mike Murphy, senior strategist of McCain's earlier campaign, put it best in his reaction to the appointment of Sarah Palin as McCain's running mate, as reported in *The Huffington Post*: "The greatness of McCain is no cynicism, and this is cynical."[3] Murphy's remarks, it should be noted, were unguarded, post interview comments inadvertently broadcast live. "No cynicism, and this is cynical": however unwittingly, Murphy had captured Wallace's sense of the McCain paradox.

In 2000, things had seemed a little different. Seemingly able to cross generational and party divides alike, McCain portrayed himself as the candidate to challenge the money politics at the root of his own party's power. He represented a genuine challenge, in particular, to GOP establishment candidate George W. Bush. (And Wallace's passing description of Bush—"patrician smirk and mangled cant" [*McCain* 53] —would certainly stand the test of time.) After McCain's surprise victory in the New Hampshire primary, the race moved to South Carolina. With voting open to independents, Democrats and

---

2 From "McCain Counters Obama 'Arab' Question" video file, YouTube.com. See Works Cited for full reference.

3 See Works Cited for full reference.

Republicans alike, McCain suddenly looked capable of causing a major upset. Something of a media darling during this period, McCain's "abnormal honesty" and openness proved disarming and attractive to political commentators and a wider national audience.[4] McCain's famous POW heroism seemed to underwrite his political integrity and lent his campaign slogans credibility or, as Wallace puts it, "reverb" (*McCain* 20). For a time, then, McCain appeared to represent something new in American national politics, generating what Wallace refers to as a "brief weird excitement" that becomes the focus of his essay. Wallace is interested, he tells us, in what McCain's campaign "might reveal about how millennial politics and all its packaging and marketing and strategy and media and spin [...] actually makes us US voters feel, inside" (*McCain* 9)

Wallace's account works in a number of key themes and preoccupations: mediation, McCain's paradoxical status as an anti-candidate, political apathy. Interestingly it also serves now to capture a particular moment in the development of digital culture. As Wallace describes one journalist: "he's got digital photos [...] in his Toshiba laptop and has his cell phone plugged into both the wall and the laptop (which is itself plugged into the wall)" (*McCain* 40-41). Cute as this description is, what it actually describes doesn't seem all that remarkable. In its precision, though, the description anticipates Wallace's insistence on refusing to portray the production of spectacle surrounding McCain as anything other than the collective product of individual decisions and specific actions. (How else to construe Wallace's reassurance with regard to the press: "don't forget they're human." [*McCain* 120-121]) He wants to resist, that is, the idea that once spectacle or simulation is installed it becomes self-sustaining, reified and out of reach. Mainly, though, Wallace's depiction of McCain seeks to capture the feeling that Thoreau identified as quiet desperation—a mood updated in Wallace's famous essay on television

---

[4]Jacob Weisberg's article, a review of McCain's *Faith of My Fathers*, may be taken as representative of the type of press attention McCain received in his first bid: "After reading his gripping book, I'm more convinced than ever that his abnormal honesty isn't a calculated strategy for winning over the press. It has that effect, of course, but it's the authentic expression of a remarkable personality." (Weisberg)

to "passive unease and cynicism" (*Supposedly* 50).[5] Wallace tracks the passivity and cynicism he found rife in televisual culture to the sphere of national politics, imagining his Rolling Stone readers leading lives of quiet desperation or, at least, staying "at home doing one-hitters and watching MTV on primary day" (*McCain* 84).

My title, "don't compare, identify," derives of course from *Infinite Jest* and is an Alcoholics' Anonymous injunction for audiences to listen to personal narratives of addiction and struggle not only with respect, but with an empathy ("identification") that manages to quiet a certain habitual cynicism and negativity of audience response, cynicism and negativity that are themselves both symptoms of addiction and obstacles to recovery (*Jest* 345). Within Alcoholics' Anonymous, then, the phrase calls for an ethics of attention or, to use the philosopher Stanley Cavell's favored term, calls for the audience to acknowledge the speaker, in this case at least as a condition of self-knowledge. Wallace finds McCain to be genuinely adept at identification; the problems begin when he discovers that he cannot, finally, identify McCain.

Wallace's preliminary question and task is just that: an attempt to "identify" McCain in the sense of asking whether he is as it were "for real," whether we can take his apparent difference and sincerity at face value. To a significant extent, of course, and inevitably, this entails a study in mediation, detailing the way that McCain can only be identified through a series of media constructed layers. We know of Wallace's admiration for DeLillo's *White Noise*, and at times McCain resembles the most photographed barn in America—no one sees McCain anymore, in the accumulation of nameless energies, the weird excitement. Within Wallace's essay, this is expressed in terms of the idea that his campaign consists of a series of mediating and constrictive boxes. The thought reaches its ontological extreme as Wallace watches two journalists run through film of McCain in order to find a suitable daily sound bite:

---

[5] The essay refers to "your normal, hardworking, quietly desperate species of American." Since the phrase appears on the same page as a reference to Cavell's *Pursuits of Happiness*, we can infer that Wallace's taking up of Thoreau here is inspired by Cavell's re-readings of American transcendentalism.

CNN's tape and editing equipment are digital, so what happens on FF is that the shoulders-up view of McCain against eight of the big flag's stripes doesn't speed up and get silly but rather just kind of explodes into myriad little digital boxes and squares, and these pieces jumble wildly around and bulge and recede and collapse and whirl and rearrange themselves at a furious FF pace, and the resultant image is like something out of the very worst drug experience of all time, a physiognomic Rubik's Cube's constituent squares and boxes flying around and changing shape and sometimes seeming right on the verge of becoming a human face but never quite resolving into a face, on the high speed screen. (*McCain* 52)

It might be assumed that we could refocus this play of surfaces by keeping in mind that other box, the tiny prison cell in which McCain spent his POW years in Hanoi. Does McCain's principled refusal to violate a military code of honor and accept early release not settle the question of whether he is "for real," representing as it does "something underneath politics [...] something riveting and unspinnable and true" (*McCain* 15)? In a justly celebrated stretch of prose—with echoes of New Journalistic style interiority—Wallace imagines the thought processes involved in that refusal. Still, he is unable to call or decide McCain's campaign in either/or terms: salesman or leader, straight talk or bullshit. As he acknowledges:

watching John McCain hold press conferences and -Avails and Town Hall Meetings [...] and be all conspicuously honest and open and informal and idealistic and no-bullshit and say "I run for president not to Be Somebody, but to Do Something" and "We're on a national crusade to give government back to the people" in front of these cheering crowds just seems so much more goddamn complicated than watching old b/w clips of John Kennedy's speeches. It feels impossible, in February 2000, to tell whether McCain is a real leader or merely a very talented political salesman, an entrepreneur who's seen a market-nice and devised a way to fill it. (*McCain* 115–116)

What sort of discipline could address this complication? Perhaps "something horseshit sounding like social historicity or historical sociality" (*Jest* 272)? Even if we were to set the question of mediation aside, McCain's POW experiences guarantee at most the possibility of his present sincerity, no more. Our attention is directed away from McCain to elsewhere: the contextualized feeling of impossibility, the cultural contours that condition the American political scene. McCain's candidacy becomes significant for dragging into the foreground absences and needs that his popularity helps to identify but does not alleviate. The crowds that turn out for McCain "are cheering not for him so much as for how good it feels to believe him. They're cheering the loosening of a weird sort of knot in the electoral tummy" which is to say, "cheering their own ability to finally really fucking cheer" (*McCain* 58).

The underlying question provoked by this instructive failure to identify, then, and the true focus of Wallace's study, pertains to his interesting misgivings over the emotional and experiential landscapes of postmodernity. As he puts it: "the only thing you're certain to feel about John S. McCain is a very modern and American type of ambivalence, a sort of interior war between your deep need to believe and your deep belief that the need to believe is bullshit, that there's nothing left anywhere but sales and salesmen" (*McCain* 117). This intersects, of course, with the question of political apathy, and Wallace offers a wonderful (and necessarily brief) negative phenomenology of disinterest: "it's next to impossible to get someone to think hard about why he's not interested in something. The boredom itself preempts inquiry; the fact of the feeling's enough" (*McCain* 53). To borrow an interesting distinction that recurs in *Infinite Jest*, Wallace's exploration of apathy is in part exploring what happens when a signal becomes an environment—perhaps we can say when a signal deteriorates into an environment. Which is to say, when a signal or meaning no longer communicates, loses its sharp focus and becomes merely background. One example of this happening in *Infinite Jest* is a persistent phone call that becomes mere background as Don Gately and his associate binge on Dilaudid:

> When the phone rang it was just a fact. The ringing was like an environment, not a signal. The fact of its ringing got more and more abstract. Whatever a ringing phone might signify was like totally overwhelmed by the overwhelming fact of its ringing. (*Jest* 936)

And what if truth no longer rings true? What if an already extant background precludes or absorbs the possibility of communication? These questions take us closer to Wallace's goal in *McCain's Promise*: to drag a habitual and generalized background of apathy into the foreground, placing it under an examination that can only take the form of representative, exemplary self-interrogation.

Instead of pushing the question of McCain's sincerity or otherwise into a reified world of autonomous simulacra beyond our reach, Wallace portrays it as the sum total of personal, individual decisions and struggles between idealism and sincerity, comparison and identification. The penultimate sentence of his essay proposes that "Salesman or leader or neither or both, the final paradox—the really tiny central one, way down deep inside all the other campaign puzzles' spinning boxes and squares that layer McCain—is that whether he's truly "for real" now depends less on what is in his heart than on what might be in yours." (*McCain* 124) This is a counter-intuitive turn. Wallace implicates himself and the reader as if the issue were in our own hands, something over which we have control; not so much in our hands, even, as in our hearts. The term calls to mind Tocqueville's sense of democratic culture as contingent upon habits of the heart. It also suggests a certain stubborn corporeality: insisting on biology promises to sidestep post-structuralist worries over whether the self is substantial or stable enough resource to provide any kind of resistance to the accumulated, nameless energies of postmodernity. Locating feelings in the heart rather than the head makes it harder perhaps for them to be cashed out in terms of mere data, information.

This is all in keeping, of course, with Wallace's care to do justice to the dizzying complexities of postmodern terrain without ceding the human scale: agency, intentionality and the integrity of the self. Part of what makes *McCain's Promise* of interest is its insistent incongruity between, on the one hand, a very precise, persuasive description of the postmodern character of the American political process, and its attempt to unpick and begin to overcome some of the problems and dilemmas identified by or as postmodernism through an appeal to categories and resources that, for the postmodernist, are culturally and theoretically unavailable. So what we find in Wallace is a self-aware attempt to stake a claim, enter into finite meaning, but an attempt that, if we still take postmodernism seriously, will remain symptomatically difficult: not impossible, but next to impossible. Wallace's combination of humanism and attentiveness to postmodernity is as engaging as it is unstable.

Such considerations hardly lessen the counter-intuitive feel of Wallace's suggestion. The key to the paradox—why McCain's heart should in any way depend on ours (a formulation that McCain's advanced age in his 2008 bid lent an unwelcome, darkly comic sense) —can be found in the distinction between what is true and what sounds true in a particular period. This is why Wallace is so fond of Cavell's phrase "an audience's willingness to be pleased," capturing as it does the conventions and sensibilities against which communication does (and does not) take place. As the matter is expressed in *Infinite Jest*, "How do trite things get to be trite? Why is the truth usually not just un- but anti-interesting?" (*Jest* 358) The sensibility that Wallace targets is the assumption that cynicism and naivety are mutually exclusive. In *Infinite Jest*, Pemulis has a poster of a paranoid king in his dorm room with the caption "YES, I'M PARANOID—BUT AM I PARANOID *ENOUGH?*" (*Jest* 1035, emphasis original). We might rephrase this to articulate Wallace's position on cynicism: "Yes, we are cynical, but are we cynical enough?" Specifically, should we be cynical about our own cynicism? Wallace notes that he has almost come to fear his cynicism as much as his own credulity but, far from endorsing some pre-critical return to credulity, *McCain's Promise* turns cynicism upon itself. Although he does not allow himself a single unqualifiedly positive assessment of McCain, one can see nonetheless why the predicaments arising from McCain's aspirations to straight talk so captivated Wallace. He directs our attention to the generalized epochal cynicism that, although it presents itself as a compelling political mode and critical stance, can also function as an obstacle to the political with some distinctly conservative implications. *McCain's Promise* works, then, to bracket the structuring ideologies of cynicism itself. This is the sense in which his essay is "about ideology": an attempt to awaken us from our dogmatic cynical slumbers.

In considering Wallace's approach to McCain, we might keep in mind an almost Wittgensteinian remark from Mario Incandenza's cartridge *Tennis And The Feral Prodigy*:

> Please learn the pragmatics of expressing fear: sometimes words
> that seem to express really *invoke*. (*Jest* 175, emphasis original)

The comment seems to capture something about Wallace's own words. The long sentences that distinguish Wallace's journalism no less than his fiction are, in their care to express rather than invoke—and perhaps despite appearances—in part deflationary. That is, they set themselves the task of trying to accurately identify the cultural and psychological stakes but without needlessly raising or aggravating them. And this is one way in which Wallace's prose seems to me unambiguously philosophical: engaged in rigorous attempts to make sure that our solutions and names for what ails us don't turn out to be worse than the problems themselves. Far from evasive, the tendency for Wallace's sentences and topics to spiral and become expansive suggests what we might call a Wittgensteinian, therapeutic care to retrieve daily experience from its distortions and unsettle our sense of the necessary. It is, in fact, easy to see why references to Stanley Cavell recur in Wallace's nonfiction, and one imagines Wallace relating to Cavell's seminal suggestion that "the writing of philosophy is difficult in a new way" (*Must We* xxii). Amid all the infinite jesting in Wallace, there is a ceaseless willingness to risk finite meaning.

This is Water and the Ethics of Attention: Wallace, Murdoch, and Nussbaum

Daniel Turnbull

In *This is Water*, David Foster Wallace makes a convincing case for the importance of the direction of attention, and the terms in which we choose to conceive of situations, in our moral lives. Despite the attractiveness of the picture for which Wallace argues, the concerns that animate it have not been much examined within the mainstream of analytic moral philosophy. One figure in this tradition that has addressed these issues, however, is Iris Murdoch. The fact that both Murdoch and Wallace are very well known writers of fiction is, I will argue, no coincidence. Using resources from the philosopher Martha Nussbaum's work on the role of fiction in informing and shaping our moral sensibilities, I will suggest that fiction can, at least some of the time, both show us how attention and imagination may be used in ways that are essential for a deeper moral responsiveness, and lead us to use our own faculties in this way. The aim will be to show that it should be no surprise that Wallace and Murdoch emphasize the role of attention and imagination in moral life, as this is a central part of what, as writers of fiction, they were engaged in doing in their 'day jobs'. Furthermore, I will try to show that the major concerns Wallace explores in *This is Water* are also present elsewhere in his fictional work.

The claim at the crux of *This is Water* is articulated most clearly where Wallace says:

> 'Learning how to think' really means learning how to exercise some control over how and what you think. It means being conscious and aware enough to choose what you pay attention to and to choose how you construct meaning from experience. Because if you cannot or will not exercise this kind of choice in adult life, you will be totally hosed. (*Water* 53-55)

Moving away from the default way of viewing and conceptualizing situations—seeing people in front of us in the supermarket queue or other drivers in a traffic jam as mere obstacles, preventing us from doing what we want, for example—towards a richer conception of these people as having, like us, genuine inner lives, takes work, Wallace tells us. We need to choose to focus our attention and use our imagination to move beyond our overwhelming concern with our own needs and difficulties, to gain a sense of the reality of others' situations (*Water* 67-81).

Wallace is keen to assure us that his point should not be read as a moral one: "None of this is about morality, or religion, or dogma, or big fancy questions of life after death" (*Water* 128). I want to argue, however, that his point is absolutely a moral one. Why should we think it justified to make this claim, despite Wallace's categorical denial? There are two reasons why this might be the case.

First, Wallace's concern might be about the narrowness of the conception of morality as it is commonly conceptualized, both in mainstream moral philosophy and in the popular imagination. Where morality is seen as purely about what we owe to others, what we are required to do and what we are forbidden to do, then it is natural to say that questions about the direction of attention do not fall within the domain of morality. However despite its widespread, albeit often unthinking, acceptance, this conception of morality is not the only one available. A wider conception of morality, of whom the standard-bearer is Aristotle, sees no sharp moral/non-moral distinction, but instead is concerned about how we can live in a way that allows us to flourish as whole people; this includes, but is by no means exhausted by, our actions that affect others. If we accept this wider conception of the domain of moral concern, questions about attention and conceptualization of situations will be seen as having moral relevance. This is a point to which I will return in my discussion of Nussbaum's picture of the texture of moral life, below.

Second, as well as the question about the scope of morality, there is also an ambiguity in the notion of being "about morality." The sense of being about morality that Wallace employs in claiming that his argument is not to do with morality may be different to the one I am using when I claim that it is. Wallace may be making the point that his argument is not a moralizing one; it is not about first-order morality, in the sense of telling us what concrete actions we ought or ought not to be taking. It is, however, a metaethical one; it is an argument about the nature of morality, saying that the way we choose to attend to and see situations is absolutely central to the way we react to the world. While he is not trying to point to some particular moral fact, he is trying to point to some fact about the nature and requirements of morality in general.

As I mentioned, the consideration of the type of issue that concerns Wallace here is largely absent from mainstream analytic moral philosophy. The usual method of moral philosophers is to take the description of the situation in question as a given, and ask, on the basis of this situation, so described, what is the right or wrong, the required or forbidden, thing to do. If we take Wallace's claim about the importance of attention seriously, however, we can see that this approach misses an important part of moral activity. By focusing only on the decision of how to act, it ignores completely the more pressing issue of how one chooses to see a situation.

One notable exception to this trend in moral philosophy, however, is Iris Murdoch. In an article entitled 'The Idea of Perfection' she argues for the vital moral importance of questions of what we choose to attend to, and how we choose to conceptualize things. In this, she sets her face against the view, prevalent in moral philosophy both when she was writing and now, that it is impossible to take a merely 'contemplative attitude to the good', the idea that it is only action that can be morally judged, and therefore be of moral worth (Murdoch 15). She diagnoses this as a misapplication of Wittgenstein's private language argument, involving a slide from the (correct) idea that any putative private language would be meaningless to the (incorrect) idea that any purely mental action is morally 'meaningless' (Murdoch 12).

Against this view, she gives the example of a mother, M, who regards her daughter-in-law, D, in a negative light, perhaps believing that her son has married beneath him. In spite of her negative perception, M always behaves impeccably towards D. Over time, however, and through an effort of moral willpower, she attends to different aspects of D's personality and behavior, so coming to see different things about her as salient, and so regarding her in a new light. "D is discovered to be not vulgar but refreshingly simple, not undignified but spontaneous, not noisy but gay, not tiresomely juvenile but delightfully youthful, and so on." In this situation, Murdoch argues, it is natural and correct to regard M as making moral progress, as in the light of a loving attention she comes to see D in both a more accurate and a more loving way (Murdoch 17-23).

For Murdoch—as, I have argued, is the case for Wallace—this type of direction of one's attention is a distinctively moral activity: "I have used the word 'attention' . . . to express the idea of a just and loving gaze directed upon an individual reality. I believe this to be the characteristic and proper mark of the active moral agent" (Murdoch 34). In other words: if you can't do this, you are totally hosed.

Like Wallace, Murdoch regards the ability to properly direct one's attention as a pre-requisite of a certain important type of freedom. Without making the moral effort to attend one is left merely looking, to use Murdoch's terminology, and when we merely look, the world is "compulsively present" to us (Murdoch 37-39) (a thought echoed in Wallace's claim about default settings). As Murdoch notes, this picture puts a different slant on the place of choice and the notion of freedom that we ought to seek:

> Moral change and moral achievement are slow; we are not free in the sense of being able suddenly to alter ourselves since we cannot suddenly alter what we can see and ergo what we desire and are compelled by. In a way, explicit choice seems now less important: less decisive (since much of the 'decision' lies elsewhere) and less obviously something to be 'cultivated'. If I attend properly I will have no choices and this is the ultimate condition to be aimed at (Murdoch 39-40)

This type of concern, investigating different conceptions of freedom, often finds expression in Wallace's fiction, for instance in Marathe and Steeply's discussion of different conceptions of freedom in *Infinite Jest* (320-321), as referenced in David Hering's paper in this volume.

We should note here one possible point of disagreement between Murdoch and Wallace: Murdoch believes there is only one proper way to attend whereas Wallace, I think, would believe there is a multiplicity of ways (but, of course, this is definitely not to say he would think anything goes when it comes to attending).

Considering this notion of freedom makes us confront the fact that will and reason are not entirely separate faculties for human beings, but instead are hopelessly entwined. When we employ reason to decide what to do, we do this on the basis of reality as we apprehend it, which, as both Murdoch and Wallace have suggested, is itself in large part down to how we choose to attend to the world. Again, this seems to be something that Wallace explores quite often in his fiction—a clear instance being *Infinite Jest*'s central focus on substance addiction and the various possible means of recovery.

On the question of why it should be two celebrated novelists who pick out this important facet of moral life, Murdoch offers an interesting comment, writing that:

> One of the great merits of the moral psychology which I am proposing is that it does not contrast art and morals, but shows them to be two aspects of a single struggle. . . Virtue is au fond the same in the artist as in the good man in that it is a selfless attention to nature: something which is easy to name but very hard to achieve. Artists who have reflected have frequently given expression to this idea (Murdoch 41).

This gives us the tantalizing suggestion that the reason Murdoch and Wallace are particularly well-placed to articulate the importance of the direction of attention in morality is that it mirrors one of the things they get up to in their day jobs as writers of fiction.

This line of thought is developed by the philosopher Martha Nussbaum, over a series of articles. Taking the example of Henry James, Nussbaum argues that direction of attention is an essential part of seeing moral reality, and certain works of fiction are able to both illustrate and develop this capacity for us.

Nussbaum starts from the idea that in moral life, perceptions of concrete situations are explanatorily prior to general rules. She gives three reasons why this is the case.

First, in a Wittgensteinian vein, even if we were to have a comprehensive set of rules to tell us how to act, we would need to be able to perceive when these rules apply. If a rule told us "one should never betray one's friends" (or more plausibly, "betraying one's friends is always morally costly") then we would still need to be able to see reliably the right sort of situations as cases of betraying one's friends in order to follow the rule properly. As Nussbaum says, situations "do not present themselves with duty labels on them" (*Love's Knowledge* 156).

Second, Nussbaum argues that no conceivable set of rules could possibly suffice to tell us how to act in every situation, in any case (156). When we consider that acting correctly in a situation may not just be a matter of whether we do the right thing, but also of how we do the thing—in what tone of voice we make our apology, for instance —this seems a credible point.

Finally, she argues that there are situations which could not, even in principle, be captured in standing principles, because they are just irreducibly particular (157). Another philosopher, Gabriele Taylor, making a slightly different, but related point, uses a wonderful example from the James Joyce story "The Dead." Just how, she asks, is one supposed to react when one's wife's remembrance of a long-dead former lover makes one see how oafish one has made oneself with one's self-satisfied speechifying? (Taylor 8-12) To suppose that there is any rule, laid out in advance, that could give us a concrete answer to this question just seems absurd.

Nussbaum uses this picture of morality to argue for the importance of fiction both as an illustration, and as a catalyst, of the sensibility it requires:

> If this view of morality is taken seriously and if we wish to have texts that represent it at its best (in order to anticipate or supplement experience or to assess this norm against others), it seems difficult to conclude that we will need to turn to texts no less elaborate, no less linguistically fine-tuned, concrete, and intensely focused, no less metaphorically resourceful, than this novel (*Love's Knowledge* 157).

Here, Nussbaum is concerned specifically with *The Golden Bowl*, but I would certainly make the case that the same conclusion can be drawn about much of Wallace's fiction (and certainly his two published novels). If morality requires us to develop our powers of choosing what to attend to, and how to attend to it, then much fiction will have a role to play. The writer of fiction typically directs our attention to salient features of situation and, to some extent, pre-conceptualizes them for us. She says to us both 'look at this' and 'look at it this way'. By presenting situations to us in this selective way, she both illustrates and develops the human capacity for moral perception. Of course, in order to have our capacity for moral vision developed by fiction we must have eyes to see. If we have eyes, however, fiction can help us use them by illustrating different ways of choosing where and how to attend.

Of course, we can have our capacity for moral vision developed by guidance in the real world, by a more virtuous or morally insightful person helping us come to see a situation in a particular light. There are, however, good reasons why this process may often be better achieved through works of art.[1]

Just as Nussbaum claims that the novels of Henry James both display and elicit this capacity, as I mentioned earlier, I think we can say the same of Wallace's fiction. One particularly stark example of this, for me, is "Brief Interview #42" where Wallace describes for us, in almost loving detail, the sights, sounds and smells of a toilet attendant's daily grind. Like most of us, I imagine, before reading this I had been guilty of thinking as little as possible what life must be like for someone with such a job. There are good reasons of psychic self-protection for reacting like this, but it does turn us away from the moral reality of the situation. Wallace's vignette cuts through all this, focusing relentlessly on the sensuous reality of the situation and makes such willful moral inattentiveness impossible in the future.

All this is not to say, however, that fiction, even fiction as acute as Wallace's, should or could replace moral philosophy. There is a value in the systematic and explicit nature of the best moral philosophy. What moral philosophy lacks, and what fiction can provide, though, is sufficiently rich descriptions of particular situations, drawing our eye to the salient factors about them. While philosophy does use examples, these tend to be far too schematic to capture the felt texture of moral reality. At certain points in his oeuvre, Wallace seems to be grappling with the uneasy relationship between these two areas of intellectual endeavor. His piece "Octet" resembles in some ways a work of moral philosophy, particularly in the Aristotelian tradition, in the

---

[1] While I need not go into these here, I would direct the interested reader to Aristotle's discussion of catharsis in his *Poetics*.

use of examples to try to get us to catch on to some underlying moral point of similarity.

To illustrate this resemblance, compare this passage from "Octet":

> A lady marries a man from a very wealthy family and they have a baby together and they both love the baby a lot, although as time goes by they become less and less keen on each other, until eventually the lady files divorce papers on the man. The lady and the man both want primary custody of the baby, but the lady assumes she'll ultimately be the one to get primary custody because that's how things usually shake out in divorce law. . . Q: (A) Is she a good mother. (*Brief Interviews* 113-4)

with this passage from a philosophical piece by Martha Nussbaum:

> X works for General Motors. All day long he performs a single repetitive task. The things he helps to make are not under his control. And yet he feels good. He is proud of the bustling capitalist economy; he may even be convinced that the capability to perform simple repetitive tasks is the only capability he possesses, that he could not handle a larger demand. Does his inner sense of worth count as genuine self-respect, and is GM therefore a successful distributor, in his case, of that primary good? ("Shame" 398-9)

The examples Wallace gives in "Octet," especially the later ones, are far richer than any I have come across in work from the mainstream of analytic moral philosophy. Even so, Wallace seems to chafe against the restrictions implicit in such brief sketches, abandoning one as "too shot through with ambiguity" (*Brief Interviews* 113) to serve his purpose, and asking questions about the others that it might seem absurd to try to answer without demanding further information. The question, then, of the boundaries between philosophical and literary approaches, and the limitations of both, seem to be at the forefront of what Wallace is trying to do with this piece. In the two complete novels, issues like these don't quite make it to the surface in the same way, but do seem to be an animating concern for Wallace.

Having said all this then, it should come as no surprise that Wallace and Murdoch address the moral importance of the direction of attention in their non-fiction, because this reflects an important part of what they are doing, and what they take themselves to be doing, in their fiction. For Wallace at least, this role and capabilities of the fiction-writer in this regard also seems to be something he directly addresses, both obliquely in some of his fiction as well as more directly in semi-fiction pieces like 'Octet'. This suggests something about how we should view *This is Water* within Wallace's wider oeuvre. Rather than regarding it as a piece that, while rich and strange, is detached from his fictional work, we should see it as much more integrated than that as it both flows from, and illustrates, the concerns that Wallace suggests are central to his wider artistic and moral mission.

ACKNOWLEDGMENTS

I would like to thank a number of people for their kind assistance in making this collection possible. Firstly, I thank David Seed, Mark Llewellyn, Nick Davis, Chris Williams, Marcus Walsh, Hana Leaper and Cathy Rees at the University Of Liverpool for their assistance with and support for the conference which led to the creation of this book. I thank Matt and John Bucher for being such enthusiastic and helpful publishers every step of the way. I thank Greg Carlisle for coming over to Liverpool to give the keynote address and for his introduction to this volume. I also thank Nick Maniatis for his tireless enthusiasm and promotion of both the conference and this collection. Jean Cannon and Richard Workman at the Harry Ransom Center in Texas provided invaluable assistance with the clearance of certain extracts, for which I am extremely grateful. I would also like to thank all of the contributors to this volume for their many useful discussions during both the conference and the editing process, as well as the people of wallace-l, who are a veritable Wallace wellspring and have consistently provided helpful information. A few contributor acknowledgements: Adam Kelly would like to thank Tony Hutchinson and Ben Williamson for their advice, Thomas Tracey thanks Anna Harpin for her assistance on trauma theory, and Christoph Ribbat thanks Stefan Haase.

I offer my profound thanks to Bonnie Nadell for kindly granting me permission to use certain extracts of Wallace's work on behalf of the David Foster Wallace Literary Trust. Finally, I would like to thank my mother Jill for her encouragement in my pursuing of an academic career, and my partner Claire for her limitless support, love and patience during the creation of this book.

CONTRIBUTOR NOTES

ABOUT THE EDITOR

DAVID HERING, editor of *Consider David Foster Wallace: Critical Essays*, is a PhD student at the University Of Liverpool, where he is currently researching the works of David Foster Wallace and Mark Z. Danielewski in relation to ideologies of choice, freedom and labyrinthine motifs and narratives. He tutors courses on Close Reading and Literary Theory, and lectures on 19th and 20th century American Fiction. His literary reviews have appeared in the *Journal Of American Studies* and *Moveable Type*, and he has given papers and spoken on Wallace and Danielewski at Harvard University, Trinity College Dublin, Strathclyde University, and the University Of Liverpool.

ABOUT THE CONTRIBUTORS

KIKI BENZON is an Assistant Professor in English Literature at the University of Lethbridge, Canada. Her chief areas of scholarship are contemporary American fiction, text and image, and the medical humanities. She is the Fictions Present thread editor of the *Electronic Book Review* and has published articles on Wallace's *Oblivion* and depictions of mental illness in *Infinite Jest* and *Brief Interviews With Hideous Men*.

GREG CARLISLE is an instructor of theatre at Morehead State University in Morehead, Kentucky, where he teaches acting, voice and articulation, and dramatic literature and recently directed plays by Beckett and Moliere. He is the author of *Elegant Complexity, A Study of David Foster Wallace's Infinite Jest*, published by Sideshow Media Group Press in 2007. He contributed to the 2009 Wallace tribute issue of the *Sonora Review* and was a panelist and reader at the associated tribute event hosted by the University of Arizona in May 2009. He has taught courses in theatre and speech, presented theatre workshops, directed productions, and acted throughout the Southern and Midwestern United States. He is currently working on a study of Wallace's story collection, *Oblivion*, and a study of the plays of Edward Albee.

DR PHILIP COLEMAN is a Lecturer in English Studies in Trinity College Dublin, where is also Director of the MPhil in the Literatures of the Americas programme. He has edited *On Literature and Science: Essays, Reflections, Provocations* (2007) and *"After Thirty Falls": New Essays on John Berryman* (with Philip McGowan, 2007). His book *John Berryman and the Public Sphere: Reception and Redress* will be published by UCD Press in 2010.

CHRISTOFOROS DIAKOULAKIS is completing his DPhil in English in the University of Sussex. He has a strong interest in deconstruction and his current research centers on William James and Edgar Allan Poe. David Foster Wallace's *Brief Interviews with Hideous Men* was the primary focus of his MA dissertation while in the University of York.

GRAHAM FOSTER is a PhD Student at Manchester Metropolitan University. His history of research is in 20th Century American Literature. His specialist area is the North American Literature of Generation X, and he is currently researching the evidence of a literary *fin de siècle* in the millennial fictions of David Foster Wallace and Douglas Coupland.

DR IANNIS GOERLANDT studied English and German in Ghent and Rostock and obtained an MA in American Studies from The University of Antwerp. With a dissertation on national imagery and utopianism in the work of Arno Schmidt, he earned his PhD in German Literature from Ghent University (*Schulen zur Allegorie*, Aisthesis 2008). His main research topics include literary ethics, narratology, translation studies, paratextuality and imagology. Currently, he holds a part-time position as Assistant Professor at K.U.Leuven (Belgium). Together with his partner, he also owns a translation agency. His Dutch translation of Wallace's essay "A

Supposedly Fun Thing I'll Never Do Again" was published in November 2009.

CLARE HAYES-BRADY is a doctoral candidate at Trinity College Dublin, where her research interests center around contemporary American literature, with a particular focus on David Foster Wallace. She has presented papers in various academic fora on different aspects of Wallace's work .

DR. PAUL JENNER is a lecturer in North American Literature and Film, Department of English and Drama, Loughborough University. His principal research area is in American intellectual and cultural history, with particular focus on the philosopher and critic Stanley Cavell. His Ph.D. was a comparative study of Stanley Cavell, Richard Rorty and Thomas Kuhn, considering their work in relation to logical positivism and early forms of analytical philosophy. More broadly, he is interested in intersections between philosophy, literature and film.

ADAM KELLY is a PhD Candidate and IRCHSS Government of Ireland Scholar at University College Dublin, where he is currently completing a dissertation entitled "Moments of Decision in Contemporary American Fiction." He received his MA from the University of York. He teaches courses on American Modernism and contemporary American fiction, and his articles have appeared or are forthcoming in *Critique*, *Philip Roth Studies*, *Irish Journal of American Studies*, and *Phrasis*.

CONNIE LUTHER is a PhD. Candidate at the University of Calgary, Alberta, Canada. Connie is interested in contemporary culture, post-postmodern literature, and philosophy. She thinks that David Foster Wallace's work is an important response to the heritage of postmodernism, the philosophical underpinnings of which he finds difficult if not impossible to accept.

GREGORY PHIPPS is currently pursuing his PhD at McGill University in Montreal, Quebec. He is writing his dissertation on

Henry James and the American intellectual movement of Pragmatism, exploring the links between James' later novels and Pragmatist writers such as Charles Peirce, Oliver Wendell Holmes Jr., and his brother William James. He also has a strong interest in contemporary American literature.

CHRISTOPH RIBBAT is a professor of American literature and culture at the University of Paderborn, Germany. His research focuses on contemporary US literature, cultural history, and photography. He has taught at universities in Switzerland and Germany and conducted research as a Humboldt Fellow at MIT and Boston University and as a Fulbright Scholar at The Cooper Union, New York. He is currently working on a research project on non-fiction books and their readers.

CHRISTOPHER THOMAS is a graduate student at The City College of New York (CUNY). His research has focused mainly on drawing connections between the American Postmodern era and the Enlightenment in Britain—specifically on the works of David Foster Wallace and Laurence Sterne. Other research interests include Critical Theory, Psychoanalysis, and art history.

THOMAS TRACEY completed his undergraduate degree in English Literature and Philosophy at Trinity College, Dublin (his hometown). He received an Interdisciplinary MA in the Culture of Modernism from the University of York (UK), where he became interested in the relation between ethics and literature, and where he first discovered David Foster Wallace. His MA thesis was on Wallace and realism. He is currently reading for a DPhil in English & Related Literature at Oxford University, where he is working on the oeuvre of David Foster Wallace, considering him as a moralist.

MATT TRESCO is a PhD student at the University of Manchester. He is currently writing on "encyclopedism" in contemporary U.S. fiction, focusing on texts by Gaddis, Pynchon, Wallace, Jenny Boully and Robert Altman. His MA dissertation was on adapting Immanuel Wallerstein's world-systems analysis as a means of interpreting *Gravity's Rainbow*.

DANIEL TURNBULL is a PhD student in the Dept. of Philosophy, Birkbeck College, University of London. He works in the area of moral philosophy, and specifically moral psychology. He is currently working on the role of emotions in moral judgement, aiming to make an argument for the importance of shame as a moral emotion, alongside guilt.

Works Cited

A Note On Works Cited
The vast majority of Wallace's books have the same pagination, though there have been noted discrepancies, specifically in some different editions of *Brief Interviews With Hideous Men*. The Boston Little, Brown edition cited by Marshall Boswell apparently has 336 pages, while I have also heard from people who have a 321-page U.S. paperback. The version used here is the 273-page 1999 London Abacus printing, and all references in the collection refer to the pagination of that edition.

Aarseth, Espen. *Cybertext: Perspectives on Ergodic Literature.* Johns Hopkins University Press, 1997. Print.

Asperger, Hans. "Autistic Psychopathy in Childhood."*Autism and Asperger Syndrome.* Trans. and Ed. Uta Frith. Cambridge: Cambridge University Press, 1993. Print.

Bachelder, Chris. *Bear V Shark.* London: Bloomsbury, 2002. Print.

Barth, John. *The Friday Book: Essays and Other Nonfiction.* New York: G.P. Putnam's Sons, 1984. Print.

Barthes, Roland. *A Lover's Discourse: Fragments.* Trans. Richard Howard. London: Vintage, 1979. Print.

Baskin, Jon. "Death is Not the End: David Foster Wallace: His Legacy and His Critics." *The Point* 1 N.p. Spring 2009. n.pag. Web. 17 Aug. 2009. <www.thepointmag.com/death1.html>

Baudrillard, Jean. *America.* Trans. Chris Turner. London: Verso, 1988. Print.

---. *Simulacra and Simulation.* Trans. Sheila Faria Glaser. Ann Arbor: The University of Michigan Press, 1994. Print.

Bercovitch, Sacvan. *The Puritan Origins of the American Self.* New Haven and London: Yale University Press, 1975. Print.

—. *The Rites of Assent: Transformations in the Symbolic Construction of America.* New York and London: Routledge, 1993. Print.

Berkeley, George. *The Works of George Berkeley, Bishop of Cloyne,* Vol. 7. Eds. A. A. Luce

Bilton, Alan. *An Introduction to Contemporary American Literature.* Edinburgh: Edinburgh University Press, 2002. Print.

Blumenbach, Ulrich. "Am Fuß vom Text, oder: Wie ich David Foster Wallace' *Infinite Jest* lieben und trotzdem übersetzen lernte: Ein (vorläufiger) Werkstattbericht." *Schreibheft* 68 (2007): 169-77. Web. Jul 14, 2010 <http://www.schreibheft.de/docs/pdfs/Ulrich-Blumenbach-Am-Fuss-vom-Text.pdf>.

Borges, Jorge Luis. *Fictions.* Trans. Anthony Kerrigan. London: Calder Publications Limited, 1998. Print.

Boswell, Marshall. *Understanding David Foster Wallace.* Columbia: University of South Carolina Press, 2003. Print.

---. "Heading Westward." *Sonora Review* 55 (2009): 28-32. Print.

Boully, Jenny. *The Body: An Essay.* Athens, Ohio: Essay Press, 2007. Print.

Boynton, Robert S., ed. *The New New Journalism: Conversations with America's Best Nonfiction Writers on Their Craft.* New York: Vintage, 2005. Print.

Buell, Lawrence. "American Pastoral Ideology Reappraised." *American Literary History* 1.1 (1989): 1-29. Print.

Burgess, Anthony. "Endtime." Homage to QWERT YUOIP: Selected Journalism, 1978-1985. London: Sphere Books, 1987: 12-16. Print.

Burn, Stephen. *David Foster Wallace's Infinite Jest: A Reader's Guide*. New York: Continuum, 2003. Print.

Cahoone, Lawrence, ed. *From Modernism to Postmodernism: An Anthology*, 2nd ed. Malden: Wiley-Blackwell, 2003. Print.

Campbell, John. "David Foster Wallace Stranded on a Desert Island." Cartoon. *Pictures for Sad Children*. Web. Jul 14, 2010 <http://www.picturesforsadchildren.com/index.php?comicID=122>.

Carlisle, Greg. *Elegant Complexity: A Study of David Foster Wallace's Infinite Jest*. Los   Angeles/Austin: Sideshow Media Group, 2007. Print.

---. "Wallace's Infinite Fiction." *Sonora Review* 55/56 (2009): 33-37 of Wallace section. Print.

Carr, George. "Posting on Wallace-l." *Wallace-l Listserv*. Waste.org. n.d. Web. 17. Aug. 2009. <http://waste.org/mail/?list=wallace-l>

Caruth, Cathy. *Unclaimed Experience: Trauma, Narrative, and History*. Baltimore and London: The Johns Hopkins University Press, 1996. Print.

Caruth, Cathy, ed. *Trauma: Explorations in Memory*. Baltimore and London: Johns Hopkins University Press, 1995. Print.

Cavell, Stanley. *Must We Mean What We Say?* New York: Charles Scribner's, 1969. Print.

---. *Pursuits of Happiness: the Hollywood Comedy of Remarriage*. Cambridge, MA: Harvard University Press, 1981. Print.

Chabon, Michael. *Maps and Legends: Reading and Writing along the Borderlands*. San Francisco: McSweeney's, 2008. Print.

Cioffi, Frank. "An Anguish Become Thing: Narrative as Performance in David Foster Wallace's *Infinite Jest.*" *Narrative* 8.2.(2000): 161-181. Print.

Coetzee, J. M. "Confession and Double Thoughts: Tolstoy, Rousseau, Dostoevsky." *Doubling the Point: Essays and Interviews.* Ed. David Attwell. Cambridge, MA: Harvard UP, 1992. 251-93. Print.

Collins, Jim. "Genericity in the Nineties: Eclectic Irony and the New Sincerity." *Film Theory Goes to the Movies.* Ed. Jim Collins, Hilary Radner and Ava Preacher Collins. London: Routledge, 1993. 242-63. Print.

Connor, Steven. Introduction. *The Cambridge Companion to Postmodernism.* Ed. Connor. Cambridge: Cambridge University Press, 2004. 1-19. Print.

Conte, Joseph. *Design and Debris: A Chaotics of Postmodern American Fiction.* Alabama University Press, 2002. Print.

Coupland, Douglas. *Generation X: Tales for an Accelerated Culture.* London: Abacus, 1992.

---. *Polaroids from the Dead.* Toronto: HarperCollins, 1996. Print.

Crain, Caleb. "Approaching Infinity." *The Boston Globe.* Christopher M. Mayer, 26 Oct. 2003. Web. Jul 14, 2010.

Cronon, William. "The Trouble with Wilderness: Or, Getting Back to the Wrong Nature." *Uncommon Ground: Rethinking the Human Place in Nature.* Ed. William Cronon. New York: W.W. Norton & Company, 1995. Print.

Danielewski, Mark Z. *House of Leaves.* New York: Pantheon, 2000. Print.

Davidson, Harriet. "Improper desire: reading The Waste Land." *The Cambridge Companion to T.S. Eliot.* Ed. A. David Moody. Cambridge: Cambridge University Press, 1994: 121-131. Print.

Deleuze and Guattari. *Anti-Oedipus.* Trans. Robert Hurley, Mark Seem and Helen R. Lane. London: Continuum, 2007. Print.

DeLillo, Don. *White Noise.* London: Picador, 1985. Print.

Derrida, Jacques. *The Gift of Death and Literature in Secret.* Trans. David Wills. 2nd edition. Chicago: University of Chicago Press, 2008. Print.

---. *Given Time: 1. Counterfeit Money.* Trans. Peggy Kamuf. Chicago: U of Chicago P, 1995. Print.

---. *Languages of the Unsayable: The Play of Negativity in Literature and Literary Theory.* Trans. Ken Frieden. Ed. Sanford Budick and Wolfgang Iser. New York: Columbia University Press, 1989. Print.
---. "The Law of Genre." Trans. Avital Ronell. Critical Inquiry 7.1 (Autumn 1980): 55-81. Print.

---. *On Cosmopolitanism and Forgiveness.* Trans. Michael Hughes. London: Routledge, 2001. Print.

---. *On the Name.* Trans. David Wood. Ed. Thomas Dutoit. Stanford, California: Stanford University Press, 1995. Print.

----. "Signature Event Context." Trans. Samuel Weber and Jeffrey Mehlman. *Limited Inc.* Ed. Gerald Graff. Evanston, IL: Northwestern University Press, 1988. 1-23. Print.

---. *Spectres of Marx: The State of the Debt, the Work of Mourning, and the New International.* Trans. Peggy Kamuf. London: Routledge, 1994. Print.

---. "'This Strange Institution Called Literature': An Interview With Jacques Derrida." Trans. Geoffrey Bennington and Rachel Bowlby.

Acts of Literature. Ed. Derek Attridge. London: Routledge, 1992. 33-75. Print.

Didion, Joan. "On Keeping a Notebook." *Slouching towards Bethlehem*. New York: Farrar, Straus and Giroux, 1981. 135-44. Print.

Dilsaver, Lary M. "Geographical Record Note: Research Perspectives on National Parks." *The Geographical Review* 99.2 (2009): 268-278. Print.

Eco, Umberto. *Faith in Fakes: Travels in Hyperreality*. London: Vintage, 1998. Print.

---. *Semiotics and the Philosophy of Language*. Indiana: Indiana University Press, 1986. Print.

Eggers, Dave. *What is the What: The Autobiography of Valentino Achak Deng*. Harmondsworth: Penguin, 2007. Print.

Eliot, T.S. The Waste Land. Ed. Michael North. New York and London: W.W. Norton & Company, 2001. Print.

Ellis, Bret Easton. *Less Than Zero*. London: Picador, 1986. Print.

Esposito, Scott. "My Infinite Summer: "Westward the Course of Empire Takes Its Way," from Girl with Curious Hair." conversationalreading.com. N.p. 5 Aug. 2009. n.pag. Web. 24 August 2009.

Favre, Alexandre, et al. *Chaos and Determinism: Turbulence as a Paradigm for Complex Systems Converging toward Final States*. Trans. Bertram Eugene Schwarzbach. Baltimore: Johns Hopkins University Press, 1995. Print.

Felman, Shoshana, and Laub, Dori (M.D.). *Testimony: Crises of Witnessing in Literature, Psychoanalysis, and History*. New York and London: Routledge, 1992. Print.

Ferris, Joshua. *Then We Came to the End*. Harmondsworth: Penguin, 2008. Print.

Fishbein, Paul. "AVN's Response to 'Neither Adult Nor Entertainment.'" *Adult Video News*. AVN Media Network. August 14 1998. n.pag. Web. 23 Jan. 2010. <http://www.thehowlingfantods.com/avn.htm>

Fishkin, Shelley Fisher. *From Fact to Fiction: Journalism and Imaginative Writing in America*. Oxford: Oxford University Press, 1985. Print.

Frus, Phyllis. *The Politics and Poetics of Journalistic Narrative: The Timely and the Timeless*. New York: Cambridge University Press, 1994. Print.

Giles, Paul. "Sentimental Posthumanism: David Foster Wallace." *Twentieth Century Literature* 53.3 (Fall 2007): 327-344. Print.

Goerlandt, Iannis. "'Put the Book Down and Slowly Walk Away': Irony and David Foster Wallace's *Infinite Jest*." *Critique* 47.3 (Spring 2006): 309-328. Print.

---. "'This is the sort of shit we waste our lives thinking about.'" *Yang* 41.4 (2005): 549-58. Web. Jul 14, 2010 <http://www.yangtijdschrift.be/editorhtml.asp?page=20054L5>.

---. and Luc Herman. "David Foster Wallace." *Post-War Literatures in English: A Lexicon of Contemporary Authors*. Eds. Hans Bak et al. Groningen: Martinus Nijhoff. Supplement 56 (2004): 1-16; A1-A2; B1-B2. Print.

---. and Daniël Rovers. "Het jaar van de Whopper©. Onvolledige encyclopedie bij het oeuvre van David Foster Wallace (1962–2008)." *Yang* 44.4 (2008): 617-47. Print.

Grafton, Anthony. *Die tragischen Ursprünge der deutschen Fußnote*. Trans. H. Jochen Bußmann [*The Footnote: A Curious History*]. München: dtv, 1998. Print.

Hägglund, Martin. "The Necessity of Discrimination: Disjoining Derrida and Levinas." *Diacritics* 34 (2004): 40-71. Print.

Hartsock, John C. *A History of American Literary Journalism: The Emergence of a Modern Narrative Form.* Amherst: University of Massachusetts Press, 2000. Print.

Hayles, N. Katherine. "The Illusion of Autonomy and the Fact of Recursivity: Virtual Ecologies, Entertainment, and *Infinite Jest.*" *New Literary History* 30.3 (1999): 675-97. Print.

Hegel, G. W. F. *The Philosophy of History.* Trans: J. Sibree. Mineola, New York: Dover, 1956. Print.

Heise, Ursula. *Chronoschisms: Time, Narrative and Postmodernism.* Cambridge: Cambridge University Press, 1997. Print.

Hellmann, John. *Fables of Fact: The New Journalism as New Fiction.* Urbana: University of Illinois Press, c1981. Print.

Hofstadter, Douglas. *Gödel, Escher, Bach: An Eternal Golden Braid.* New York: Vintage, 1980. Print.

Holland, Mary K. "The Art's Heart's Purpose: Braving the Narcissistic Loop of David Foster Wallace's *Infinite Jest.*" *Critique* 47.3 (Spring 2006): 218-242. Print.

Hyde, Lewis. *The Gift: Imagination and the Erotic Life of Property.* New York: Vintage, 1983. Print.

Jacobs, Timothy. "American Touchstone: The Idea of Order in Gerald Manley Hopkins and David Foster Wallace." *Comparative Literature Studies* 38.3. (2001): 215-30. Print.

---. "The Brothers Incandenza: Translating Ideology in Fyodor Dosto-evsky's *The Brothers Karamazov* and David Foster Wallace's *Infinite Jest.*" *Texas Studies in Literature* 49.3 (2007): 265-292. Print.

Jameson, Fredric. *The Political Unconscious: Narrative as a Socially Symbolic Act.* Ithaca: Cornell University Press, 1981. Print.

---. *Postmodernism, or, the Cultural Logic of Late Capitalism.* Durham: Duke University Press, 1991. Print.

Kerouac, Jack. *Selected Letters, 1940-1956.* Ed. Ann Charters. New York: Viking, 1995. Print.

Kipp, Jeremiah. "Looking for One New Value But Nothing Comes My Way: An Interview with Film Critic Glen Kenny about David Foster Wallace." *The House Next Door.* Slant Magazine. 8 April 2009. n.pag. Web. 23 Jan. 2010.

Klein, Naomi. *No Logo.* London: Flamingo, 2000. Print.

Kramer, Mark and Wendy Call, eds. *Telling True Stories: A Nonfiction Writer's Guide from the Nieman Foundation at Harvard University.* New York: Plume, 2007. Print.

Kunkel, Benjamin. *Indecision.* London: Picador, 2005. Print.

Ladyga, Zuzanna. Technology, Temporality, and the Postmodern Mimesis in David Foster Wallace's "The Suffering Channel." *Vitalpoetics: A Journal of Critical Literary Theory* 1:3 (2008). N.p., n.pag. Web. 1 September 2009. <http://www.vitalpoetics.com>.

LeClair, Tom. *The Art of Excess: Mastery in Contemporary American Fiction.* Urbana: University of Illinois Press, 1989. Print.

---. "The Prodigious Fiction of Richard Powers, William Vollmann, David Foster Wallace." *Critique: Studies in Contemporary Fiction* 38:1 (1996): 12-37. Print.

Lipsky, David. "The Lost Years & Last Days of David Foster Wallace." *Rolling Stone.* Rolling Stone, 30 Oct. 2008. Web. 24 Aug. 2009.

Lyotard, Jean-François. *The Postmodern Condition: A Report on Knowledge.* Trans. Geoff Bennington and Rian Massumi. Minneapolis: University of Minneapolis Press, 1984. Print.

Martone, Michael. "Footnotes[i] & Endnotes[ii]." *Sonora Review* 55/56 (2009): 51-5 of Wallace section. Print.

Marx, Leo. *The Machine in the Garden: Technology and the Pastoral Ideal in America.* Oxford: Oxford University Press, 1964. Print.

Max, D. T. "The Unfinished." *The New Yorker.* Conde Nast, 9 Mar. 2009. Web. 17 Aug. 2009.

"McCain Counters Obama 'Arab' Question." YouTube. YouTube LLC, 11 Oct. 2008. Video file. Web. 23 Jan 2010.

McCain, John and Mark Salter. *Faith of My Fathers: A Family Memoir.* New York: Random House, 1999. Print.

McHale, Brian. *Postmodernist Fiction.* New York: Metheun, 1987. Print.
McCrum, Robert. "A Cult Above the Rest." *The Guardian.* Guardian Media Group, 11 Dec. 2005. Web. Jul 14, 2010 <http://books.guardian.co.uk/print/0,,5352939-99939,00.html>.

Mendelson, Edward. "Encyclopedic Narrative: From Dante to Pynchon," in *MLN: (Modern Language Notes)* 91. 6, Comparative Literature (1976): 1267-1275. Print.

Messud, Claire. "Crushed by a Killing Joke." Rev. of *Infinite Jest. The Times* 6 Jul. 1996: n.pag. Print.

Metz, Bernhard and Sabine Zubarik, eds. *Am Rande bemerkt: Anmerkungspraktiken in literarischen Texten.* Berlin: Kulturverlag Kadmos, 2008. Print.

Miller, J. Hillis. *Speech Acts in Literature.* Stanford, California: Stanford University Press, 2001. Print.

Moore, Steven. "In Memoriam David Foster Wallace." *Modernism/ Modernity.* Volume 16, Number 1 (January 2009): 1-24. Print.

Moretti, Franco. *Modern Epic*, Trans. Quintin Hoare. London: Verso, 1996. Print.

Motte, Warren F. *Oulipo: A Primer of Potential Literature.* Lincoln: University of Nebraska Press, 1987. Print.

Mundaca, Marie. "The Influence of Anxiety: Wading In." *hipsterbookclub.com.* June 2009. Web. Jul 14, 2010 <http://hipsterbookclub.com/features/influenceofanxiety/June09/index.html>.

---. "Posting on Wallace-l." *Wallace-l Listserv.* Waste.org. n.d. Web. 17. Aug. 2009. <http://waste.org/mail/?list=wallace-l>

Murdoch, Iris. *The Sovereignty of Good.* London: Routledge & Kegan Paul, 1970. Print.

Nichols, Catherine. "Dialogizing Postmodern Carnival: David Foster Wallace's *Infinite Jest.*" *Critique* 43.1 (2001): 3-16. Print.

Nussbaum, Martha. "Shame, Separateness, and Political Unity: Aristotle's Criticism of Plato." *Essays on Aristotle's Ethics.* Ed. Amélie Oksenberg Rorty. Berkeley: University of California Press, 1980. 395-435. Print.

---. *Love's Knowledge.* New York: Oxford University Press, 1990. Print.

Olsen, Lance. "Termite Art, or Wallace's Wittgenstein." *The Review of Contemporary Fiction* 13.2 (1993): 199-215. Print.

Patterson, Troy. "Infinitely Sad: David Foster Wallace, Self-Absorbed Genius." *Slate Magazine*. Washington Post. 15 September 2008. n.pag. Web. 24 July 2009.

"Peggy Noonan, Mike Murphy Caught On Tape Disparaging Palin Choice: "Political Bullshit," "Gimmicky."" *The Huffington Post. HuffingtonPost.com, 4 Oct. 2008. n.pag. Web. 23 Jan 2010.*

Powers, Richard. Interview. *Bookworm*. KCRW, California. 15 Mar. 2001. Radio.

Raban, Jonathan. *Bad Land: An American Romance*. London: Picador, 1996. Print.

Raizman, Noah. "Call It Something I Ate: Language-games, Addiction, and Dialogic Possibility in David Foster Wallace's *Infinite Jest.*," n.d., n.pag. Web. 23 Jan. 2010. http://www.thehowlingfantods.com/vitru3.html

Ricoeur, Paul. "Narrative Identity". *On Paul Ricoeur: Narrative and Interpretation*. London: Routledge, 1992. Print.

Robbe-Grillet, Alain. *For a New Novel: Essays on Fiction*. Trans. Richard Howard. Evanston, IL: Northwestern UP, 1989. Print.

Rorty, Richard. *Contingency, Irony and Solidarity*. New York: Cambridge University Press, 1989. Print.

---. *Philosophy and the Mirror of Nature*. Oxford: Basil Blackwell Publisher, 1980. Print.

---. *The Consequences of Pragmatism*. Sussex: The Harvester Press Limited, 1982. Print.

Sánchez, Yvette. "Titel als Mittel: Poetologie eines Paratextes." *Arcadia* 32.2 (1999), 244-61. Print.

Serres, Michael. "Dream." *Disorder and Order. Proceedings of the Stanford International Symposium* (September 14-16, 1981). Trans. and Ed. Paisley Livingston. Saratoga: Anma Libri (1984): 225-39. Print.

Scott, A. O. "The Panic of Influence." *The New York Review of Books* 47. NYREV, Inc., 10 Feb. 2000: 39-43. Web. 17 Aug. 2009.

Shakespeare, William. *Hamlet*. Ed. John F. Andrews. London: Everyman, 1996. Print.

Sheenan, Michael. "Interview with Tom Bissell on *Brief Interview with Hideous Men*." *Sonora Review* 55/56 (2009): 13-22 of Wallace section. Print.

Smith, Zadie. "Brief Interviews with Hideous Men: The Difficult Gifts of David Foster Wallace." *Changing My Mind: Occasional Essays*. London: Hamish Hamilton, 2009. 257-300. Print.

----. Introduction. *The Burned Children of America*. Ed. Marco Cassini and Martina Testa. London: Hamish Hamilton, 2003. xi-xxii. Print.

Sterne, Laurence. *The Life and Opinions of Tristram Shandy, Gentleman*. London: Penguin, 1997. Print.

Stewart, Kathleen, and Susan Harding. "Bad Endings: American Apocalypsis." *Annual Review of Anthropology* 28 (1999): 285-310. Print.

Tate, Andrew. *Douglas Coupland*. Manchester: Manchester University Press, 2007. Print.

Taylor, Gabriele. *Pride, Shame and Guilt: Emotions of Self-Assessment*. Oxford: Oxford University Press, 1985. Print.

Taylor, Jane. "'Why do you tear me from Myself?': Torture, Truth, and the Arts of the Counter-Reformation." *The Rhetoric of Sincerity*. 19-43. Print.

Thoreau, Henry David. *Walden, or Life in the Woods. The Norton Anthology of American Literature.* Ed. Julia Reidhead. Fifth Edition ed. Vol. I. London: W.W. Norton & Company, 1998. Print.

Trilling, Lionel. *Sincerity and Authenticity.* London: Oxford University Press, 1972. Print.

Ulrich, John M. & Harris, Andrea L., ed. *Genxegesis: Essays on Alternative Youth (Sub)Culture.* Madison: The University of Wisconsin Press/ Popular Press, 2003. Print.

Updike, John. "Problems." *Problems and Other Stories.* New York: Knopf, 1979: 150-3. Print.

Van Alphen, Ernst, Mieke Bal and Carel Smith, eds. *The Rhetoric of Sincerity.* Stanford, CA: Stanford University Press, 2009. Print.

Wallace, David Foster. *Brief Interviews with Hideous Men.* London: Abacus, 1999. Print.

---. *The Broom of the System.* New York: Penguin, 1987. Print.

---. *Consider the Lobster.* London: Abacus, 2005. Print.

---. "Deciderization 2007: A Special Report." *The Best American Essays 2007.* Series Ed. Robert Atwan. Boston & New York: Houghton Mifflin Company, 2007. xii-xxiv. Print.

---. "The Empty Plenum: David Markson's Wittgenstein's Mistress." *Review of Contemporary Fiction* 10.2 (1990): 217-39. Print.

---. *Everything and More: A Compact History of* ∞. New York: W.W. Norton, 2003. Print.

---. "Fictional Futures and the Conspicuously Young." *Review of Contemporary Fiction* 8 (1988): 1-27. Web. 26 Jan. 2010. <http://www.theknowe.net/dfwfiles/pdfs/ffacy.pdf>

---. *Girl with Curious Hair*. New York: W.W. Norton, 1989. Print

---."Good People." *The New Yorker.* Conde Nast, 5 Feb 2007. Web. 17 Aug. 2009.

---. *Infinite Jest*. Boston: Little, Brown, 1996. Print.

---. Interview. *The Believer*. McSweeney's, Nov. 2003. Web. 17 Aug. 2009. http://www.believermag.com/issues/200311/?read=interview_wallace

---. Interview. *Bookworm*. KCRW, California. 11 Apr. 1996. Radio.

---. Interview. Bookworm. KCRW, California. 15 May 1997. Radio.

---. Interview. *Bookworm*. KCRW, California. 3 Aug. 2000. Radio.

---. Interview. *Bookworm*. KCRW, California. 2 Mar. 2006. Radio.

---. Interview with Larry McCaffery. *The Review Of Contemporary Fiction* 13.2 (Summer 1993): 127-150. Print.

---. Interview with Laura Miller. *Salon.com*. Salon Media Group, 15 Feb. 1996. n. pag. Web. 24 Aug. 2009. <http://www.salon.com/09/features/wallace2.html>

---. Interview. *The Charlie Rose Show*. PBS, New York. 27 Mar. 1997. Video file. Web. 24 Aug. 2009. <http://www.charlierose.com/view/interview/5639>

---. Interview. *Whiskey Island* Magazine. Cleveland State University, Spring 1993. n.pag. Web. 23 Jan. 2010.

<http://www.thehowlingfantods.com/dfw/news/upcoming-public ations/news-galore---and-a-new/old-dfw-interview.html>

---. "Letter to Don DeLillo." 21 March 2000. Don DeLillo Collection. Harry Ransom Humanities Research Center, University of Texas at Austin. Box 101, folder 10. Used by permission of the David Foster Wallace Literary Trust. Print.

---. *McCain's Promise*. New York: Little Brown, 2008. Print.

---. *Oblivion: Stories*. New York; Boston: Little, Brown and Co, 2004.

---. "Shipping Out: On the (Nearly Lethal) Comforts of a Luxury Cruise." *Harper's*. Harper's Magazine Foundation, Jan. 1996. Web. Jul 14, 2010.

---. "Solomon Silverfish". *Sonora Review* 55/56 (Summer 2009): 67-96 of Wallace section. Print.

---. *A Supposedly Fun Thing I'll Never Do Again*. London: Abacus, 1997. Print.

---. "The Depressed Person." *Harper's*. Harper's Magazine Foundation, Jan. 1998. Web. Jul 14, 2010

---. *This is Water: Some Thoughts, Delivered on a Significant Occasion, about Living a Compassionate Life*. New York: Little, Brown and Company, 2009. Print.

---. "Wiggle Room." *The New Yorker*. Conde Nast, March 9, 2009. Web. 17 Aug. 2009

Weisberg, Jacob. "Campaign Book Report: John McCain." *Slate.com*. Washington Post. 8 September 1999. n.pag. Web. 8 September 1999.

Wieland, Magnus. "Fußnoten über Fußnoten: Am Beispiel von Renaud Camus, David Foster Wallace und Michael Stauffer." Workshop "Den Rahmen sprengen – Anmerkungspraktiken in literarischen Texten II". University of Erfurt (Germany). 9 Oct. 2008. Presentation.

Wittgenstein, Ludwig. *Philosophical Investigations.* Trans. G.E.M. Anscombe. 2nd ed. Oxford: Blackwell, 1958. Print.

---. *Tractatus Logico-Philosophicus,* Trans. G.E.M. Anscombe. 3rd ed. Oxford: Blackwell, 1978. Print.

---. *Tractatus Logico-Philosophicus.* Trans. D. F. Pears and B. F. McGuiness. London and New York: Routledge, 2001. Print.

---. *Zettel.* Ed. & trans. G.E.M. Anscombe. Oxford: Blackwell, 1981. Print.

Wood, David, ed. *On Paul Ricoeur.* London: Routledge, 1991. Print.

Wood, James. *How Fiction Works.* London: Jonathan Cape, 2008. Print.

Wolff, Tobias. "Hunters in the Snow". *Hunters in the Snow.* London: Macmillan, 1983. Print.

Wolfe, Tom. *The New Journalism.* New York: Harper and Row, 1973. Print.

Zelizer, Barbie, ed. *The Changing Faces of Journalism: Tabloidization, Technology, and Truthiness.* New York: Routledge: 2009. Print.

Index